UNEMPLOYMENT IN HISTORY

Unemployment in History

ECONOMIC THOUGHT
AND PUBLIC POLICY

JOHN A. GARRATY

HARPER & ROW, PUBLISHERS

NEW YORK

HAGERSTOWN

SAN FRANCISCO

LONDON

1817

FIRST EDITION

Designed by Sidney Feinberg

Library of Congress Cataloging in Publication Data

Garraty, John Arthur,
  Unemployment in history.
  Includes index.
  1. Unemployed—History. I. Title.
HD5706.G33 1978   331.1'379   76–26227
ISBN 0–06–011457–6

78 79 80 81 82 10 9 8 7 6 5 4 3 2 1

And about the eleventh hour he went out, and found others standing idle, and saith unto them, Why stand ye here all the day idle?

They say unto him, Because no man hath hired us. He saith unto them, Go ye also into the vineyard; and whatsoever is right, that shall ye receive.

Matt. 20: 6–7

For Gail

Contents

Preface

To the best of my knowledge, no one has ever before written a general history of unemployment, or even the history of unemployment in one country over any substantial period of time. But I have called this book *Unemployment in History* instead of *A History of Unemployment* because it does not attempt to describe or analyze in any depth the reasons why there was unemployment at various times, or to determine the number of persons who have been unemployed in different periods, or for the most part to discuss the effects of unemployment in particular situations. Rather it is a study of how the condition of being without work has been perceived and dealt with in different societies from the beginning of recorded history to the present, and of how the idea "unemployment" has been understood and evaluated, both before and after the term itself was invented. Thus it deals with what economists and others who have written about economics have said about work and idleness, and with the impact of these views on public policy, and also with the effects of actual conditions and of public policies on the development of economic ideas.

Although I believe my work has considerable relevance for an understanding of current economic problems, it has evolved out of interests far removed from contemporary affairs. In the late 1960s I began the research for a comparative history of the Great Depression. Unemployment is obviously a subject no student of the depression can ignore, and I had soon accumulated a great deal of material about joblessness during the 1930s. But when I began to write what I intended to be a chapter on unemployment during the depression, I found myself being forced, in the effort to understand the subject, to look back into earlier periods. I soon became fascinated by the evolution of certain concepts and problems, and when I realized how little had been written directly about unemployment, I decided to undertake the present study.

Needless to say, I have called upon many scholars for advice and guidance; the project has led me into a large number of areas where I lacked specialized knowledge. I am especially in the debt of David Brody, Donald Dewey, William V. Harris, Andrzej Kaminski, Daniel J. Leab, Walter P. Metzger, John H. Mundy, Hugh Neuberger, Marc Raeff, Eugene F. Rice, Jacob W. Smit, and Isser Woloch, all of whom read the manuscript of this book in whole or in part at various stages of its evolution. They have saved me from many errors of omission and commission, and much of whatever merit this book has is the result of their wisdom and generosity. I also wish to thank Cass Canfield, Jr., my editor, who encouraged me to put aside my original project in order to undertake this one, and who has supported my efforts with his enthusiasm at moments when my energies, mental and physical, have flagged. To my wife, Gail, to whom this work is dedicated, I owe a similar debt. She has provided loving support and encouragement, and her keen critical eye and ear have often forced me to think through more carefully and phrase more intelligibly ideas that if left to my own devices I would have failed to make properly clear.

—JOHN A. GARRATY
Columbia University

UNEMPLOYMENT IN HISTORY

1

The Nature of Unemployment

Of the economic perils that threaten the Western world, one of the most alarming is the persistence of unemployment. Increases and decreases in unemployment are commonly thought to be connected to changes in the level of prices, the relationship being, according to modern theory, inverse. Inflation is supposed to reduce unemployment, deflation to cause it to go up. The relationship produces considerable social tension because while individuals, faced with a choice between a gradual erosion of their purchasing power and the loss of their jobs, opt unhesitatingly for the former, the tendency of those not directly threatened is to feel greater concern about inflation. Governments, attempting to mediate between these conflicting attitudes, tend to avoid all-out assaults on either unemployment or inflation. Their vacillation, paradoxically, results not from lack of conviction about the desirability of either objective, but out of fear lest by curing one disease they will increase the virulence of the other.

However, popular attitudes toward unemployment and inflation are sometimes quite irrational. It is usually assumed that conservatives fear inflation, liberals unemployment, the argument being that conservatives place security of their property ahead of concern for the suffering of others. But even if this most dubious generalization is correct, many of those who see inflation as the greater threat actually profit from it. Probably their fear grows out of the uncertainty that rising prices entail rather than from the effect on their pocketbooks. (Such persons cannot escape from their awareness that inflation may "run away," that a price explosion of nuclear magnitude like that which swept across Germany after World War I might again occur.) But almost equally remote dangers loom large in the thinking of those who see unemployment as a greater threat to the stability of society. The memory of the Great Depression, when, worldwide, the ranks of the jobless reached heights never approached before or since, haunts such people. (Indeed, that depression shapes the attitudes of nearly everyone toward unemployment.) Yet the possibility that such mass unemployment could recur is remote, and the capacity of society to cope with unemployment has increased enormously since the 1930s.

What made the unemployment of the thirties so disastrous and caused it to last so long was principally a lack of understanding of the dynamics of early-twentieth-century capitalism. Unemployment during the depression was caused directly by a decline in production. The concomitant steep and prolonged decline of profits and of the prices of goods and services inspired a general mood of belt tightening. The deflation was exacerbated by the efforts of governments, faced with shrinking revenues, to balance their budgets by cutting expenses and raising taxes, a policy that most bankers, economists, labor leaders, and other supposed experts strongly supported. One of the most curious and indeed dismaying aspects of the Great Depression for those who study it today is the mountain of evidence in the record of governments deliberately doing things in an effort to end the depression that only made it worse.

Out of the experience of mass unemployment in the depression came the general theory of John Maynard Keynes, a new total view of the capitalist economy that described the relationships between employment, interest rates, and government monetary and fiscal policies. By providing a rationale for deliberate deficit spending, Keynes made it politically possible for a nation to stimulate its lagging economy and thus reduce unemployment. After the exigencies of World War II had demonstrated the effects of massive government deficits on the practical level, the industrial nations adopted the Keynesian techniques with a rush. The Great Depression became the bad old days, unemployment, its trademark, a symbol of ignorance and official incompetence.

And so the postwar era, whatever its difficulties, appeared to have solved the problem of unemployment. The standard way of handling economic downturns was for governments to stimulate consumption and investment, either by increasing their own expenditures or by reducing taxes and interest rates in order to encourage private citizens to increase theirs. The mixtures of these techniques were almost endless but by the 1960s just about everyone had joined the Church of Keynes, a fact highlighted by President Richard Nixon's famous admission: "I am a Keynesian." Economists boasted that they could manipulate an economy by delicately shifting from expansive to restrictive policies, trends being anticipated through an enormous statistical network that measured every nuance of production, employment, and consumption almost on a day-to-day basis. There were, periodically, minor slumps called recessions, but even in these recessions unemployment remained minuscule in most of the European countries, and in the United States it seldom approached 6 percent. The word "depression" disappeared from the vocabulary of economists and politicians, retaining currency chiefly among psychiatrists. In the public mind it lingered in memory only as the name of a dark decade in the bad old days before World War II.

This Age of Keynes, however, was also an age of inflation. And with the passage of time inflation made it increasingly painful to apply the Keynesian stimulants when economic growth slackened and unemployment began to rise. If prices were falling (as during the thirties) or controlled by law (as during the war), large infusions of spending power worked wonders; when prices were already rising, however, the infusions caused them to soar and the resulting dislocations hurt at least as many innocents as unemployment had during the Great Depression. As governments backed away from "stimulants," unemployment increased to levels not approached since 1940, and what to do about it again became an important public issue. Consumers, businessmen, legislators, and even many economists began to call the marvelous Keynesian mechanisms into question. Vague but pervasive fears for the future of the economic system once more shook the confidence of millions.

Of course this was not the first time that smugness had given way to disillusionment and uncertainty or that "laws" based on logic and experience had inexplicably ceased to describe the actual workings of the economy.

Unemployment has always been a complex and elusive phenomenon. Superficially it seems an unmitigated evil, but because of its relationship to trends in the price and consumption of goods and services, which Keynes did so much to clarify, most economists and political leaders are prepared deliberately to create unemployment when circumstances warrant. Working people fear unemployment, but for many it also has its charms. Manufacturers associate it with a decline in demand for what they produce (which is bad), but also with an increase in the supply of available labor (which is good). How these and other interests perceive unemployment at any particular moment depends on their individual and group needs and expectations. Little wonder that throughout history unemployment has played a continuing but changing role in the development of economic and social thought, in the formulation of public policy, and in the shaping of popular attitudes toward work, government, life itself.

The apparently straightforward idea "unemployment" is replete with ambiguities. To be unemployed can signify, in addition to the common meaning of being without a job, merely to be at leisure, or when applied, say, to capital, to be unused or idle. The English word "unemployment" did not come into general use until the mid-1890s. Before that time those concerned with the subject (and many were, for the phenomenon certainly existed) fell back upon such circumlocutions as "want of employment" and "involuntary idleness," which indicates that they saw the phrase as meaning "unused" or "at leisure." The usual German word for unemployment, *Arbeitslosigkeit* (literally "the state of being without work"), was also rarely used before the 1890s; when Karl Marx discussed the unemployed in *Das Kapital* he referred to them not as *die Arbeitslosen* but as *die Unbeschäftigen,* (the idle, or not busy).

The concept "unemployment" in its ordinary sense has a social dimension; the lack of the word therefore suggests that the condition of being without work was seen as a personal rather than a social problem, and reflects the opinion of most nineteenth-century economists (certainly of Marx) that "involuntary idleness" was a necessary element in the capitalist system of production. "*Want* of employment" surely indicates an individual-centered view of the term—who other than the idle worker "wants" employment? The point is reinforced by the fact that the French word for unemployment, *chômage*, has existed since the Middle Ages, although French attitudes toward the unemployed were no more humane and socially oriented than those of their contemporaries. But *chômage* derives from the Greek *kauma* (burning heat), via the medieval Latin *caumare,* which meant "to take one's ease during the heat of the day." The English "calm" has the same origin. Thus *chômage* was rooted in the idea "at leisure"—in modern French *un jour chômé* is merely a day off.[1]

Another ambiguity in the concept is that in its ordinary usage it presumes a curious mixture of freedom and dependence. Slaves cannot suffer from unemployment, although kind masters may allow them periods of leisure and inefficient ones cause them to be idle. Being bound to labor for life, they cannot lose their "jobs," as ante-bellum apologists for American slavery were at pains to point out. That from the point of view of employment there are worse states than slavery is suggested in the Old Testament. When Moses described to the Israelites what the Lord would do to them if they broke His commandments, he concluded with the warning: "And the Lord shall bring thee into Egypt again . . . and there ye shall be sold unto your enemies for

[1] *Chômeur,* an unemployed person, seems, however, to be a late-nineteenth-century invention.

bondmen and bondwomen, and no man shall buy you."[2]

But truly independent workers cannot be unemployed either. Novelists and sculptors may find it difficult or impossible to earn a decent living but they are never unable to work. Doctors, lawyers, and other professionals are a special case. They are not quite so immune as writers and artists because they are licensed by the state—removal of their right to practice would result in unemployment. Farmers, shopkeepers, and similar types perform labor but are actually capitalists. And capitalists, that is, the owners of businesses, cannot be unemployed. Historically, unemployment has been distinctively associated with free-enterprise capitalism—in a sense it is a disease of capitalism—precisely because under capitalism labor is free (neither employer nor employee is permanently obligated one to the other) and because, on the other hand, the system has increased the dependence of labor by separating workers from the ownership of the means of production. In short, only those who work for wages or a salary, who are at liberty to quit their jobs yet who may also be deprived of them by someone else, can become unemployed.

The vagueness of the word "unemployment" is compounded by the ambivalent attitude that most people have toward work. The desire to work, earning a living aside, is a powerful human need, an ego drive related to self-expression, power, creativity. So, however, is the desire to be idle and free of responsibility. These coexistent urges vary in strength within individuals, between cultures, and within individuals and cultures over time, which is another way of saying that they have an environmental as well as a physiological or psychological dimension.

Changes in economic conditions affect the desire to work; when the demand for labor is great and wages good more people want jobs, while in bad times many become discouraged and (as the economists say) drop out of the labor market. Social policies also shape attitudes toward work and leisure. Generous public welfare systems and unemployment insurance not only make joblessness more tolerable materially but, at least for many persons, they reduce the psychological pressure to labor. When unemployment relief is hedged about with demeaning qualifications, accepting it is less likely to have this result.

Levels of expectation affect the balance too, and these are influenced by such things as education, tradition, and the relative rigidity of class boundaries, as well as by economic conditions. During his travels in Latin America in the early nineteenth century, Baron Alexander von Humboldt noted a difference between the industrious laborers of Lima

[2] *Deuteronomy*, 28:68.

and the lazy *guachinangos* of Mexico City. Mexico City was far richer, but in Lima wealth was more equitably distributed. Artisans and free blacks there lived well because they worked hard, whereas the *guachinangos* "work one or two days a week" and then loll about, sleeping under the stars, content if they have enough for *pulque* and something to eat.[3]

On the other hand, when, early in the 1960s, the French sociologist Pierre Bourdieu asked rural Algerians to describe their condition, about three-quarters of those in the southern section of the country reported themselves as *agriculteurs* and only about 6 percent as unemployed. In the Kabylia district, however, only a quarter of the respondents said they were *agriculteurs* and nearly half claimed to be unemployed. Since economic conditions in the two regions were not noticeably different, Bourdieu was forced to conclude that "either the unemployed Kabylians are in reality agricultural workers who say they are unemployed or the southern agricultural workers are unemployed but do not know it."[4] A dispassionate observer might be able accurately to determine the "true" status of each of these Algerians; nevertheless, such subjective self-evaluation often influences unemployment statistics and (more important) how people react to changing economic conditions.

Genesis tells us that work is punishment for sin and the fate of humankind, that idleness is the normal condition of the blameless soul (it was the Lord, not Adam, who planted the Garden of Eden), and that even the Lord, despite his omnipotence, felt the need to take a day off. Historically, the tension between the wish to work and the wish to be idle has been a source of confusion to statesmen, employers, social workers, and others concerned with the problem of unemployment. Aside from persons physically unable to work, there appear to be in any society numbers of individuals who for emotional, cultural, or perhaps even philosophical reasons are simply unwilling to work. Separating these "unemployables" from the rest of the jobless has always been difficult, in large measure because every person is in a sense "unwilling" to work. Because of this human ambivalence toward labor, policy makers have for centuries debated the relative merits of the carrot and stick approaches to the unemployed. To the extent that the work ethic predominates, it pays to encourage and sustain them;

[3] Alexandre de Humboldt, *Essai politique sur le royaume de la Nouvelle-Espagne* (Paris, 1811), II: 36–38.

[4] Pierre Bourdieu, *Travail et travailleurs en Algérie: étude sociologique* (Paris, 1963), pp. 52, 303–304. According to Bourdieu, for years many Kabylians had been emigrating to France. Thus the people of the region were familiar with the concept of work as a productive, money-making activity, whereas the southern population, lacking this notion, "had not discovered the idea, unemployment."

if it does not, then leaving them to their own devices or even punishing the idle may appear reasonable.

The unemployment problem is at once part of and separate from the problem of poverty, which is still another of the ambiguities that enmesh the subject. Unemployment is a cause of poverty, often also a result, yet many poor people have steady work and not all who do not are unemployed in the technical sense of the term. Only some people, rich, poor, or middling, who are not working are properly described as unemployed. In many instances the distinction is easy to make. We do not count children in enumerating the unemployed, although some children work—even infants may earn wages as performers and models. Nor do we include the retired, the mentally deficient, the physically handicapped, and the "idle rich," again despite the individuals in these categories who hold down jobs. Workers on vacation and those who are not working because of illness are not unemployed, although the former are certainly at leisure and the latter involuntarily idle.

But beyond these common-sense limits, classification becomes more difficult. Is a youth looking for a job for the first time unemployed? What of a bricklayer idle because of bad weather, or an assembly-line worker laid off while the factory is retooling for a new model? Certain types of labor are not ordinarily thought of as work; those who engage in such activities are not counted as unemployed when their labor stops. (Consider the thief who lies low during an anti-crime crusade or the beggar driven from the streets by a policeman.) More importantly, housewives work hard yet are not counted as part of the labor force and thus cannot be unemployed. But what of the working married woman who loses her job, cannot find another, and so discharges her housekeeper and takers care of her home herself? Clearly two persons have lost jobs, but how many are added to the ranks of the unemployed?

Then there is the concept "*under*employment." Factory workers on short time because of production cutbacks are underemployed, so are workers in seasonal industries, and in a somewhat different sense so are persons who work long and hard at jobs that do not make efficient use of their skills and energies—a college graduate driving a taxi, a mechanic pumping gasoline, a labor gang building a highway with no tools but picks and shovels are examples. Underemployment is particularly prevalent in underdeveloped countries. Indeed it is usually a major reason why they are underdeveloped; no doubt most of the Algerians Pierre Bourdieu queried could better have been described as underemployed than as either agricultural workers or jobless. But underemployment is common among disadvantaged groups in heavily industrialized societies too, especially among newcomers, whether they be recent immigrants or merely young people recently arrived at working age. In part, however, the idea of underemployment depends upon convention. Workers on vacation, even teachers during the long summer recess, are not considered underemployed. Two hundred years ago a person working only eight hours a day would have seemed grossly underemployed if the term had then existed.

In the last analysis governments decide who is unemployed and who is not. That their decisions are in large measure arbitrary is demonstrated by the fact that definitions of unemployment vary from nation to nation and have varied in all countries at different periods: currently in the United States a jobless person is considered unemployed only if able to work and actively seeking to find a job; in France during the Great Depression, a person was not listed until he had lost a job—technically, young people entering the labor market for the first time were not unemployed.

National differences in how governments define unemployment have shrunk substantially since the 1930s (although quite different methods of counting the unemployed remain). All governments, however, influence in many ways, some deliberate, others not, how many of their citizens and of resident aliens are jobless. In the first place, governments are employers who hire and (less frequently) discharge workers as their funds allow and as the needs of their bureaucracies change. Welfare programs probably have no impact on the number of people working, but they do reduce unemployment, since if they did not exist many who benefit from them would enter the job market. Child-labor legislation and laws fixing the retirement age of workers affect *who* works rather than the number of persons employed, but they reduce unemployment, again by removing potential workers from the market. Protective tariffs, import quotas, subsidies, and restrictions on immigration tend to reduce domestic unemployment. Minimum-wage laws, however, may increase it by discouraging employers from hiring unskilled and inefficient labor.

Indeed, any legislation that influences economic activity will indirectly cause unemployment to rise or fall. This generalization seems so obvious as scarcely to merit mention, but it is no commonplace because economists and political leaders have taken widely different positions on the question at different times. In the seventeenth century the dominant opinion was that proper state action could reduce unemployment, while in the nineteenth century most authorities believed that any regulation of the economy would either add to the number of idle workers or at best cause shifts within the work force between one industry or region and another. Keynes demolished the latter line of reasoning once and for all in 1936 with his *General Theory of Employ-*

ment, Interest, and Money, which explained how government monetary and fiscal policies affected savings and investment and thus employment. The post-Keynesian inflation has called into question the ultimate results of policies aimed at permanent full employment, but that the policies have effects is beyond argument.

Attitudes toward unemployment have shifted many times over the years. It has always been incorrect to assume that all who are without work want it, but for reasons I have mentioned the relative strength of the desire to work has varied greatly from time to time and from place to place. Nor is it safe to assume that workers invariably favor efforts to reduce unemployment. They fear the loss of their jobs but also the competition of the jobless. Given the choice between having fellow workers discharged or sharing limited opportunities with them and thus accepting a reduction in income, relatively few individuals and still fewer labor organizations have willingly accepted the second alternative. Yet there have been times when the labor force has shown a remarkable solidarity.

Modern economists and political leaders put a high priority on keeping unemployment low. (But not too low—their opinions of how high is low enough can change very quickly.) But there have been periods when substantial unemployment was believed to be a necessary evil, and others when any unemployment at all was seen as a national disaster.

What to do about the unemployed has always been a difficult and controversial public issue. Unemployed persons have been treated as criminals who must be isolated from society or driven to hard labor, and as sinners to be regenerated by exhortation and prayer (their own as well as those of their betters). They have been viewed as wayward children who must be taught how to work, as lazy incompetents best left to suffer the consequences of their sloth, and as innocent victims of forces beyond their control. Nearly every scheme for both improving their lot and sustaining them in their misery that is currently in vogue, along with many no longer considered workable, was known and debated at least as far back as the sixteenth century. What actually has been done for the unemployed and about unemployment has depended upon the interaction of moral and religious attitudes, the sense of what is economically possible, the locus of political power in society, and the extent to which those who possess the power are aware of how unemployment affects both its victims and their own interests.

I seek here to trace the development of these perceptions from ancient times to the present day. This is the history of a concept, not of people, although many individuals—Keynes is an obvious example—have greatly influenced the concept and will thus play large roles in my account. What people thought about unemployment even before they had invented the term and how their circumstances shaped that thought and their consequent behavior are my central concerns. The reality behind the thought cannot, of course, be ignored. To understand how one generation could look upon the jobless as pariahs, another as "children of Christ," still another as slightly subhuman creatures suitable for dispassionate scientific analysis, one must examine closely the unemployed, their judges, and the worlds in which both lived. But my main purpose is not to count the jobless, or to describe their misery, or to explain why they were unemployed, or to pass judgment on what was done about unemployment. In short, my approach is eclectic. I deal with economics, for example, as a branch of intellectual history, not as a social science. But I place economists, and also politicians, philanthropists, and labor leaders in a social context, seeing them primarily as products of their surroundings.

Discussing the history of unemployment before the condition received that name presents problems. I do not use the word as precisely as it is employed by the technicians of the Bureau of Labor Statistics and other modern experts because in historical perspective their "unemployment" is a special case. For my purposes unemployment means "the condition of being without some socially acceptable means of earning a living," and the unemployed are persons capable of labor, in need of its rewards, but idle, without regard for their willingness to work or the suitability of what they can do to the needs of society. These definitions are of course too broad to describe modern conditions accurately, but narrower ones would force the exclusion of material relevant to the history of the subject.

Moreover, any definition of these terms involves judgmental elements. For example, with the occasional exceptions I have noted, we do not consider young children capable of work, the desirability of their working aside. Yet at various times and places millions below the age of ten have worked long and hard as a matter of course, and in the seventeenth century it was seriously advanced that four-year-olds could earn their daily bread and that it was in the public interest that they do so. At various times there have been guilds of beggars in Europe, in India and China, and throughout the Muslim world. As late as the eighteenth century, cities all over Europe licensed individuals with certain carefully spelled-out qualifications to "earn their living" by begging in the streets. Prostitution may not actually be the oldest profession, but whether a prostitute is a legitimate worker or a parasite depends upon the attitudes of society and indeed of the individual prostitute.

I shall therefore use the terms "unemployment" and "the unemployed" rather imprecisely, though not without forethought. My perspective will shift back and forth between the present and the past, as any historian's must. Beggars and how they were viewed by their contemporaries are part of my concern, whether they saw themselves as workers or work seekers, whether others saw them as God's poor or the scum of the earth, however a modern labor economist would classify them in their particular situations. Since begging is related to unemployment, it falls within the scope of this study. So also do children, the superannuated, the dissolute, and the ordinary worker discharged because times are hard. In sum, I write about Marx's *Unbeschäftigte,* those who are not busy but who need, and about what has been done and said, to and about them.

2

In the Beginning

In the ancient world the concept, unemployment, did not exist, nor for that matter did such concepts as production, capital, demand, market, and investment, for none of which, in its abstract sense, is there a Greek or Latin word. But, just as capital was invested and goods produced and sold, so workers were sometimes unemployed in Greek and Roman times and no doubt earlier still in Egypt and the Near East. Since most ordinary labor was performed by slaves, whose idleness would be at the expense of their owners, unemployment was probably not a major social problem. But free workers certainly experienced it at times. No one can say how many or, except in the most general way, why workers were unemployed, but substantial and widely dispersed evidence of the condition exists.

It has been suggested, for example, that the great monuments of antiquity, such as the pyramids and the Temple of Karnak in Egypt and the Temple in Jerusalem, may have been built as public work-relief projects. The case for the pyramids is particularly persuasive (although still speculative), the reasoning being that during the late-summer flooding of the Nile, when the enormous limestone blocks could be floated to the site, the pharaohs employed tens of thousands of peasants idled by the flood as laborers, paying them in kind. It might also be argued that when projects requiring the concentration of so many laborers in one place were completed, what we would now call "frictional unemployment" would be bound to occur before the work force could be reabsorbed into other activities. It is beyond argument that the typical sculptor or worker in bronze and precious metals lived a peripatetic existence, moving from place to place as one or another center prospered and declined. The skills of these artisans were in great demand, but seldom in one city for very long. The fifth-century sculptor Myron, creator of the Discobolus, is known to have worked in places as distant from his native Greece as Asia Minor and Sicily. Greek smiths fashioned the fabulous Scythian gold in southern Russia and still-more-remote regions. The defeat of Athens by Sparta resulted in an exodus of craftsmen from the city. Traveling in ancient times being slow, expensive, and not without danger, probably few skilled workers undertook long journeys except in search of work not available nearby.

It is not, however, necessary to rely upon this kind of reasoning to demonstrate that unemployment existed in antiquity. In Athens, Plutarch tells us, Pericles undertook "vast projects of buildings and designs of work," supervised by the sculptor Phidias, "it being his desire and design that the undisciplined and mechanic multitude . . . should not go without their share of public salaries, and yet should not have them given them for sitting still and doing nothing."[1]

In Rome during the time of Tiberius Gracchus there were many homeless wanderers who managed a precarious existence by casual labor on the docks, supplemented during the harvest season by farm labor, an indication that they suffered from chronic unemployment. According to the historian P. A. Blunt, "it is likely that there was much unemployment and under-employment" during the late republic, the probability being strengthened by the fact that during this period free grain was first distributed to the Roman populace, a practice that in the next century had become so commonplace as to inspire Juvenal's famous comment that "the people of Rome . . . yearn for two things only—bread and circuses." Suetonius reports that the Emperor Vespasian, who ruled Rome from A.D. 69 to 79, refused to make use of a mechanical device for moving heavy stone columns on the ground that it would "take from the poor commons the work that fed them," proof at least of concern about unemployment, if not of its actual existence.[2]

Other sorts of evidence throw light on the question of joblessness in the ancient world. Pericles systematically dispatched expeditions to found colonies in places like Naxos and Thrace in order (again according to Plutarch) to "discharge the city of an idle, and, by reason of their idleness, a busy meddling crowd of people; and at the same time to meet the necessities and restore the fortunes of the poor townsmen." Later, in 346 B.C., Isocrates urged Philip of Macedon to establish colonies for "those who now, for lack of the daily necessities of life,

[1] Alison Burford, *Craftsmen in Greek and Roman Society* (Ithaca, 1972), pp. 62, 65–66; Plutarch, *The Lives of the Noble Grecians and Romans* (New York, [n.d., Modern Library]), pp. 192–93.

[2] P. A. Blunt, *Italian Manpower: 225 B.C.—14 A.D.* (Oxford, 1971), pp. 106–10, 140; Juvenal, *Satires*, X:81; Suetonius, *The Lives of the Twelve Caesars* (New York, 1931), pp. 332–33.

are wandering from place to place and committing outrages upon all they meet." A modern scholar concludes that under the Athenian Empire "the colony was seen as the answer to the problem of surplus citizens without means of livelihood." The Roman practice of giving land to discharged veterans was surely a means of preventing unemployment.[3]

Still another kind of evidence comes from the Gospel of Saint Matthew, Jesus' parable of the householder hiring men to work in his vineyard, which concludes with the lines: "So the last shall be first, and the first last: for many be called, but few chosen." When the householder went to the marketplace for the last time at the eleventh hour "he found others standing idle, and saith unto them, Why stand ye here all the day idle? They say unto him, Because no man hath hired us." The story not only offers an example of unemployment but also suggests that marketplaces served as labor exchanges where employers and laborers could seek each other out. Certainly unemployed Athenian day laborers regularly gathered on a certain hill in hopes of being hired, the practice being well established in the fifth century B.C.[4] Then too there is a mass of evidence about beggars and vagrants in the records of antiquity: the *Odyssey* mentions beggars, as do the poet Hesiod's *Work and Days*, written in the eighth century B.C., both the Old and the New Testament, the plays of Aristophanes, Plato's *Republic*—the list is endless.[5]

The common attitude toward beggars and indeed toward idle persons generally was very harsh. In the Greek city-states, civic honor was felt to be compromised by the mere existence of beggars.[6] Solon repealed the Draconian death penalty for idleness in Athens, but substituted chastisement. The Spartan Lycurgus decreed that to prevent idleness laborers should "be kept down with continual toil and work." The unemployed person, to the classical mind, was responsible for his own idleness; to give him alms, as the Roman playwright Plautus put it, was "to do him an ill service." A Spartan's response to a beggar's appeal was typical: "If I gave to you, you would proceed to beg all the more; it was the man who gave to you in the first place who made you idle." Philanthropy, even pity, did not pass across class lines. "Pity,"

[3] Plutarch, *Lives*, p. 191; Isocrates, *To Philip*, section 120; A. R. Hands, *Charities and Social Aid in Greece and Rome* (Ithaca, 1968), p. 68.

[4] *Matthew* 20:1–16; Alexander Fuks, "Labour Exchange in Classical Athens," *Eranos*, 49 (1951), 171–73.

[5] Alexandre Vexliard, *Introduction à la sociologie du vagabondage* (Paris, 1956), p. 28; Hendrick Bolkestein, *Wohltätigkeit and Armenpflege in vorchristlichen Altertum* (Utrecht, 1939), pp. 202–10.

[6] Looking back on the golden age of Athens, Isocrates wrote: "At that time no citizen lacked the necessities of life, and no one dishonored the city by begging." Quoted in Bolkestein, *Wohltätigkeit in Altertum*, p. 207.

says the demagogue Cleon in Thucydides' history, "is appropriately given on an exchange basis to men of like character."[7] Nevertheless, the continuing presence of beggars is proof presumptive that some people were giving them alms.

If unemployment was relatively insignificant in classical times it was, if possible, even less important in the life of the Middle Ages; the condition remained literally inconceivable in the sense, already mentioned, that the term itself did not exist, and also in the sense that it was difficult for a person of the period to envisage a situation in which large numbers of willing and able workers had nothing to do. Medieval methods of production remained simple and by modern standards technologically primitive. Farming was the principal occupation, industry small-scale and localized, considerable regional self-sufficiency the rule. Agricultural output varied with the vagaries of climate, not because of the decisions of individuals. Moreover, and in this respect they differed radically from the ancients, medieval people had a powerful commitment to the ideal of the interdependence of all members of society. Rich and poor, lord and peasant alike possessed traditional perquisites and accepted traditional obligations, being "bound to service" without regard for their social positions or material state. In such a structured system, the labor force appeared to be a fixed quantity.

On the medieval manor, the lord could not easily increase or decrease the number of serfs in accordance with his hope or fear of profit or loss because he was obligated to employ and protect them. For their part, the serfs were bound to the land and to their lord, owing him part of their labor. Serfdom was a condition intermediate between slavery and freedom; serfs were neither dependent in the sense of being subject to dismissal, nor free in the sense of having the right to leave their work. Hence they could not become unemployed.

Town artisans did not have the restraints and protections of serfs, but they too suffered little from unemployment. By the end of the thirteenth century, the members of most crafts in the towns had joined together in guilds. However imperfectly, these organizations reflected the medieval view of society; they existed to moderate rather than to bring into focus adversary relationships between employer and employee, and between producer and consumer. Masters and their workers made up the membership, the assumption being that their interests were the same. In addition to their economic functions, guilds served as political institutions of a kind, since belonging made one a citizen of the community with the privileges and obligations that entailed, and

[7] Plutarch, *Lives*, pp. 107, 110; Hands, *Charities*, pp. 65, 80.

they also played educational, recreational, and religious roles in town life. To the extent that they promoted both social harmony and economic stability, and especially the latter, they were major protections against unemployment. More directly, guilds sought to guarantee their members adequate work by limiting entry into the craft, a policy characteristic of organized labor in nearly every era. No one not a guild member could practice a trade, and often only relatives of members were admitted. Still more frequently, "foreigners," a term usually meaning anyone not of the town, were kept out.[8]

Restricting the number of workers made sense because in stable and encapsulated communities the demand for goods fluctuated but little. Both prices and wages were controlled by regulations, not by competition. If the "just" price of a product (that is, its "normal" market price) tended in fact not to change, it was because the price was fixed by rules, and the "just wage" as well. Since prices and wages did not change much from year to year or even from lifetime to lifetime, people came to assume that tradition was the controlling force that determined "just" rates. In reality, neither custom nor guild regulations but the level of productivity of the system set the standard of living of everyone. The price charged for an article multiplied by the volume of the seller's business equaled the cost of production plus enough profit to enable the seller to live at a level considered appropriate for persons of his calling, and the wage of a craftsman was that sum sufficient to keep a craftsman's family in a manner suitable to its station. Stability was, however, directly responsible for the rarity of unemployment.

The economist Joseph Schumpeter once wrote that the "structural design" of medieval society "excluded unemployment." This statement is correct according to the modern technical definition of the term, which requires that the jobless be actively seeking work. But if few who were able-bodied could not find jobs, more did not work, although just how many no one can say. When the hardest labor could not be expected to produce much more than a bare subsistence, some persons sought alternative ways of subsisting. These became the beggars, vagabonds, and outlaws, types that in Schumpeter's words had "broken loose from their environment or been cast off by it."[9] Outlaws and those beggars who made mendicancy a way of life ought perhaps to be thought of as working people, and among the wanderers were troubadours, magicians, and entertainers, who in their unstructured way practiced highly skilled trades. But most authorities would agree that beggars and vagrants are properly classified as unemployed. And

[8] Emile Coornaert, *Les corporations en France avant 1789* (Paris, 1968), pp. 181–87, 191, 217–21, 236–40, 251.

[9] Joseph Schumpeter, *History of Economic Analysis* (New York, 1954), p. 270.

if the settled majority could count on a secure place in the economic structure, all working people were far from immune to economic hazards. Farming is an occupation fraught with uncertainty, never more so than in the Middle Ages. Drought, flood, and the ravages of insects and plant diseases often wiped out crops, leaving those dependent upon agriculture both without sustenance and idle. Wars and plagues could also disrupt the economy; while either raged ordinary business came almost to a halt. When epidemics like the Black Death of 1348–49 swept through a medieval town, those who could fled and those who remained cowered in their homes or were kept from their work by stringent quarantine regulations. When the scourge had passed, the demographic balance of the region would be slow in readjusting to the loss of life, and until it had the economy suffered.

Medieval society, therefore, had to deal with unemployed people, though it had no unemployment problem in the modern sense. Its way of doing so was shaped by the ambiguities I have mentioned. Underlying the medieval approach and separating it most distinctly from the Graeco-Roman view of society was a powerful commitment to caring for the unfortunate, Christian in origin, which was predicated on the beliefs that poverty was a holy state, accepting alms no disgrace, and charity both a proof of piety and a key to eternal salvation. Jesus, by his earthly example, had sanctified poverty. A poor person was preeminently a child of the Lord, as the French put it, *"un membre souffrant de Jésus Christ,"* and was presumed to have a special influence with God, so much so that princes and great nobles often admitted beggars to their feasts, and the friends of a dead person often gave alms to poor people on condition that they pray for the soul of the departed. Beggars were not merely inevitable but necessary elements in the community, their relationship with almsgivers symbiotic—"if there were no beggars, one could not give alms." It was also assumed—paradoxically but with the same result so far as attitudes toward poverty were concerned—that except for members of religious orders who had taken vows of poverty, no one was poor on purpose. To ask why an individual could not support himself seemed to humane people contemptible, and to others immaterial, since it was widely believed that giving alms was a form of penance for one's sins, meritorious in the eyes of God without regard for the worthiness of the recipient.[10]

On the other hand the conviction that to live by the sweat of one's brow was the fate of humankind after Adam's fall was ingrained. Since

[10] J. P. Gutton, *La société et les pauvres: l'example de la généralité de Lyon, 1534–1789* (Paris, 1971), pp. 215–17; Lotte Koch, *Wandlungen der Wohlfahrtspflege im Zeitalter der Aufklärung* (Erlangen, 1933), pp. 27–28; Brian Tierney, "The Decretists and the 'Deserving Poor,' " *Comparative Studies in Society and History,* 1 (1958–59), 361.

a society that did not need the labor of everyone seemed beyond imagination, it followed that an idle person was not so much morally inadequate as antisocial.[11] The conflict between the duty to give alms to the poor and this attitude toward work tended to produce certain compromises. The charitable principle was upheld, but resources being limited, priorities were established. The main distinction drawn was that separating the "deserving" from the "undeserving"—no less an authority than St. Augustine suggested that charity should not be given to those who "neglected righteousness."

An undeserving poor person might not necessarily be an idle one; hard-working sinners have never been rare. Willful idleness, however, was presumptive evidence of lack of worth and therefore ground for discrimination for those interested in drawing a line. Many medieval writers went no further than to argue that the undeserving must wait until those with better claims were relieved, and do without if there was not enough to go round, and most thought that a starving person should be fed no matter how disreputable. But by the twelfth century some canon law experts were taking the position that anyone who was able to work but unwilling to do so should be denied help no matter what the circumstances. Related questions were whether alms given the undeserving should be accompanied by efforts to make them mend their ways, and if so, whether this end could better be accomplished by punishment or by education and persuasion. Making the idle work appealed to some as a form of punishment, to others as a means of redeeming them from vice.[12] All these questions continued to puzzle philanthropists and social workers long after the Middle Ages had passed into history. They persist, indeed, in our own day.

While European society was relatively stable during the High Middle Ages, it was far from static. The twelfth and thirteenth centuries were prosperous times compared with what had gone before; the population increased steadily and the economy expanded. New land was brought under cultivation as swamps were drained and forests cleared. Towns increased in number and size, although few had more than 10,000 inhabitants and only Paris, Venice, and Milan approached 100,000 in the early fourteenth century.

This order and prosperity, however, rested upon a fragile base. In the towns expansion led to economic and social stratification. The flourishing cloth industry became more specialized; merchants gained

[11] Paradoxically, the landed nobility (and the urban upper class, professional people, and clerics who aped it) looked down on any kind of manual labor. This had been equally true in the ancient world, where, when mentioned at all by writers, ordinary workers are seen as so lowly as to be almost subhuman. See Bolkestein, *Wohltätigkeit in Altertum*, p. 411.

[12] Tierney, "The Decretists and the Deserving Poor," pp. 367–69.

control of the manufacturing process and the guilds excluded from their benefits and protections unskilled washers and carders and even semiskilled workers such as dyers (marked by their blue fingernails, stained by constant immersion in the dye) and the fullers who washed and stretched the finished cloth. In other trades as well, the gap between rich and poor spread, breeding resentments and increasing the percentage of the populace that lacked political influence. The simple economic relations of the "feudal" rural society broke down. The result was widespread disorder. A series of uprisings swept through the textile towns of Flanders in the late thirteenth century, sparked by hatred of the big merchants and the magistrates who were their allies. In 1307, Parisian workers rioted against high food prices brought on by a devaluation of the currency, and during the following decades there were many similar outbreaks—for example, in Amiens, Rouen, and other French towns; in Barcelona; in Venice, Florence, and elsewhere in Italy.[13]

Agricultural prosperity was brought to an end by climatic changes. Prolonged and severely cold winters, periods of drought and of crop-destroying downpours caused repeated bad harvests and much suffering, for the population had been steadily increasing. In Languedoc, as the researches of Emmanuel LeRoy Ladurie have shown, between 1302 and 1348 twenty harvests failed or fell short; in the worst times the peasants had nothing to eat but grass.[14] Famine swept across all Europe during three consecutive bad years in 1315–17, thousands dying of starvation. Then came the deadly epidemics that began at mid-century with the Black Plague, "the massacre of the undernourished," and continued sporadically thereafter, each outbreak further reducing the population. As time passed, farms and whole villages were abandoned. Hard times bore heavily on the towns. Wars, civil and foreign, further disrupted the medieval balance, destroying property and lives, and causing massive economic and social dislocations.

In these chaotic times wages rose because of the labor shortage caused by famine and pestilence, but so did the number of unemployed. Some regions suffered from the plague more than others; when the danger had passed, many people drifted toward these empty areas, unemployed but hopeful of improving their lot. Rural depopulation drove landlords to shift to less labor-intensive agriculture, principally by converting to sheep raising; in the process they dispossessed many of their tenants, who joined the rootless element wandering in search of work.

[13] Coornaert, *Corporations*, pp. 245–47; Michel Mollat and Philippe Wolff, *The Popular Revolutions of the Late Middle Ages* (London, 1973), pp. 16, 44–46, 93–107.
[14] Emmanuel LeRoy Ladurie, *Les Paysans de Languedoc* (Paris, 1969), p. 17.

This same combination of labor scarcity and unemployment existed in the towns. The plagues took a fearful toll among workingmen, for though they spared no class, the poor suffered most by far. Thus merchant entrepreneurs and master artisans were in great need of additional hands. In Florence, for example, real wages in the 1350s were more than double what they had been in the 1340s. But the newcomers who flocked to the towns were mostly unskilled and unfamiliar with city ways. Employers took advantage of them, paying them as little as possible and trying to keep them in subservient positions by tightening still further restrictions on entry into the guilds. The gap between employer and wage worker widened, and as the workers became more and more dependent and subject to the vagaries of changing economic conditions, writers and jurists began to refer to them as base *(vils mécaniques)*, a different order of being. Many of these laborers wandered from town to town, seeking work and a chance to set themselves up as independent artisans. To protect themselves, they often formed mutual-aid societies, with secret rituals and religious overtones. Each member, called in France *un compagnon*, carried a kind of membership card *(un viatique)*, which identified him to his fellows, who were committed to providing him food and shelter and to helping him find work.[15]

The amount of movement, the rapidity of change, the precariousness of life seemed all without precedent. Able-bodied vagrants crowded the roads. Armed bands roamed the countryside. There were beggars everywhere. How to tell an honest artisan trudging to a nearby town in search of work from a renegade soldier or an ordinary tramp, a displaced tenant from a runaway serf, a mendicant monk from a sturdy beggar became increasingly difficult, for indeed the unsettled times were bringing out the ambivalent attitudes of people toward work. Everyone realized that the population had declined precipitously. The obvious shortage of labor raised workers' hopes and tempted them to seek self-improvement by pulling up stakes, whatever their legal status or contractual obligations. Yet, when the most industrious laborer, hemmed in by guild restrictions, could not expect to improve his status, with his mere subsistence subject to a hundred unpredictable hazards, the temptation to live by begging or thievery also became powerful. Many displaced peasants, unaccustomed to freedom, found the easgoing life of the road a heady experience. On the other hand, the sight of able-bodied idlers when the need for labor was so great hardened the hearts of landlords, merchants, and master

[15] Michel Mollat, ed., *Etudes sur l'histoire de la pauvrété* (Paris, 1974), II: 505–10, 673–83; Emile Coornaert, *Les compagnonnages en France du Moyen Age à nos jours* (Paris, 1966), pp. 31–35; Mollat and Wolff, *Popular Revolutions*, p. 247.

artisans. A London proclamation of 1359 expressed the attitude of such people, denouncing the "many men and women, and others, of divers Counties . . . [who] go about begging . . . so as to have their own ease and repose, not wishing to labour or work for their sustenance . . . and also, do waste divers alms, which would otherwise be given to many poor folks, such as lepers, blind, halt, and persons oppressed with old age." The line between the deserving and the undeserving was drawn more sharply when apparently capable loafers, as a later English ordinance put it, "counterfeit the begging poor."[16]

Kings and princes sought to deal with this problem by keeping people in their place. The King of Denmark forbade serfs to seek work in the herring fisheries. In Prussia, similar efforts were made to hold the rural population on the land. In Sweden the authorities rounded up peasants who had gravitated to the towns. In England, while the Black Death still raged in 1349, Edward III issued an Ordinance of Labourers, buttressed in 1350 by a parliamentary Statute of Labourers, which denied workers the right to leave their employment in search of higher pay, and at the same time prohibited anyone from giving alms to "valiant" beggars, "so that thereby they may be compelled to labour for their necessary living." In 1350 Jean le Bon of France decreed that beggars and other idle persons able to work be punished by banishment or imprisonment, and that no charity be given to such types by the clergy. The next year, Pedro the Cruel of Castile issued decrees providing for the flogging of sturdy beggars and fixing wages and prices in all his Spanish domains.[17]

None of these measures could be enforced. In such times, people reacted in strange and unpredictable ways. The uncertainty of life made many heedless of the morrow. Such persons abandoned themselves to pleasure seeking. Others saw the endless plagues, wars, and famines as signs of God's displeasure and of impending doom, and retreated into prayer. Groups of Flagellants roamed about beating one another with barbed ropes, denouncing humanity as hopelessly corrupt, refusing to labor, living on alms. But others sought merely to survive, while still others found in the instability of the times the excuse to cast off old restrictions and grasp whatever advantages they could. This confusing state of affairs explains the ambivalence of the Ordinance of Labourers, in which in a single sentence King Edward condemned both those who "will not serve unless they may receive

---

[16] C. J. Ribton-Turner, *A History of Vagabonds and Vagrancy and Beggars and Begging* (London, 1887), pp. 51–52.

[17] Jacques Heer, *L'occident aux XIVe et XVe siècles: aspects économiques et sociaux* (Paris, 1963), p. 94; Ribton-Turner, *Vagabonds and Beggars*, pp. 43–47; Gutton, *Pauvres de Lyon*, pp. 94–96, 218.

excessive wages," and those "rather willing to beg in idleness than by labour to get their living."

As time passed, the political disorder and social upheaval became if anything still worse. The Hundred Years' War between England and France continued into the mid-fifteenth century, while dynastic conflicts raged between rival cliques in these nations, in Italy, and in other areas, disrupting the lives of millions of ordinary people. Uprisings of town laborers and peasants flared sporadically. In 1378 in Florence, during the *tumulto dei Ciompi* artisans and laborers burned the houses of the rich, looted the grain supply, hanged the public executioner, occupied the seat of government. In 1381 in England there was Wat Tyler's rebellion—an army of peasants from Kent and Essex marched on London, burning and looting in the city and compelling (temporarily) the youthful Richard II to abolish serfdom and repeal the Statute of Labourers. In the next century serious riots broke out in France, Catalonia, Scandinavia, Bohemia, and many other regions—between 1413 and 1453, there were fourteen revolutions in the city of Genoa.[18]

The European economy eventually recovered from the catastrophes of the fourteenth century; the population began to increase again, farmland was reclaimed from the encroaching forest, industry expanded. This recovery, which extended with minor interruptions to about 1620, did not, however, bring back social stability; rather, by strengthening the trend toward large-scale production and specialization, notably in textiles, it widened the gap between merchant and artisan and between artisan and wage earner. More land was converted to sheep raising, and the consequent uprooting of rural labor added to the floating population. Although workers were not yet class-conscious in the modern sense, an industrial proletariat was emerging, in the cities and in rural areas where merchant entrepreneurs were utilizing peasant labor in the cloth industry on a putting-out system. This work force was poor; it lived from hand to mouth and had little hope of improving its position; it was vulnerable in every way. In the towns it was made up to a considerable extent of deracinated peasants, villagers, and mountain people, more often than not men without families, alone and disoriented. Master artisans welcomed these people for their cheap labor but, fearing them, as guild statutes were wont to put it, as possible sources of "conspiracy and tumult," they excluded them from membership in their organizations. The guilds became, in the words of their historian, Emile Coornaert, "little islands of privilege in a world of unregulated labor."[19]

[18] Mollat and Wolff, *Popular Revolutions, passim;* Coornaert, *Corporations,* pp. 97–99; Heer, *Occident,* pp. 99–100; Fernand Braudel, *The Mediterranean and the Mediterranean World in the Age of Philip II* (New York, 1972), p. 339.

[19] Coornaert, *Corporations,* pp. 100, 111–31.

Gradually, "the poor" came to mean "those who have only their work." That being the case, unemployment meant instant destitution. Idle people therefore seemed inherently dangerous to the better off because it was so obvious that social upheaval could only improve their lot, and often repulsive, because, living in brutish poverty, they appeared to be little better than animals. As always, however, social attitudes toward the unemployed were mixed and confused. The church still preached the virtues of charity, and distributed alms, and denounced the exploitation of the poor. (But to those who would not accept their assigned places in the social order it turned a face of flint. Endure in this world, it taught; your reward will come in the next.)

Laymen were also touched by so much suffering. Some were at least dimly aware of the social causes of unemployment, poverty and vice. In his introduction to *Utopia*, Sir Thomas More reflected upon current conditions in England, upon the "great flocke or traine of idle and loyterynge servyngmen" who were disturbing the peace and rousing so much public concern. The unemployed were ex-soldiers, many of them disabled, the retainers of the rich thrown on their own resources by the deaths of their lords, and rural people uprooted by the enclosure movement. ("Your shepe," More wrote, "eate up, and swallow downe the very men them selfes.") Such persons "go aboute and worke not: whom no man wyl set a worke, though thei never so willyngly profre themselves thereto." Soon they become unemployable—"when they have wandred abrode so longe, untyl they have worne thredebare their apparell, and also appaired their helth, then gentlemen, because of their pale and sickley faces, and patched cotes, will not take them into service." The inevitable result was that the idle turned to begging and stealing; the solution was to find work for "this idell sort to passe their tyme in profitablye."[20]

More's argument, while not strictly speaking "utopian"—he advanced it by way of preface to his description of his ideal society—was far more enlightened than that of the majority of his contemporaries, but many recognized the social costs of poverty: crime; disease; disorder; the incessant importuning of the citizenry by beggars. "Suppose," wrote a Spanish scholar who had observed conditions in Paris, London, and the cities of Flanders, "suppose there is at some church or other a high festival drawing great crowds: one has to make one's way into the building between two lines of disease, vomitings, ulcers, or other afflictions disgusting even to speak of." One would have to be "made of iron" not to be disturbed, "especially when ulcers of this sort are not only forced upon the eyes, but upon the nose and mouth,

[20] Thomas More, *Utopia* (New York, 1910), pp. 21–28.

and are almost touched by the hands and bodies of passers-by, so insolent are they in begging."[21]

By the early sixteenth century it had become clear that new public policies must be devised and institutions established to help those who for whatever reason could not help themselves, and to restrict and punish vagrants and beggars. Spontaneously, or so it seemed, a kind of "international movement for welfare reform" erupted. In towns and cities from the Low Countries to Italy, from Nuremberg to Paris and Lyons, magistrates and councils began to enact ordinances for the control of the poor.[22]

The new regulations were not uniform, but differences from city to city were relatively minor. The basic idea was to set up a comprehensive system of relief for the old, the sick, and the incompetent and then to ban begging. A general fund (called *aumône générale* in French, *gemeine Kasten* in German) was established and all local citizens deemed worthy of aid were registered. Thereafter, anyone caught asking for alms could be considered a criminal or a fraud and either driven out of town if a "foreigner" (vagrant) or jailed or put to forced labor if a local idler.

The new system was not in principle repressive. It gave the force of law to the obligation of society to care for those who could not support themselves, and reflected the humanist ideas that poverty was not a holy state but a handicap limiting the development of the individual's capacities, and that people's attitudes and prospects could be advanced by education. Provision for the education and training of foundlings, orphans, and the children of the very poor was incorporated into most of the new ordinances. In keeping with tradition, relief funds came mostly from private and church sources, freely given. But the main purpose was to protect the better-off elements—against crime, against disease (beggars and vagrants were thought to be the chief spreaders of plague), against revolution.

The Aumône Générale of Lyons, the most advanced in France and perhaps in all Europe, may serve to illustrate why the new poor relief came into being and how it functioned. Lyons was growing at a very rapid rate; the figures are not precise, but it had about 30,000 inhabi-

[21] F. R. Salter, ed., *Some Early Tracts on Poor Relief* (London, 1926), p. 8.

[22] N. Z. Davis, "Poor Relief, Humanism, and Heresy: The Case of Lyon," *Studies in Medieval and Renaissance History*, 5 (1968), 258. Spain was an exception; religious and other private foundations appear to have provided support for the poor throughout the sixteenth century and beyond. Writing of Valladolid, the historian Bartolomé Bennassar reports: "It is because the city is the abode of the rich that it is also the abode of the poor." At the end of the century, in 1597 a census of beggars in Valladolid was ordered, but merely to see that worthy ones were properly cared for. Bartolomé Bennassar, *Valladolid au siècle d'or: une ville de Castille et sa campagne au XVIe siècle* (Paris, 1967), pp. 435–37, 447–49.

tants in 1500, between 40,000 and 50,000 in the 1530s, and perhaps 65,000 in 1560. As a major center of trade and commerce, it attracted large numbers of poor peasants from the surrounding countryside and artisans from as far away as Flanders and Italy. There were many opportunities but not enough by far for all who came, and the resulting "urban crisis" was exacerbated during food shortages or when pestilence struck. The problem came to a head with a bloody uprising, the Grande Rebeine (riot) of 1529, during which mobs of destitute people pillaged the homes of the rich, broke into the municipal granary, and occupied the city hall in protest against the soaring price of bread. The Grande Rebeine caused profound concern in Lyons, and over the next few years the new system of poor relief was put into effect.

The Aumône Générale was managed by a board of eight unpaid rectors, who supervised a staff of money collectors, bakers, nurses, and police. Applicants for aid were visited in their homes. If found qualified, they received tickets (printed on parchment if their need was long term, on paper if presumed to be temporary) entitling them to weekly distributions of bread and money at assigned points in the city. Each ticket bore the name of the recipient, the amount of the weekly grant (twelve pounds of bread and one sou for an adult male), and the length of time for which it was valid. Orphans and the children of the indigent were housed in hospital asylums, where they were taught reading and writing and "all the other good habits that can and should be taught to young children," given some vocational training, and then apprenticed or placed in domestic service. The town authorities made great efforts to develop industries that could absorb these wards, the most important by far being the Lyons silk manufactory—Etienne Turquet, one of the founders of that industry, also played a major role in the establishment of the Aumône Générale. The money to run the program came from private contributions, from the clergy, which turned over foundations for alms to the rectors, from a royal subvention, from police fines, and, when necessary, from local taxation.

Begging of any kind was then forbidden—even lepers, whose special right to beg was everywhere traditional, were thenceforth restricted to their hospitals. Anyone found soliciting alms was to be arrested by the poor-relief police, called *chasse-coquins* (rascal hunters), and put to work at hard labor or thrown into jail. Guards were stationed at the entrances to the city to keep out vagrants, and innkeepers were ordered not to put up strangers for more than one night. These coercive powers were confirmed by letters patent from the king in 1560 as necessary to prevent "loafers and vagabonds" from "eating the bread of the poor and the sick." Legitimate poor travelers were entitled to one week's support, given in money, but to prevent outsiders from flocking into Lyons residence of from three to seven years was required before anyone could qualify for aid.[23]

What was distinctive about the Aumône Générale and the other municipal poor laws of the period was their effort to organize and centralize assistance and the fact that they were controlled by civil, not clerical authorities. Leviathan, as the English historian Christopher Hill has put it, was coming to replace the Good Samaritan.[24] The changes, however, were neither revolutionary, nor resisted by the church, nor much influenced by the contemporary ideological controversies growing out of the Protestant Reformation. Lay involvement in charitable administration long preceded the sixteenth century. In Italy, for example, fraternal groups called *Scuole* had been aiding the poor, operating hospitals and almshouses, and even providing casual employment for the needy since the fourteenth century. City authorities, not the clergy, supervised these organizations. Nuremberg, Frankfurt, Louvain, Poitiers and other towns had nonreligious and even publicly managed assistance organizations long before 1500, and begging was banned, or at least subject to regulation, in many towns in Flanders as early as the fourteenth century.

Although certain mendicant orders resisted both civil administration of relief and the idea that begging was not a basic human right, most of the Catholic clergy cooperated with the new approach; indeed, in 1587 Pope Sixtus V even banned begging in Rome. Probably local priests and bishops were relieved to be free of primary responsibility for care of the poor; distinguishing between the deserving and undeserving certainly caused them few qualms. On the other hand, the municipal authorities retained a sincere interest in the spiritual welfare of their charges. And, while it is true that Luther and Zwingli drafted two of the early municipal poor-relief ordinances, and along with other religious radicals of the period decried begging, saw work as a necessary punishment for original sin, and advocated state rather than clerical control of social policy, many leading Catholic thinkers of the time held similar views.[25] The first carefully worked out theoretical justification of state-run poor relief, *De Subventione Pauperum* (1526), was the work of Juan Luis Vives, a Spanish humanist, disciple of Erasmus, who, while a religious reformer, rejected Lutheranism and remained an

[23] Gutton, *Pauvres de Lyon*, pp. 229–30, 273–84; Davis, "Poor Relief," pp. 217–69.

[24] Christopher Hill, *Society & Puritanism in Pre-Revolutionary England* (New York, 1972), p. 270.

[25] Brian Pullan, *Rich and Poor in Renaissance Venice: The Social Institutions of a Catholic State, to 1620* (Cambridge, Mass., 1971), pp. 12, 44–45, 63–64, 76–77; Paul Bonenfant, "Les origines et la charactère de la réforme de la bienfaisance publique aux Pays-Bas sous le règne de Charles-Quint," *Revue Belge de Philologie et d'Histoire*, 6 (1927), 208–12; J. P. Gutton, *La société et les pauvres en Europe* (Paris, 1974), p. 119.

ardent Catholic.[26] When the mendicant friars of Ypres challenged the poor-relief system of that town, the magistrates submitted the dispute to the faculty of theology of the Sorbonne in Paris, and these learned Catholic authorities upheld the plan provided that its public relief provisions "be administered with . . . diligent care." "The system . . . is severe but valuable," their judgment ran. "It is healthy and pious, and not inconsistent either with the Gospel or with the example of the Apostles or of our forefathers."[27]

At the root of the system was not a change in moral attitudes or a new theory of government but the practical problem of unemployment. That poverty per se ceased to be considered a holy state did not mean that society had turned its back on the helpless, or that charity was no longer considered a virtue. The Sorbonne professors were at pains to insist that no one be allowed to suffer serious privation and that paying taxes to support public aid did not relieve the rich of their obligation to help anyone "submerged in extreme, or nearly extreme, destitution."[28] The number of poor people was increasing; hence, organized, centralized, more rationally financed poor aid was necessary. The deeply devout Pope Pius V, at his coronation in 1566, broke with the tradition of tossing coins to the crowd from the loggia of St. Peter's. Instead the money was distributed to the poor in an orderly fashion. Toward those of the poor who could not work (the old, the ill, orphans) and those who, working, could not support their families because they had too many children or because shortages had caused the price of bread to rise beyond their means, attitudes had not changed.

Sturdy beggars and vagabonds were the villains. The new laws were an attempt, the first of many, to separate these types from the unemployable and others that society considered deserving of public assistance. The problem was very real, for what one English chronicler with a penchant for alliteration called "lousey leuterars," another a "ragged rabblement of rakehelles" were on the move everywhere. Tales circulated of robbery and murder on the highways, and every town and city was plagued by hordes of beggars. Sturdy beggars scoffed at working people, boasting that they collected more in alms in a day than a laborer could earn in a year. If this was an absurd exaggeration, it nonetheless reflected reality: an English doctor, writing in 1555, recalled that when he had offered "for Goddes sake" to cure beggars with the marks of certain horrible diseases they refused his help, saying

[26] Salter, *Tracts*, pp. 1–31; Friedrich Kaufer, "Johannes Ludwig Vives (1492–1540)," *Historisches Jahrbuch* 15 (1894), 307–53.
[27] Salter, *Tracts*, p. 76.
[28] Gutton, *Pauvres de Lyon*, pp. 250–51.

that they preferred being sick and idle to being healthy and having "with great payne and labour" to earn a living. (Nearly four hundred years later, an American doctor reported an identical experience with a Chinese beggar in Chungking.)[29]

Beggars often feigned illnesses, for example, by eating some soap and then throwing themselves on the ground in convulsions, as though epileptic. A French doctor reported a beggar who had cleverly attached to his person the rotting arm of a dead man in order to attract sympathy. Sir Thomas More complained of "sturdy and valiaunte beggers, clokinge their idle lyfe under the colours of some disease or sickness." In Rome, Pope Sixtus V denounced beggars "who simulate illness or feign poverty that is caused only by their laziness and spinelessness," and a beggar named Pompeo confessed to the police that his evil confrères—they were "worse than Lutherans" he admitted—were organized into nineteen secret societies, each specializing in a particular trick—*gonsi,* who act like gibbering idiots; *sbasiti,* who fake illnesses; *barons,* who claim to be honest tradesmen who have lost their jobs, and so on.[30] Other beggars actually mutilated or otherwise injured themselves to appear more pitiable to potential almsgivers. Methods of causing skin diseases became so common that a name, "the leg of God," was invented to describe the condition. A number of books were written about the many devices used by professional beggars to increase their appeal; Martin Luther's *Liber Vagatorum* (1528) is a notable example of this genre.

It is impossible to discover whether a greater percentage of the wandering poor and urban beggars were loafers, thieves, and mountebanks than had been the case in the Middle Ages, but that the number of beggars and vagrants was larger is incontestable. This fact explains the growing public alarm and the brutal treatment afforded them: whipping, the stocks, labor on chain gangs, branding and mutilation, even in countries like England where begging was legal until 1536. (An act of Henry VIII in 1531 required justices of the peace to issue begging licenses to aged and other deserving paupers in their districts and provided that unlicensed persons caught seeking alms be tied naked to a cart and whipped through town till bloody.)

[29] Ribton-Turner, *Vagabonds and Beggars,* p. 71; W. K. Jordan, *Philanthropy in England, 1480–1660: A Study of the Changing Patterns of English Social Aspirations* (New York, 1959), p. 79; Gideon Sjoberg, *The Preindustrial City* (New York, 1965), p. 204.

[30] Gutton, *Pauvres de Lyon,* pp. 242–43; Jean Delumeau, *Vie économique et sociale de Rome dans le second moitié du XVIe siècle* (Paris, 1957), pp. 404–407. In 1627 an Italian monk published a description of thirty-three types of false beggars, including such specialists as *Allacrimati,* who were able to burst into tears at will; *Attarantati,* who pretended to have gone mad as a result of a tarantula bite; and *Affarinati,* who begged for flour supposedly to be made into communion wafers. Ribton-Turner, *Vagabonds and Beggars,* pp. 577–80.

Why so many able-bodied men and women lived in this way, however, was rarely understood. The medieval assumption that work was available for all who would labor was not challenged. In the influential *De Subventione Pauperum*, Vives defended vocational training for the unskilled with the argument: "Workshops will not be lacking in which all these people can be employed." Vives also thought that blind people could find profitable employment with a little help. "Laziness and listlessness are the causes of their declaring themselves unable to do anything." Even in Utopia, though hours were short, everyone worked, for as Sir Thomas put it, "busie labors and good exercises" were the "key to felicity."

Being based upon such an attitude, the new public-assistance techniques, rational and humane as far as they went, left a large gap in their classification of the population. By taking responsibility for those who could not care for themselves under any circumstances and giving help to "respectable" folk temporarily in need, the magistrates assumed that no one would any longer need to beg. Therefore, anyone who did was a shirker or worse. Idleness was evil (and as contagious as the plague). Even one of the most enlightened and appealing reformers of the period, the Venetian Girolamo Miani, who devoted himself to the care and training of that city's orphans, fulminated against "inert and slothful mendacity" and invested as much effort in inculcating disciplined work habits in his wards as in seeing to their material needs.

One way to discourage idlers was to make them work. In Paris, any healthy poor person who was not employed (those, according to one document of the period, who were bad workers, lazy, or "somewhat feeble") were ordered to labor at "reasonable and moderate" wages on town projects, such as repairing walls and fortifications. If they refused they were whipped or imprisoned; "incorrigibles" ended up chained to oars aboard galleys. In Venice, beggars were made to serve on merchant ships at half pay and drafted as oarsmen in the city's navy.[31]

Optimists expected that forced labor would cause professional loafers and wastrels to repent and reform their ways. Less sanguine people hoped that the harsh treatment afforded these types would discourage others from straying from the path of righteous living. But the chief purpose of these "public works projects" was to rid the community of public nuisances.

The vocational training given pauper children was more constructive in purpose, as were such other modest efforts as that of Strassburg,

[31] Salter, *Tracts*, p. 13; More, *Utopia*, pp. 15, 57; Pullan, *Renaissance Venice*, pp. 252–53, 259–61; Ernest Coyecque, "L'assistance publique à Paris," *Bulletin de la Société de l'Histoire de Paris et de l'Ile de France*, 15 (1888), 114–18.

where poor women were given wool and flax by the town to spin into cloth, and the aforementioned silk manufactory of Lyons. But even the apprenticing of poor children often ran into stiff opposition from the guilds, and in any case it did not reflect a real attempt to create jobs. To most sixteenth-century authorities, what an English writer called "that loathsome monster idleness" was the cause, not the result, of poverty. The unemployed were, as another Englishman wrote, "unprofitable persons"; they contributed nothing to society and their failure was assumed to be willful.[32] Thus the English Statute of Artificers of 1563, a codification of earlier legislation, began with the principle that everyone had an obligation to work, the assumption being that work for all was available.

This statute also contained elaborate restrictions on the entry of apprentices into the crafts and other provisions aimed at checking the flow of rural labor to the towns, implicit, if not necessarily recognized, indications that there were not enough jobs to go round in urban centers. The universal stress in all communities on keeping out vagrants and providing help only for local residents is a further reflection of this reality. That it was a reality seldom seen from this perspective helps explain why the legislation of the sixteenth century failed to achieve its objectives.

[32] Koch, *Wohlfahrtspflege*, p. 37; Pullan, *Renaissance Venice*, pp. 305–307; E. F. Heckscher, *Mercantilism* (London, 1955), II: 154; I: 227–28.

3

The Struggle
for Full Employment

Working people were becoming steadily poorer and unemployment—idleness, begging, vagabondage in the language of the times—was as widespread as ever. The persistence of these problems seemed baffling. The sixteenth century marked the culmination of the great age of discovery, the century of Columbus (who made his last voyage to the New World in 1502–1504), of Balboa and Magellan, of Cortez and Pizarro, of Verrazano, de Soto, Cartier, Drake, Frobisher, and Sir Humphrey Gilbert, the beginning of the spread of European influence across four continents. What this expansion would mean in new wealth and new opportunities was imperfectly understood at the time, but it stimulated the imaginations and released the energies of thoughtful people across all western Europe. (Utopia means "nowhere" but More placed his ideal community on an island in the New World.)

Very early in the century it was clear that the expansion was bringing enormous new resources into Europe. First came the slaves and gold of Africa, then the spices and other riches of the Orient, then the gold and silver of Mexico and Peru, then fish, sugar, tobacco, lumber, and other agricultural products from the North American colonies. As colonies were founded the New World became a market too, increasing the demand for European goods and for the labor needed to produce them. Each European peasant or artisan who migrated to the Americas left behind a job for someone else; every beggar or vagabond who made the journey, freely or under compulsion, reduced by one the number of Europe's unemployed. The international trade that developed also increased employment by providing work for sailors and stevedores, for shipwrights, sailmakers, and other craftsmen, for clerks and accountants and customs collectors. And the stimulus of overseas expansion was only a small part of the picture—the economic growth that had begun in the fifteenth century continued with only minor setbacks through the sixteenth.

More wealth yet more destitution, progress and poverty—how could such things be? The trouble was that the great social and economic forces that had made the poor-relief system necessary had not ceased to function, and indeed they increased steadily in strength and complexity. Warfare, rising now from religious as well as political and economic conflicts and fought with ever-larger armies, raged almost incessantly, devastating broad regions and disrupting the activities of peasants and townspeople. The trend toward capitalist control of manufacturing also continued, with its consequent unsettling effects on the labor force: low wages, lack of opportunity to rise, and rapid fluctuations in the level of output, leading to unemployment. Inflation made the situation still worse; prices rose astronomically, pushed up by the flow of precious metals from America but also by the pressure of an expanding population on agricultural prices, by the devaluations decreed by debt-ridden monarchs, and by the debasing of the coins of copper and other metals used by the common people. Wages, as is nearly always the case at such times, rose much more slowly.

Even the overseas discoveries caused damaging side effects. Setting apart as not germane to our subject the ruinous impact of the European invasion on the people of the conquered lands, the opening of the whole world to Europe meant additional reasons for making war; more epidemics and plagues, and a new scourge, syphilis, which was a far more virulent disease in the sixteenth century than today. Colonization also led to the further development of capitalist methods of doing business and to greater dependence of each craft and of whole communities on uncontrollable and unpredictable economic forces in distant lands.

But the most important reason for the persistence of unemployment was probably the very one that had triggered economic revival in the fifteenth century: the growth of the population. By 1600 there were between 60 and 70 million people in Europe, roughly double the number a hundred years earlier. A "biological revolution" had taken place, more significant in its immediate effects than the discovery of America or the rise and fall of empires. "This increase," the historian Fernand Braudel writes, "lay behind all the triumphs and catastrophes of a century during which man was first a useful worker and then, as the century wore on, a growing burden." The situation was especially serious in the cities, for people were flocking to them constantly— Corsicans into Marseilles for example, Moors ejected from Granada into Valladolid, rural people from the Midlands and the southeastern counties into London, nearby villagers into Venice.[1]

Even before it became obvious that the municipal welfare systems were not stamping out begging and vagrancy, royal authorities had put their weight behind the effort. As early as 1531 Charles V issued an edict banning begging throughout the Hapsburg empire and ordering towns to establish relief funds on the model of the Flanders cities, and in 1540, in his capacity as king of Spain, he obtained a law authorizing local officials to compel beggars and vagrants to work without pay.[2] The French king François I issued a similar order in 1536, and around the middle of the century his successor, Henri II, enacted harsh punishments for begging and vagabondage. In England, without waiting for municipal ordinances, the central government attempted to deal with the problem with the laws against beggars of the 1530s, and by ordering local officials, beginning in the 1570s, to tax residents for the support of their poor. Little was accomplished, however, until the end of the century, when, with the famous Elizabethan poor law of 1601, a system of parish relief financed by local taxation (the poor rate), was finally made effective.

The trend, clearest in England, toward substituting taxation for voluntary giving reflects the seriousness of the effort to make the systems work, and considering the resources available they succeeded quite well in caring for those whom no one expected to perform useful labor. But the Elizabethan poor law also sought to put the able-bodied unemployed to work, principally by supplying them with a "stock" of raw material, such as wool, which they could turn into goods for sale. In theory the fund of capital raised by the community to purchase the stock would be self-replenishing; in practice it tended to shrink because of the inefficiency of the workers and the inadequate supervision provided by local administrators. The system did, however, keep many idle people alive and occupied, and whatever they produced at least lessened the burden on the community of supporting them.[3]

Both population growth and the rate of economic expansion leveled off early in the seventeenth century, but thereafter times were hard. As in earlier periods, bad harvests caused much direct suffering and compelled many agricultural workers to abandon the land. These people

[1] Fernand Braudel, *The Mediterranean and the Mediterranean World in the Age of Philip II* (New York, 1972), pp. 430–37, 521–25.

[2] Religious resistance to cracking down on beggars was, however, so strong in Spain that the law of 1540 could not be enforced. The mendicant orders insisted that begging was a basic human right and local support of their position made the law "virtually a dead letter." J. H. Elliott, *Imperial Spain: 1469–1716* (New York, 1977), p. 187.

[3] Sidney and Beatrice Webb, *The Old Poor Law* (London, 1927), pp. 32–67; J. P. Gutton, *La société et les pauvres: l'exemple de la généralité de Lyon, 1534–1789* (Paris, 1971), p. 253; Emanuel Chill, "Religion and Mendacity in Seventeenth-Century France," *International Review of Social History* 7 (1962), 402n.

straggled into the towns, but they could seldom find enough work to support themselves. In the worst years, soaring food prices triggered massive urban unemployment that spread the suffering still further. The historian Pierre Goubert has calculated, for example, that in the region of Beauvais northwest of Paris, there were thirteen years between 1609 and 1725 when crop failures caused the price of bread to double, five others when the price tripled, three when it rose to four times its normal level. In such years the textile workers of Beauvais could not feed their families adequately. But they were also thrown out of work and reduced to destitution because the ordinary people of Paris, where most of the cloth made in Beauvais was sold, were so impoverished by the soaring cost of bread that they could afford nothing else. Paris cloth merchants stopped buying; manufacturers in Beauvais laid off their weavers. A chain reaction followed swiftly. "If the food crises became sharp and prolonged," Goubert writes, "nearly all the crafts shut down, nearly all the workers were unemployed." An English historian, A. L. Beier, makes the same point about the "classic" form taken by economic crises in the seventeenth century. Harvest failures led to high food prices and thus to "the fall in effective demand for consumer goods such as textiles," the textile workers becoming "increasingly unemployed as depression became general."[4]

Man-made disasters caused even more dreadful problems. In Central Europe the horrors of the Thirty Years' War produced poverty beyond the resources of the municipal relief systems and destroyed much of the social-mindedness that had played a large part in their creation. Soon tens of thousands of starving displaced persons were following the armies, and when the fighting ended, jobless ex-soldiers joined these hordes aimlessly roaming the countryside. Landless Polish peasants called *ludzie luzni* drifted in unrecorded numbers in and out of the towns in search of work. In England, with the demobilization following the Civil War in 1656, "the whole country—and the Metropolis in particular—swarmed once more with beggars and vagrants," an estimated eighty thousand "wandering up and down the land." In 1655 the town clerk of London issued a proclamation denouncing the "vermine" (defined as rogues, vagabonds, and beggars) who "swarme in and about this City" pestering the inhabitants with their "clamorous begging at the doores of Churches and private Houses, and in the Streets." A diarist in Florence noted in 1650 that the local textile industry had come to a standstill and that beggars "naked and covered

[4] Pierre Goubert, *Cent mille provinciaux au XVIIe siècle: Beauvais et le Beauvaisis de 1600 à 1720* (Paris, 1968), pp. 340–42; A. L. Beier, "Poor Relief in Warwickshire: 1630–1660," *Past & Present*, 35 (1966), 86.

with sores" were so desperate that they were importuning worshipers in the churches even during the mass.[5]

Amidst the so-called Golden Age of Philip II, Spanish beggars and vagrants had crowded the roads and practically taken over certain quarters in the cities—the Puerto del Sol in Madrid, the Slaughterhouse district in Seville—and in the seventeenth century conditions were probably worse. The municipal authorities of Paris had become so alarmed by the hordes of vagrants in the city that they petitioned the Estates General in 1614 to authorize the hanging of second offenders. But in 1642 Paris was still swarming with what one observer called an "infinity of beggars." At the other end of Europe, Istanbul was jammed with a large floating population "attracted by the mirage of Constantinople"—peasants, gypsies, people from all over eastern Europe and the Near East, who "sought to attach themselves to some powerful person or grand bourgeois who would support them without demanding too much effort."[6]

The bad times made caring even for the most blameless poor more difficult; as for any idle person who seemed capable of work, the general response was brutal. Paradoxically, with jobs becoming scarcer, not having one became a more heinous offense. An English law of 1603 extending the late-Elizabethan acts against vagrancy provided for branding "incorrigible" rogues on the shoulder with a large "R" and executing offenders already branded without benefit of clergy.[7] At the same time, in an action reflecting monumental frustration, the Privy Council called for banishing such types to Newfoundland, the Indies (East or West), or to France, Germany, Spain, or the Low Countries, all, of course, places where they would never be accepted.

The establishment of English settlements in America made expulsion more practicable and it was soon attempted. In 1618 James I ordered the colonization in Virginia of "divers idle young people . . . havinge noe ymploymte," an early example of a long-continued if

---

[5] Lotte Koch, *Wandlungen der Wohlfahrtspflege im Zeitalter der Aufklärung* (Erlangen, 1933), pp. 43–51; Andrzej Kamiński, "Neo-Serfdom in Poland-Lithuania," *Slavic Review*, 34 (1975), 266; Webb, *Old Poor Law*, p. 96; Beier, "Warwickshire," pp. 91–92; C. J. Ribton-Turner, *A History of Vagabonds and Vagrancy and Beggars and Begging* (London, 1887), p. 160; Braudel, *Mediterranean World*, p. 735.

[6] Braudel, *Mediterranean World*, p. 740; Gutton, *Pauvres de Lyon*, p. 311, C. W. Cole, *Colbert and a Century of French Mercantilism* (New York, 1939), I: 263; Robert Mantran, *Istanbul dans la seconde moitié du XVIIe siècle: essai d'histoire institutionelle et sociale* (Paris, 1962), pp. 165–66.

[7] Branding such people was not, however, a new development. An English law of 1360 amended the Statute of Labourers to provide that runaway "Labourers and Artificers" were to be branded on the forehead with an "F" for falsity, and in the 1580s a law called for branding a "V" on the chests of vagrants. Ribton-Turner, *Vagabonds and Beggars*, pp. 50–51; F. M. Eden, *The State of the Poor* (London, 1928), p. 11.

sporadic English policy. The logic seemed irrefutable. "If we should imagine we have in England employment but for one hundred People," wrote Sir Josiah Child, an important early economist, "and we have born and bred amongst us one hundred and fifty People; I say the fifty must away from us, or starve; or be hanged to prevent it." A clergyman, Richard Eburne, was more specific. If every year two persons from each parish in England were forced to emigrate to the colonies, the land would be rid of 16,000 vagrants, petty criminals, pauper children, and other "superfluous" types, he wrote in *A Plaine Path-way to Plantations* (1624). French writers had made the same argument as early as the 1580s, when the Seigneur de La Popellinière claimed that France could expel a fifth of the entire population "without any inconvenience," and in the early 1600s numerous proposals were advanced for sending sturdy beggars, idlers, and "all bad actors" (*toutes les mauvaises humeurs*) to Canada.[8]

Some unemployed men and a larger number of women, who were more welcome in the predominantly male colonial societies, were sent to the French colonies, but there were formidable pressures militating against forced migration, in France and in other nations with overseas posessions. While it was easy to lose patience with dissolute and criminal types and to envisage packing them all off to some distant howling wilderness, most seventeenth-century analysts who gave serious thought to the problem took the position that the way to deal with unemployment was to put people to work right at home. By putting people to work, however, a sensible and humane concept from the modern point of view, they did not mean what the phrase came to mean three hundred years later.

They began with two uncontested facts of seventeenth-century life: the population had increased and prices had risen. The former caused the latter, they believed, because it had led to shortages of food and other necessaries. The objective, therefore, must be to increase production, and the obvious way to do this was for more people to work harder. They saw—with perfect accuracy in that pre-machine-age society—that labor was the most important element in production, and this insight led them to the conclusion that there could be no such thing as too many people. The more people the more work, the more work the more output, the more output the more wealth—such was their reasoning. Where labor was concerned they had no conception of the law of diminishing returns.

This attitude was almost universal among writers on economics in

[8] Ribton-Turner, *Vagabonds and Beggars*, pp. 133, 143; W. K. Jordan, *Philanthropy in England, 1480–1660* (New York, 1959), pp. 71–72; E. F. Heckscher, *Mercantilism* (London, 1955), II: 158; Gutton, *Pauvres de Lyon*, pp. 289–91.

the seventeenth century, and for the first time large numbers of men were putting their minds to the subject, an indication of the seriousness of conditions all over Europe. Both positive and negative pressures were affecting their thinking and that of many other intellectuals, merchants, and statesmen. Confronting mind-expanding opportunities and mind-boggling social problems, they began to break free from medieval, feudal perspectives. The possibilities for acquiring wealth and power seemed enormous, if only human energies could be properly marshaled and focused. The one agency that could accomplish this organizational task was the state, which they conceived of in something approaching modern terms—a secular, geographically concentrated administrative unit charged with setting national goals and devising policies for achieving them.

This point of view highlighted the importance of labor. "Laborers are the feet of the state, for they sustain and carry all the weight of the body. . . . They enable the nobility to exist and cities to be nourished." So wrote the French hardware manufacturer Antoine de Montchrétien, inventor of the term "political economy," in 1616. Around 1630, in *England's Treasure by Forraign Trade*, Thomas Mun, a wealthy merchant, one of the directors of the East India Company, praised "the multitude, in whom doth consist the greatest strength and riches both of King and Kingdom." "Where the people are many, and the arts [manufactures] good, there the traffique must be great, and the Countrey rich."[9] The leading German economic writer of the period, Johann Joachim Becher, defined a nation as a "populous productive community" *(volckreiche nahrhaffte Gemein)*, adding, "the more populous a nation is, the more powerful it is." Numerous other German commentators took the same position, recommending tax relief for heads of families and the encouragement of immigration, as well as measures making life difficult for confirmed bachelors. Even Sir Josiah Child, although he argued for sending the unemployed to the colonies, accepted the importance of a large population—"the Riches . . . of a Nation [consists of] the multitude of Inhabitants"—and some writers even favored importing foreign workers as a way to add to a country's wealth.[10]

Since labor seemed so central to prosperity, unemployment was not a personal tragedy but a national one. This view reinforced the already

[9] Antoine de Montchrétien, *Traicté de l'oeconomie politique* (Paris, 1889), p. 43; Thomas Mun, *England's Treasure by Forraign Trade* (New York, 1895), p. 17. On the meaning of the word "art" in the economic writing of this period see E. A. J. Johnson, *Predecessors of Adam Smith: The Growth of British Economic Thought* (New York, 1937), pp. 259–67.

[10] Hermann Hassinger, *Johann Joachim Becher, 1635–1682: Ein Beitrag zur Geschichte des Merkantilismus* (Vienna, 1951), p. 72: Erich Frohenberg, *Bevölkerungslehre und Bevölkerungspolitik des Merkantilismus* (Gelnhausen, 1930), p. 19; Heckscher, *Mercantilism*, II: 158–61.

prevalent moral criticism of idleness with an economic argument. Beggars and vagrants were antisocial, and not merely because they lived, like drones, off the labor of workers. By failing to produce, they reduced the potential wealth of the community and "suck[ed] the Breasts of Industry." As Mun put it, were it not for "lewd" idleness, "maintenance might be much encreased, to the further wealth and strength of these Kingdomes . . . for our own safety, and terrour of our enemies." A French writer was able to list thirty-nine separate vices directly traceable, he said, to idleness.[11]

Given this attitude, the way to deal with the unemployed was to compel them to labor by, as it were, putting the work in their hands. Sir William Petty, one of the most versatile persons of the century, professor of both anatomy and music at Oxford, naval officer, member of Parliament, surveyor, and pioneer statistician, as well as a writer on economic subjects, went so far as to suggest in his *Treatise of Taxes & Contributions* (1662) that criminals be enslaved rather than thrown in jail or executed: "Being slaves, they may be forced to as much labour, and as cheap fare, as nature will endure, and thereby become as two men added to the Commonwealth, and not as one taken away from it." Writing in 1697, the philosopher John Locke advanced a similar argument. Able-bodied beggars should be drafted into the navy or sentenced to labor in houses of correction, there to work for the warden as if they were his slaves. Colonization was another possibility; Locke, it will be remembered, drafted the frame of government for the colony of Carolina.

As for those who claimed to be unable to find jobs, their bluff should be called. Local officials should advertise their availability, selling their services at wages below the going rate. ("He that cannot be set on work for twelvepence per diem," Locke wrote, "must be content with ninepence or tenpence rather than live idly.") Poor women who had children to take care of ought also to be employed "in the broken intervals of their time." Children of the poor between the ages of three and fourteen need not be a total drain on national resources either. If they were sent to "working schools" their mothers would "be at the more liberty to work," and the children not only better cared for—they would get "their belly-full of bread daily at school"—but also "inured" to labor at an impressionable age and at least partially self-supporting.[12]

[11] Heckscher, *Mercantilism,* II: 154; Mun, *England's Treasure,* p. 99; Gutton, *Pauvres de Lyon,* pp. 315–16.

[12] Johnson, *Predecessors of Adam Smith* pp. 93–97; Heckscher, *Mercantilism,* II: 297; Peter Gay, ed., *The Enlightenment: A Comprehensive Anthology* (New York, 1973), pp. 100–107; Webb, *Old Poor Law,* pp. 110–12.

It has often been said that in expressing such views the early writers on economics were merely ventilating their preconceptions and seeking their own advantage and that of their class. Nearly all of them were businessmen or merchants or government officials, people to whom such phrases as "laborers are the feet of the state" and "as much labour, and as cheap fare, as nature will endure" came naturally. They also took the position that the way to increase the efficiency of labor (and not merely that of criminals, as in Petty's argument) was to *lower* wages so that workers would have to work longer and harder to earn a bare subsistence. They thought that children should be put to work almost as soon as they could walk, that the number of holidays in the year should be sharply reduced, and they attacked poor relief as an incentive to idleness and a waste of public resources. They even believed that unemployment tended to *raise* wage rates. The "mischief" of high wages, one commentator claimed, "is occasioned by reason of the idleness of so vast a number of people . . . so that those who are industrious and will work make men pay what they please for their wages: but set the poor at work and then these men will be forced to lower their rates."[13]

But many of them, Mun and Petty among others, also criticized the idle rich and their wasteful and luxurious habits. Mun, for example, compared what he called the "general leprosie" of his countrymen— their supposedly excessive fondness for "sucking smoak, and drinking healths," and other "monstrous Fashions"—with the restraint of the "industrious Dutch," who, he claimed, had mastered these "swinish" vices. Of course many of the English writers (and they were the most numerous and in general the most thoughtful of the seventeenth-century economists) were influenced by Puritan ideas and values. This may explain their attacks on idleness and extravagant living as well as their obsession with making everyone work. Max Weber's now-classic argument that the Protestant Revolution, particularly the ideas of John Calvin and the English Puritans, which stressed the moral importance of work, thrift, diligence, and the calculating pursuit of wealth through one's "calling," created "the spirit of capitalism," is relevant in this connection.

Certainly the Puritan idea that, since most human beings were damned to roast in Hell throughout eternity, the "elect" minority fated to escape this grim future should rule them on this earth, provided a religious justification for disciplining both workers and the unemployed identical in effect with the reasoning of the economists. Both the tough-minded William Petty and Thomas Firmin, an English phi-

[13] T. E. Gregory, "The Economics of Employment in England, 1660–1713," *Economica*, 1 (1921), 44.

lanthropist who devoted his life and much of his fortune to providing jobs for the unemployed, believed that making people work was socially important beyond the material results of the labor. "It is better to lose something in a way that will make our poor people better and skilful, than to suffer them to live in idleness," Firmin wrote. Petty agreed: "Better to burn a thousand men's labours for a time, than to let those thousand men by non-employment lose their faculty of labouring." Even building "a useless pyramid upon Salisbury Plain," or hauling the "stones of Stonehenge to Tower Hill" would be preferable to allowing the unemployed to remain idle.[14]

The spirit of capitalism, however, was no stranger to Catholic societies or to Catholic writers on economic subjects, whose views are indistinguishable from those of their Puritan confrères. "Wealth in work" was the key to happiness, wrote Montchrétien. Furthermore, Puritan economists did not hesitate to denigrate "unproductive" callings, ranging from medicine and law down to shopkeeping and pawnbroking, and even, in some cases, the ministry. Sir William Petty argued for religious uniformity on economic grounds—the proliferation of sects was drawing too many men into the clergy who might otherwise be engaged in "productive" labor, and in France, Louis XIV's great minister of finance, Colbert, took a dim view of monks because of what he considered their "idle" habits.[15]

The economists may have had but limited vision and their viewpoint was surely not very humane, but they were not—certainly not consciously—apologists for the manufacturers, merchants, and farmers whom they regarded as the chief producers of wealth. Their attitude toward laboring people was in part an expression of class feelings, but feelings shared by most educated people of means at the time. And the policies they advocated for dealing with unemployment were logical extensions of those developed in the late Middle Ages and in the sixteenth century. The cold-blooded tone of their writings on these subjects resulted from the nature of what they were attempting to do: describe objectively the working of the entire economy, extract from the myriad activities of millions of people the principles that governed these activities, an extremely difficult task in which they were pioneers.

The question remains, how could so many intelligent and well-informed observers, however primitive their understanding of the complexities of economic relationships, believe that most unemployed

[14] Mun, *England's Treasure*, pp. 98–99; Max Weber, *The Protestant Ethic and the Spirit of Capitalism* (New York, 1930), *passim;* Christopher Hill, "Puritans and the Poor," *Past & Present*, 2 (1952), 38–42; Eden, *The State of the Poor*, p. 34; E. Strauss, *Sir William Petty* (Glencoe, Ill., 1954), pp. 220–21.

[15] Montchrétien, *Traicté*, p. 99; Johnson, *Predecessors of Adam Smith*, pp. 244–45, Pierre Deyon, *Le mercantilisme* (Paris, 1969), p. 24.

people were malingerers? They reasoned approximately as follows: Poverty was endemic all over Europe; even by the standards of the day those who tried to investigate the subject estimated that about a quarter of the population existed in direst need. To reduce poverty, more goods must be produced. The resources existed, but it would take much labor to develop them. If labor was in such great demand, those who were not working must be lazy loafers; their behavior was a crime against society and they ought to be driven to labor like criminals. "One should say to them, 'if you want your lunch, *mes enfants,* do such and such,' " wrote the French economist Du Noyer de Saint-Martin in 1614. "In this way you will make honest people of them by force."[16]

This explanation of unemployment was based on deductive reasoning, a most dubious method for analyzing human behavior. But the belief that the unemployed were lacking in industriousness was not without foundation. Where the analysts went wrong was in attributing the distaste for labor to defects of character. In part they were confusing cause and effect; as many studies have shown, prolonged unemployment does tend to make people "lazy," both by undermining their self-confidence and through its effects on diet—undernourished people have little energy. More importantly, the analysts were failing to take into account the character of the society in which they lived—a not uncommon error. They were deeply impressed with the need to increase production, but laborers were not. As a twentieth-century economist might put it, the "disutility" of work loomed large in the ordinary, low-paid worker's view of the world.

In the seventeenth century and probably since the beginning of time, workers were accustomed to hard labor but also to enjoying periods of idleness. To begin with, there were fifty or sixty religious holidays in the year in addition to the traditional weekly day of rest. Then too the economy was still predominantly agricultural and farmers have relatively little to do in winter. Industrial activity was less restricted by climate, but the habit of steady labor did not become ingrained easily, especially when wars, plagues, and fluctuations in business conditions so frequently interrupted work. For independent craftsmen no sharp line separated work time from leisure time, which helps explain why such people tended to feel that they were losing their freedom when they were compelled to work for wages, and also why wage workers tended to adopt the values and attitudes of independent craftsmen. Moreover, in societies where the lower orders knew their place, and where life was both hard and uncertain, what Alexander Gerschenkron has called the "time horizons" of most ordinary

16 Gutton, *Pauvres de Lyon,* pp. 313–14.

people were low. Craftsmen needed relatively little capital and the time needed to produce most goods was quite short. They had little or no incentive to make long-term investments or to plan very far ahead; they tended, rather, to live from day to day without extravagant hopes. The incentive to work steadily was therefore also small, especially, as during the seventeenth century, when times were bad. "Monday is Sundayes brother," runs a seventeenth-century rhyme. "Tuesday is such another." When the economists (whose own time horizons were by the nature of their interests higher) argued that an increase in wages would encourage idleness, they based their conclusion on much direct observation.[17]

"When the framework knitters or makers of silk stockings had a great price for their work," wrote an English scientist in 1681, "they have been observed seldom to work on Mondays and Tuesdays. . . . The weavers, 't is common with them to be drunk on Monday, have their head-ache on Tuesday, and their tools out of order on Wednesday." This may have been something of an exaggeration, but an exaggeration of a reality. As the eighteenth-century writer Arthur Young put it, "Every one but an idiot knows that the lower classes must be kept poor or they will never be industrious." Mun, Petty, Child, and many other commentators made essentially the same point. "Their unanimity," wrote the historian Edgar S. Furniss after a careful study of the literature, "would indicate that there was a marked tendency among wage-earners to negative all attempts to stimulate an increase of industry through an advancing wage scale."[18]

As a practical matter it was therefore hard for anyone interested in economic expansion to avoid the conclusion that the way to make people work harder was to lower their wages. In the language of modern economics, the seventeenth-century writers saw labor as a factor of production but almost ignored it as a factor of consumption. They were assuming an inelastic demand for goods; increasing the opportunity to earn would not increase the worker's desire to consume. The idea may seem to fly in the face of human nature, but it need not. In a society in which all but a handful were accustomed to spending everything they earned on essentials, "consumerism" was unimaginable. In eighteenth-century France, the typical wage earner spent half his income on bread and about 90 percent on food, clothing, and

[17] Emile Coornaert, *Les corporations en France avant 1789* (Paris, 1968), p. 250; E. P. Thompson, "Time, Work-Discipline, and Industrial Capitalism," *Past & Present*, 38 (1967), 38–72; Alexander Gerschenkron, "Time Horizons in Russian Literature," *Slavic Review*, 34 (1975), 692–95; Keith Thomas, "Work and Leisure in Pre-Industrial Society," *Past & Present*, 29 (1964), 58.

[18] E. S. Furniss, *The Position of the Laborer in a System of Nationalism: A Study in the Labor Theories of the Later English Mercantilists* (Boston, 1920), p. 121.

fuel. In famine years, when food prices soared, bread absorbed as much as 88 percent of a worker's income.[19]

The early writers disagreed about many things, and there were substantial national differences among them. Those from maritime powers like England and France put great emphasis on increasing exports. Those from the landlocked German principalities were more concerned as one of them put it, "to get along with their domestic products . . . except where great need leaves no alternative."[20] They were also interested in questions other than making people work. All, for example, were intensely nationalistic, and obsessed with the importance of precious metals—the criticism of luxury was motivated partly by the desire to cut down on the use of gold in the manufacture of cloth and for gilding, since in such forms the metal wore out and was lost.

But while they sometimes appeared primarily interested in prestige and power, their ultimate objective was economic expansion. Given the state of European technology, expansion required increasing the size and efficiency of the labor force. The English stress on exporting, the German on keeping foreign products out were both meant to foster labor-intensive manufacturing and thus to increase employment. In France, Barthélemy de Laffemas, Controller General of Commerce under Henri IV, sought, beginning in the 1590s, to develop silkworm culture for the silk industry, and to encourage the making of linen and other products. He proposed founding special villages on the edges of cities, where the unemployed could be put to work at simple manufacturing tasks. "By this means," he explained, "the poor will be made to work, for if we do not give them something to do they will do nothing." Montchrétien made the same point, and a few decades later Colbert wrote: "It is certain that by manufacturing, a million people languishing in sloth will be able to earn their own living." In the 1660s and 1670s Johann Joachim Becher called for founding state manufacturing companies and the establishment of commercial colleges in the industrially backward German states, and in his widely read *Oesterreich über Alles,* published in 1684, Philipp Wilhelm von Hornick wrote: "All commodities . . . which cannot be used in their natural state, should be worked up within the country; since the payment for *manufacturing* generally exceeds the value of the raw material by two, three, ten, twenty, and even a hundred fold, and the neglect of this is an abomination to prudent managers." English writ-

[19] Gregory, "Economics of Employment," 40; D. C. Coleman, "Labour in the English Economy of the Seventeenth Century," *English History Review,* 5 (1952), 287–88; George Rudé, *Paris and London in the Eighteenth Century: Studies in Popular Protest* (New York, 1971), p. 165.

[20] A. I. Monroe, ed., *Early Economic Thought* (Cambridge, Mass., 1951), p. 224.

ers were also virtually unanimous in favoring the development of manufactures in order to occupy the idle, none stating the case more categorically than Thomas Manly, who wrote in 1677: "A pound of wool manufactured and exported is worth more to us by employing our people than ten pounds exported raw at double the present rate."[21]

It had, however, proved impractical to provide such work for idle people on a piecemeal basis. Out of 447 persons who became public charges in Warwickshire in England between 1649 and 1660, the justices of the peace were only able to keep four productively occupied by supplying them with the "stock" authorized by the poor law of 1601.[22] Some way of organizing the work was necessary, and recognition of this fact in the western European countries where manufacturing was important resulted in the development of a new institution, the workhouse. A workhouse was a place where the jobless were housed and maintained and where they were employed at various tasks. The idea evolved out of earlier systems for controlling beggars and vagrants on the one hand, and orphans, the aged, and the feeble on the other, that is, from prisons, and hospitals or asylums. These prototypes had usually extracted a certain amount of labor from inmates, as modern prisons still do. The notorious Bridewell prison of London was founded in 1555 partly to put "idle and lewd people to work" and partly "for the lodging and harbouring of the poor, sick and weak, and sore people of the city." In Venice the Mendicanti, a "hospital" for beggars established in 1600, functioned as a place of work and also as "a kind of paternalistic employment agency" where unemployed paupers were housed while the authorities tried to find them jobs.[23]

The first true workhouse was apparently that opened in Amsterdam in 1596. Its founders conceived of this institution as a prison for minor offenders and they advanced the novel idea that its purpose should be to reform rather than to punish. (They called it a *tuchthuis,* or house of correction, and planned to teach weaving and a variety of other trades to the inmates.) Before very long, however, so many were employed at grinding up dyewoods with heavy rasps, a particularly arduous labor that was supposed to be good training for idlers, that the institution became known as the *Rasphuis.* Under either name it at-

---

[21] C. W. Cole, *French Mercantilist Doctrines before Colbert* (New York, 1969), pp. 81–82, 94, 99–100; Gutton, *Pauvres de Lyon,* pp. 306–308, Montchrétien, *Traicté,* pp. 26–28; Deyon, *Mercantilisme,* 101; Hassinger, *Becher,* pp. 146–59; D. C. Coleman, ed., *Revisions in Mercantilism* (London, 1969), pp. 176–77; Furniss, *Position of the Laborer,* 47n.

[22] Beier, "Warwickshire," pp. 80–82.

[23] Webb, *Old Poor Law,* pp. 49–50; Brian Pullan, *Rich and Poor in Renaissance Venice* (Cambridge, Mass., 1971), pp. 369–70, 415.

tracted a great deal of interest and was widely copied in the Low Countries, in Germany, and elsewhere.[24]

In France the pattern was somewhat different. As early as 1611 Paris had a "general hospital" where beggars and vagrants were put to work —women and children at spinning and button making, men at grinding flour, mixing cement, and other tasks. Similar institutions were created in Lyons, Toulouse, Marseilles, and other French cities. Although these hospitals were financed and operated by the church and designed primarily to care for old people and orphans, the idea of confining all the indigent in such structures was gaining popularity. In 1625, shortly after he became chief minister, Richelieu drafted a paper calling for hospitals "in all the cities of our realm" where "the able-bodied poor could be employed on public works." By mid-century, the government was trying (without expense to itself) to put this idea into practice. Royal edicts ordered all towns to set up hospitals and over the next hundred years most of them did so. In Paris a new Hôpital Général des Pauvres opened its doors in 1657 to over 4,500 inmates, most of whom entered voluntarily. By the 1670s the number had increased to 6,500 and there were nearly twice that many in a whole complex of institutions in Paris by the middle of the next century. In England John Cary, a Bristol merchant, led a group which, after obtaining parliamentary approval, built a workhouse in 1696 that became a model in that country; inmates were employed in preparing flax, hemp, wool, and cotton for weaving. To both reformers and those merely interested in pushing the problems of poverty and unemployment under the rug, they seemed a panacea. There was a workhouse at Anvers in Belgium for a brief period beginning in 1613 and more of them early in the next century, when Belgium, according to the historian Paul Bonenfant, was "obsessed by the idea of confining" the idle poor. There was also a *hôpital général* in Belgium after 1738, one noted for its strict discipline—inmates ate and worked in total silence. A few small workhouses (they were primarily almshouses) were founded in the American colonies in the eighteenth century. There was a workhouse in Bavaria as early as 1679, in Dessau early in the next century, in Turin in the 1760s. But only late in the eighteenth century, when industrialization had made more progress, did the idea catch on in Central Europe.[25]

[24] Thorsten Sellin, *Pioneering in Penology: The Amsterdam Houses of Correction in the Sixteenth and Seventeenth Centuries* (Philadelphia, 1944), pp. 9–12, 26–44, 49–59, 97–106.

[25] Gutton, *Pauvres de Lyon*, 297–8; Chill, "Religion and Mendacity," p. 404; O. H. Hufton, *The Poor of Eighteenth-Century France: 1750–1789* (Oxford, 1974), pp. 139–42, 147; D. J. Rothman, *The Discovery of the Asylum: Social Order and Discipline in the New Republic* (Boston, 1971), pp. 25–26, 38, 41, 55; Koch, *Wohlfahrstpflege*, pp. 143–44; Dorothy

At one level, the workhouse seemed a way of reducing and even eliminating the cost of maintaining those who could not support themselves, at another, a device for caring for the helpless efficiently and providing vocational training for orphans and poor children so that they would not become public charges when they grew up. At still another level, the workhouse was expected to improve the morals of inmates by separating them from the temptations of their miserable surroundings and by religious instruction in the institution. It was also seen as a powerful deterrent; rather than accept the loss of liberty involved, lazy people would "buckle to labour" and support themselves. Finally the workhouse offered a way of protecting the public—from the importunities of beggars and from the danger of infectious disease, riot, and crime. In England the reformers, mostly businessmen and merchants, tended to stress the economic advantages of workhouses, one of them calculating that even a blind, armless, one-legged man could, in a well-managed institution, earn sixpence a day. In France, where the leadership came mostly from the higher clergy, the emphasis was less on profit and more on moral regeneration; the church remained a "great buffer" for all the poor. Everywhere, however, the deterrent and social-protective purposes of the houses were important, and in all but a handful of cases, only these were achieved. Despite their high-minded intentions, the managers of the Amsterdam House of Correction were soon dealing with inmates who refused to work by putting them in a "water house," where they had the choice of manning a pump or drowning. As for enabling the unemployed to support themselves, the attempt, made in hundreds of institutions in many nations over two centuries and more, was an almost total failure.[26]

One of the earliest and best-intentioned efforts was begun in London in 1676 by Thomas Firmin, a well-to-do draper. Firmin sought to employ the poor of his parish in making linen; he accepted people ranging in age from children of three to half-blind "ancients," paying them from twopence to sixpence a day but supplementing these wages with gifts and providing humane working conditions. He gave close personal attention to the project, and the East India Company and some other customers paid more than the going rate for his coarse linen to encourage it. But the workhouse lost money steadily; when

Marshall, *The English Poor Law in the Eighteenth Century* (New York, 1960), p. 47; Paul Bonenfant, *Le problème du paupérisme en Belgique à la fin de l'ancien régime* (Brussels, 1934), 90–100, 245–47.

[26] Marshall, *English Poor Law*, p. 151; M. R. Zirker, Jr., *Fielding's Social Pamphlets* (Berkeley, 1966), p. 122; Webb, *Old Poor Law*, pp. 102–107; O. H. Hufton, *Bayeux in the Late Eighteenth Century* (Oxford, 1967), p. 102; Sellin, *Pioneering in Penology*, pp. 69–72.

Firmin died in 1697 most of his fortune was gone and the workhouse swiftly passed out of existence. John Cary's Bristol workhouse, which mobilized the resources of all the parishes of the city and which was managed by a dedicated board of guardians serving without pay, also ran continuously in the red. In France, the government expected the general hospitals to be largely self-supporting, but they never were. One of the biggest and best run, the *hôpital général* of Rouen, managed to occupy only about 500 of its 2,000 inmates, principally in sewing and spinning, and about half that number at maintenance work in the institution. In the region of Lyons during the 1720s, inmates of the smaller general hospitals often did no work at all; in Lyons itself, the directors admitted that spinners were taking two weeks to spin one pound of thread. Studies of British workhouses in 1725 and 1776 showed that none had made a profit, and another, in 1805 revealed that most of them barely produced enough to cover the cost of the materials used in manufacturing, and some not even that. "From the standpoint of making each pauper earn his own bread," the historians Sidney and Beatrice Webb concluded, "the failure of the workhouse manufactories was ludicrous in its completeness."[27]

Under the best of circumstances manufacturing by the unemployed in workhouses was unprofitable because the typical inmate was inefficient and unmotivated and because the goods produced tended, by increasing supplies, to depress the prices at which all goods of that type could be sold. And circumstances were rarely optimal. To simplify administration and cut costs, inmates were frequently hired out to contractors, who exploited them ruthlessly. Although nearly everyone with practical experience insisted that the unemployed should be housed separately from criminals and from the aged and incompetent, for reasons of economy all public charges were often combined in one building. Most workhouses soon became little more than jails or almshouses, or at best training schools for poor children. An Italian visitor in Lyons in the 1650s reported that beggars were being rounded up indiscriminately into a kind of horse-drawn cage, and carted off to the *hôpital général,* "where they are made to work hard and eat little." By the early eighteenth century an Englishman associated with the management of workhouses could write coolly: "The advantage of the workhouse . . . does not arise from what the poor people can do towards their own subsistence, but from the apprehensions the poor have of it." In 1723 Parliament permitted (but did not require) the parishes to deny relief to any claimant who refused to go to a work-

[27] Eden, *State of the Poor,* p. 34, Webb, *Old Poor Law,* pp. 119–20, 222, 233–34; Hufton, *Poor in France,* pp. 150, 155–6; Gutton, *Pauvres de Lyon,* p. 454; Furniss, *Position of the Laborer,* pp. 108–9; Marshall, *English Poor Law,* p. 146.

house. Over the next few years, about 150 English parishes built such places, not to give the unemployed an opportunity to work but to discourage them from seeking public support. The typical English workhouse became a combination of Bedlam and Bridewell, a place where idiots and lunatics, thieves and worn-out prostitutes, dotards and abandoned waifs existed side by side amid filth and chaos, and the effect was to "drive all idle poor [read, *unemployed*] out," to make of them vagabonds and furtive beggars.[28]

A similar tactic was developed a little later in France. A royal edict of 1764 ordered the arrest of all beggars. They were to be confined in *dépôts de mendicité* and made to work. But Controller General de l'Averdy ordered local officials to concentrate on rounding up "those who are known to be most dangerous" and also the most feeble. The latter "not being able to work are the most difficult to keep from begging," he explained, and "the able bodied, seeing them arrested, will become frightened and make up their minds to look for a job." Although perhaps half of the inmates of the *dépôts* were actually unemployed people capable of work, the deterrent effects were no doubt considerable, since about 14,000 of the 70,000-odd persons incarcerated in the period up to 1773 died before their short sentences had expired, most of them victims of epidemics of jail fever and other diseases which flourished in the filthy, crowded quarters assigned to the *dépôts* by a penurious government.[29]

The disappointing results of the drive to increase manufacturing by institutionalizing the unemployed stimulated much further thought among those concerned with economic expansion. That everyone had both a right and a duty to work remained axiomatic. To supply this work, some sought to improve the workhouses, clinging to the idea that they could be made to function efficiently, but more people, believing that the houses could serve only as a deterrent to idleness, argued for making them even more uncomfortable. Others favored turning them into houses of correction where the idle could be trained to habits of industry and thrift. Still others thought they should be abandoned, these dividing into those who recommended other ways of extracting work from the unemployed and those who adopted what would later be called a laissez-faire position. Whereas the workhouse idea had been first advanced at least partly with the hope of improving the condition of the unemployed, during roughly the first half of the eighteenth century the trend was toward ever-harsher repression. Only later, partly because of the work of pioneering statisticians, did

[28] Gutton, *Pauvres de Lyon,* pp. 354–55; Webb, *Old Poor Law,* pp. 243–45, 414–15.
[29] Christian Paultre, *De la répression de la mendicité et du vagabondage en France sous l'Ancien Régime* (Paris, 1906), pp. 395–97; Hufton, *Poor in France,* pp. 226–43.

an awareness of the social causes of unemployment begin to emerge and more constructive attitudes develop; the conviction that there was work for anyone willing to do it died hard.

Some suggestions for improving the workhouses were utopian in character. The English Quaker John Bellers, writing in 1695, proposed establishing "Colleges of Industry" financed by the rich. Each college should be given land on which half the residents would raise food for the group, the rest being occupied in manufacturing. Bellers thought a unit of three hundred persons could be self-sufficient, an "epitome of the world." If all the idle of England were so employed, he calculated that the profit would amount to £12,000 a day. In 1720 another Englishman, Laurence Braddon, expanded upon Bellers's scheme. In his "Collegiate Cities" of twenty thousand or more, each supported by ten thousand acres of arable land, all would labor according to their abilities—it was Braddon who insisted that a blind, armless, one-legged person could be productively employed. In France, the Abbé de Malvaux, summing up the ideas of a number of reformers, urged Louis XVI to establish houses of industry on the outskirts of every village and city, where the poor would raise their own food and manufacture "all things needed by the residents," such as stockings, shoes, hats, and cloth. "Children, old people, the infirm—all would be busy, and everyone would obtain what he needed by his own work."[30]

The most elaborate of these utopian proposals was surely Jeremy Bentham's plan of 1797, which called for building five hundred large houses, each 10 2/3 miles apart so that no one in England would be more than half a day's walk from a refuge. He would insure that inmates worked by not feeding them until their daily tasks were done. The tasks, however, would be carefully related to individual capacity. Bentham insisted that the ability to work was relative. Just about anyone could do something useful; the blind could knit, the energy expended by children at play could be harnessed through a kind of seesaw arrangement and used to pump water. To avoid competition with free labor, each "vast, populous establishment" would be self-sufficient, this system of "Self Supply" having the additional advantage of creating a community of interest that would raise morale and stimulate efficiency. The problems associated with having all kinds of people in one house Bentham attacked with an ingenious if labyrinthine plan of organization. Raving lunatics could be kept next to the deaf, prostitutes to aged women, the badly deformed to the blind.

More realistic English reformers generally took the position that

[30] Webb, *Old Poor Law*, p. 108; Zirker, *Fielding's Pamphlets*, pp. 121–22; Furniss, *Position of the Laborer*, p. 93; Abbé de Malvaux, *Les moyens de détruire la mendicité en France, en rendant les mendians utiles à l'état sans les rendre malheureux* (Châlons sur Marne, 1780), pp. 339–46.

workhouses ought to be much larger than was the case in most parts of the country, and that the able-bodied poor should be kept separate from criminals and the infirm. The novelist Henry Fielding, who as a London magistrate had much experience in dealing with the problem, offered in 1753 *A Proposal for Making an Effectual Provision for the Poor* that combined these ideas. Each county should have a large structure housing about 5,600 people. Workrooms and prison facilities should be separated (though petty criminals should be made to work), and respectable unemployed inmates should be taught trades. Fielding estimated that with the better management that a large institution could command each worker ought to be able to earn four shillings a week, but in another essay he pointed out that even if money was lost, the nation would profit because of the goods that otherwise idle people would produce. Nothing came of Fielding's plan or of other similar ones. Indeed, disillusionment with workhouses as a solution to the problem of unemployment was growing steadily. Writing about the same time as Fielding, the Reverend Thomas Alcock favored turning them into prisons. Round up all "idle, disorderly, drunken, profane, abusive persons," he urged, especially those who refuse to work, and "send them to the workhouse and there keep them to hard labor a longer or shorter time, according to the degree of their offense, and the appearance of reformation."[31]

The case for abolishing workhouses was made as early as 1704 by Daniel Defoe in a pamphlet, *Giving Alms no Charity, and Employing the Poor a Grievance to the Nation,* and in his weekly *Review,* and never much expanded. Defoe's assault was two-pronged: work was already available for anyone willing to perform it, and artificially contrived manufacturing was counterproductive, since it competed with and thus depressed the demand for goods made by private industry. There were, he wrote, two kinds of poor people, those who were lazy or improvident, and those whose poverty was owing to "infirmities merely providential," such as illness and old age. The latter were proper subjects for public assistance—indeed "begging . . . *in the Impotent* 'tis a scandal upon the Country." But the others ought to be left to their own devices —"oblige them to find themselves work and go about it." Forced to choose between honest labor and going hungry, they would quickly find jobs. The army, for example, was constantly in need of soldiers. "If men wanted employment, and consequently bread, this could never be; any man would carry a musket rather than starve." Those

[31] J. R. Poynter, *Society and Pauperism: English Ideas on Poor Relief, 1795–1834* (London, 1969), pp. 129–35; Zirker, *Fielding's Pamphlets,* pp. 110, 125; B. M. Jones, *Henry Fielding: Novelist and Magistrate* (London, 1933), pp. 182–86; Furniss, *Position of the Laborer,* pp. 112–13.

who claim they cannot find work, Defoe wrote, are dissemblers. "The reason why so many pretend to want work is that they can live so well with the pretense . . . [that] they would be mad to leave it and work in earnest." He claimed to have offered men nine shillings a week only to be "told . . . to my face that they could get more a-begging," and he described others who took their pay on Saturday night and "go with it directly to the ale-house, lie there till Monday, spend every penny, and run into debt to boot." If public aid were not available to such people, he insisted, they would have to change their ways.[32]

Workhouses, on the other hand, "tend to the Encrease . . . of the Poor" because they produce goods already in adequate supply. "Suppose now a Workhouse for the employment of poor children sets them to spinning of worsted. For every skein of worsted these poor children spin, there must be a skein the less spun by some other poor person or family that spun it before. . . . To set poor People at Work, on the same thing which other poor People were employ'd on before . . . is giving to one what you take away from another." And he denounced "*ye Hypocrites*, who Gild your Follies with Outside Shams, while Essentially and Effectually, you . . . Starve the Diligent Hands, that honestly labour for their Bread; that having first turn'd Numerous Families into the Street, you may pick up their Ruin'd Orphans for Vagrants, and boast of their Numbers, as an Instance of your Charity."[33]

Clearly no consensus emerged from these many commentaries on workhouses as a solution to the problem of occupying the idle. The institutions continued to exist in many forms; in less industrialized nations they appeared for the first time. Philip V established one in 1718 in Madrid that employed about a thousand persons. There was considerable discussion of them in Spain during the latter half of the century, much of it by writers influenced by the ideas of Colbert, which were by then a hundred years old.[34] In the 1760s a workhouse was opened on the outskirts of Madrid. Charles III ordered the confinement of vagabonds in workhouses in 1775, and by the end of the century there were *casas de misericordia,* where at least some work was done by the inmates, in most Spanish cities.[35]

Frederick the Great, who liked to refer to himself as "the attorney

[32] Daniel Defoe, *Giving Alms no Charity, and Employing the Poor a Grievance to the Nation* (London, 1704), pp. 3–28.

[33] Daniel Defoe, *A Review of the Affairs of France,* 84 (December 23, 1704), 350.

[34] Spanish economists also discovered the sixteenth-century humanist Juan Luis Vives at this time; his *De subventione pauperum* was finally translated into his native tongue.

[35] Jean Sarrailh, "Note sur la réforme de la bienfaisance en Espagne," *Hommage à Lucien Febvre* (Paris, 1953), pp. 371–80; Henri Bérindoague, *Le mercantilisme en Espagne* (Paris, 1929), p. 148; E. J. Hamilton "The Mercantilism of Gerónimo de Uztáritz," N. E. Himes, ed., *Economy, Society, and the Modern World* (Cambridge, 1935), p. 122.

to the poor," endowed a workhouse in Berlin in 1742. The Hapsburg Emperor Joseph II did the same in Vienna in 1783, placing over the entrance the words: *"Hier können Arbeitsuchende einen Verdienst finden"*—here those seeking work can find gainful employment. Most large German cities established workhouses during the last quarter of the century, some of these, according to contemporaries, extremely well managed. The most famous was the Munich workhouse, founded in 1790 by the Massachusetts-born scientist and soldier Benjamin Thompson, Count Rumford, while in the service of the Elector of Bavaria. Rumford, who held the rank of lieutenant general in the Bavarian army and was minister of police, was a stickler for efficiency. He divided Munich into sixteen districts. In each a committee was assigned the task of registering each house and assigning it a number. Then on January 1, a traditional day for distributing alms, Rumford's troops rounded up all Munich's beggars. These were carefully examined, the able-bodied ordered to report to Rumford's workhouse, the rest assigned to the proper district committee and promised aid. In the workhouse over a thousand were kept busy making army uniforms and at a variety of crafts. Conditions in Rumford's workhouse were good, efficiency was rewarded. Those without skills received training; the young were provided with a rudimentary education.

Rumford was soon boasting that his enterprise was clearing 8 percent on the goods produced. He wrote a number of widely reprinted essays explaining his methods, but few could duplicate his success. While undoubtedly an excellent manager, he was also quite ruthless. He economized rigidly on food, claiming that he could feed people for a penny a meal. He insisted that water had nutritive value and that stale bread was better than fresh, since the extra chewing it required prolonged the pleasure of eating. He specialized in soup recipes; critics spoke derisively of the "Metaphysical Soups of Count Rumford," adding that "those who can swallow the Count's dinners can swallow anything." In any case he left Bavaria in 1795 to resume his scientific work in London, and without him the workhouse swiftly declined. It closed its doors in 1799.[36]

Rumford's was not a residential workhouse; his beggars only worked and took their meals there. This was increasingly the pattern elsewhere in German-speaking countries and throughout Europe. In Great Britain Parliament passed a law sponsored by Thomas Gilbert in 1782 allowing parishes to join together to maintain hospitals and asylums

[36] Koch, *Wohlfahrstpflege*, pp. 97, 144, 239–41; Carl Jantke and Dietrich Hilger, eds., *Die Eiguntumslosen* (Munich, 1965), pp. 197–207; W. J. Sparrow, *Knight of the White Eagle: A Biography of Sir Benjamin Thompson, Count Rumford* (London, 1964), pp. 85–96, 188–91; Poynter, *Society and Pauperism*, pp. 87–90.

to care for orphans and aged and infirm indigents, the theory being that larger units would be better managed and more efficient. But Gilbert's Act forbade local authorities to confine in these institutions anyone capable of working; they must either operate separate facilities for the able-bodied, or find them work, or provide them with direct assistance—what was called "outdoor relief." This law did not mean the end of workhouses in Britain, for many parishes did not join the so-called Gilbert Unions. But the country was moving away from the workhouse system. It had never made much sense to force an indigent family into a workhouse when its distress was obviously temporary, as when the breadwinner was ill or when a bad harvest caused prices to soar beyond the means of low-paid workers. In some districts the practice developed of supplementing the earnings of poor people with sums scaled to the price of bread and family size, the idea being to keep "the poor man, verging upon indigence . . . propped up." This tactic became known as the Speenhamland system, after a district in Berkshire whose scale of assistance, established in 1795, became well known. Bad harvests in 1794 and 1795 and again after the turn of the century produced chronic hard times in some agricultural districts and caused this system to be widely adopted.[37]

The French also experimented with new methods of dealing with unemployment. In the 1770s Turgot, Louis XVI's minister of finance, began to offer agricultural laborers work in the winter months without forcing them to live in institutions. Like Count Rumford, Thomas Gilbert, and most other students of the problem, he believed in separating those who could not work from those who could. The hospital workshops continued to function, but most of the labor was done by women, children, and old people, some of them non-residents who came in daily to work in what were called *ateliers de filature*. Some even worked in their own homes, spinning and weaving with materials supplied by the hospitals. Turgot shut down most of the *dépôts de mendicité*, which had in effect become concentration camps for beggars, vagabonds, prostitutes, and idle agricultural laborers. He put the criminals among the inmates in ordinary jails, and he expanded the number of *ateliers de charité* (literally, charity workshops). These were not actually workshops, but rather public-works projects, such as road building and repair, financed partly by the state, partly by the church and by private contributions. Unemployed rural laborers, along with their wives and children, were given specific tasks (and not paid until the jobs were

[37] Webb, *Old Poor Law*, pp. 170–71, 176–80; A. W. Coats, "Economic Thought and Poor Law Policy in the Eighteenth Century," *Economic History Review*, 13 (1960), 46–51; G. W. Oxley, *Poor Relief in England and Wales: 1601–1834* (London, 1974), pp. 106–14; E. W. Martin, ed., *Comparative Development in Social Welfare* (London, 1972), pp. 85–94.

done). Recognizing that large projects required strength and skills that the unemployed could not always provide, Turgot contracted out these tasks to specialists. Unfortunately Turgot's system did not work well in practice; it was too expensive, and although he organized *ateliers de charité* in most sections of France, the projects were never numerous enough to employ even a substantial fraction of the idle poor. When he was dismissed by the king in 1776, his successor continued the *atelier* system, which by the 1780s was also functioning in the cities, but he also resumed the practice of herding beggars and vagrants into *dépôts de mendicité*.[38]

Thus the workhouse system, like the municipal relief systems of the sixteenth century, failed to accomplish its purpose, despite much effort and many ingenious experiments. Countless thousands all over Europe continued to "want" employment, yet the English expression "Saint Monday," the French *"chômage du lundi,"* the German *"blaue Montag"* reflect the persistent complaints of businessmen, economists, and government officials that laborers were still placing their own ease ahead of national needs to increase production.

Gradually, however, during the last half of the eighteenth century, many of those who struggled to understand the complexities of economic and social relationships began to question ancient assumptions. Perhaps the state ought not to meddle so much in the everyday affairs of the people. Perhaps laborers would work harder if they had more to look forward to; as one English pamphleteer remarked, "necessity will not always do . . . what may be effected by encouragement."[39] Perhaps poverty, vice, and idleness were not entirely the result of personal defects. Particularly with regard to this last uncertainty, experience had repeatedly demonstrated that neither government projects, nor repressive laws, nor the exhortations of philosophers, clergymen, and magistrates had succeeded in clearing the roads of vagabonds or the cities of beggars. Even in the Americas, where labor was in short supply, vagrancy existed, both in frontier districts where it was always tempting to live off the land aimlessly, often on the edge of the law, and in the cities. There were "loose and vagrant persons that have not any setled Residence" in seventeenth-century Virginia, and "Idle and disorderly persons, having no visible Estates or Employments" in the eighteenth. Every runaway indentured servant, indeed, nearly all westward-wandering pioneers, conformed to the definition—lack of fixed

[38] S. T. McCoy, *Government Assistance in Eighteenth-Century France* (Durham, 1946), pp. 28–30, 267; Hufton, *Poor in France,* 182–93; Hufton, *Bayeux,* pp. 106–109; Paultre, *Répression de la mendicité,* pp. 440–42.

[39] A. W. Coats, "Changing Attitudes to Labour in the mid-Eighteenth Century," *Economic History Review,* 11 (1958), 35–51, esp. 42.

abode, precise destination, income, or occupation. On the Chilean steppes and in the bustling seaport of New York, officials in the eighteenth century complained of "lost souls" and "Sloathful . . . disobedient, and Stragling Vagabonds."[40]

It was difficult to persuade ordinary people not to give these "lost souls" help. Compassion and the persistence of medieval values, along with the awareness of the masses that they might easily find themselves in similar circumstances, rendered laws against begging hard to enforce. In Switzerland, for example, an edict of 1754 provided that persons repeatedly caught begging should have their ears slit and the initials of the community branded on their foreheads, but begging and the giving of alms even to "foreign" vagabonds continued, despite the general poverty of the region. Belgian authorities found it equally difficult to enforce anti-begging laws. Even Sir William Petty, he who believed that criminals should be enslaved and who thought that charity should end as well as begin at home, left the poor £20 in his will, "to answer custom and to take the safer side."[41] French archives contain evidence showing that the police were often harassed by crowds when they attempted to arrest beggars and that time and again individuals repeatedly apprehended for begging were released by provincial judges. It is perhaps not surprising that a blind woman in Lyons reported that "important people in this city" not only allowed her to beg but even had her taken daily to a post on the Fourvière road "so that she could obtain the means to subsist." But Lyonnais officials also resisted pressure from Paris to arrest able-bodied beggars: "Poor laborers who are reduced to begging during temporary work stoppages are not the types the government wants to eradicate," they claimed. As early as 1728 the town of Bayeux in Normandy was complaining to the governor of the province that enforcing the edict requiring the arrest of beggars would mean the incarceration of 1,800 people in a community of about 6,000.[42]

There was nowhere a sudden shift in public attitudes or public policy. That laws against begging and vagrancy were hard to enforce did not mean that efforts to enforce them were without effect; indeed, thousands were thrown into jails and workhouses every year. Many writers continued to argue that the unemployed were lazy or criminal;

[40] E. S. Morgan, *American Slavery American Freedom: The Ordeal of Colonial Virginia* (New York, 1975), pp. 238, 339; Mario Gongora, "Vagabondage et société," *Annales,* 21 (1966), 161; R. A. Mohl, *Poverty in New York: 1783–1825* (New York, 1971), p. 43.

[41] A. M. Dubler, *Armen- und Bettlerwesen in der Gemeinen Herrschaft "Freie Ämter"* (Basel, 1970), *passim,* esp. pp. 63, 66; Bonenfant, *Paupérisme en Belgique,* pp. 147, 391–2; Christopher Hill, *Society & Puritanism* (New York, 1972), pp. 288–89.

[42] Paultre, *Répression de la mendicité,* p. 551; Hufton, *Poor in France,* pp. 102–103, 194–96, 227; Gutton, *Pauvres de Lyon,* pp. 120–21, 460; Hufton, *Bayeux,* p. 99.

nearly all held that more, rather than fewer people were necessary and that low wages were the best incentive to hard work and thus to national prosperity. The great thinkers of the eighteenth-century Enlightenment, despite their essential humanitarianism, their compassion for the poor, and their belief that education could expand human potentialities, tended to dismiss the mass of ordinary people as a lower order of beings. Voltaire referred to them as *"canaille,"* "two-footed animals . . . barely enjoying the gift of speech," and he accepted the prevailing belief that there were too many holidays enabling laborers to avoid work. Diderot considered them *"imbécile,"* Kant *"Idioten,"* and David Hume lent his authority to the dogma that high wages would only enable working people to "indulge themselves in idleness and riot." Peter Gay, the leading modern authority on Enlightenment thought, speaks of "the superb sneer that most of the philosophers directed, most of the time, at their less fortunate fellow beings."[43]

But the *philosophes* were ambivalent or at least inconsistent in their attitudes, as Gay points out, just as were less intellectual and high-minded people of the time. For in the last quarter of the eighteenth century massive new forces were changing the way unemployment was understood and dealt with. Two of these were so traumatic that everyone could appreciate their importance, if not their particular significance—a period of hard times exacerbated by crop failures that brought misery to Europe repeatedly during these decades, and the French Revolution. Two others began so imperceptibly as to be scarcely noticed by contemporaries, but by the early decades of the next century they had reached proportions no one could ignore—the accelerating increase in the population and the industrial revolution. From these changes would emerge an attitude toward unemployment that was almost a mirror image of the old view.

[43] Peter Gay, *The Enlightenment: An Interpretation* (New York, 1969) II: 521, 4, 46, 519, 517; Johnson, *Predecessors of Adam Smith,* p. 170.

4

The Great Transition

The hard times of the late eighteenth century were the product of famine and war. Such troubles encouraged the better-off, out of compassion or prudence, to extend more help to the suffering, and to recognize at least temporarily that the unemployed were victims of circumstances beyond their control, thus properly entitled to assistance. But the revolutions—economic, social and political, demographic—these upheavals changed the whole character of Western society. Little wonder that they altered both the way that economists, businessmen, and statesmen understood unemployment and the way that the unemployed reacted to their own condition.

The industrial revolution, that is, the application of power-driven machinery to the manufacturing process and the development of the factory system of production, reduced the relative importance of labor. Although it made possible an improvement of living standards, it made work more monotonous if less physically demanding, the workers more dependent. It further accelerated the drift of population to the cities, exacerbating urban problems that were already extremely serious. By greatly improving the efficiency of labor and by opening up new occupations to women and children, it both undermined the assumption that there could be no such thing as too many workers and put various types of workers in conflict with one another—factory hands against artisans, union labor against the unorganized. At the same time it increased the importance of capital and the power of capitalists in society.

These effects tended to make laborers more class-conscious and more militant. The growth of unions was intimately related to the revolution, although for many decades factory workers played almost no part in the union movement, which was essentially a defensive effort by skilled craftsmen to protect themselves against changes wrought by industrialization. And by causing the economic system to become much more complex and therefore more subject to dislocations (which in turn, had more, and more widespread, ramifications) it made wage earners and ultimately the rest of society aware of unemployment as a social problem distinct from poverty and idleness.

Although when viewed narrowly machines often appeared to displace workers (optimistic designers of utopias were not the only people who envisaged a system of production that functioned without human effort), the industrial revolution made more jobs than it destroyed; certainly it did not reduce the size of the labor force. This was small comfort to those who *were* displaced. The machine breaking of the early industrial age reflected genuine and, for particular skilled workers like the shearers in the English and French woolens industry, legitimate fears that their livelihoods were being eliminated. During the bad times after Waterloo, sporadic attacks on shearing machines occurred in France, and it was generally true that when manufacturers wished to install these new machines the local *gendarmerie* and sometimes even the army had to be called out to preserve order.[1]

But too much should not be made of the resistance of artisans to machinery. The industrial violence of the period had many causes, and the tactic of destroying the property of a hated employer long antedated the industrial revolution; it was part of what one historian has called "collective bargaining by riot," examples of which can be found as early as the seventeenth century. Even the bloody Luddite uprisings of 1811–13 and thereafter in the English textile districts, during which mills were repeatedly attacked and machines smashed, were as much protests against political oppression as against the factory system.[2]

The industrial revolution did, however, lead to much sharper fluctuations in economic activity. By speeding up production, vastly adding to capacity, expanding markets geographically, and stimulating the pace of technological innovation, it made the coordination of production and consumption much more difficult. When prospects seemed good, manufacturers naturally sought to produce more, and the new techniques enabled them to do so in unprecedented volume and very rapidly. But the power of the machines brought into play, as it were, the force of inertia. Once geared up, it was difficult to slow down the juggernaut. Before long goods glutted the market, and then the ma-

[1] D. Roche, ed., *Ordres et classes, colloque d'histoire sociale* (Paris, 1973), pp. 241–43; F. E. Manuel, "The Luddite Movement in France," *Journal of Modern History,* 10 (1938), 187–205.

[2] E. J. Hobsbawm, *Labouring Men: Studies in the History of Labour* (London, 1964), pp. 6–7, 11; E. P. Thompson, *The Making of the English Working Class* (New York, 1963), pp. 484–602, esp. 553.

chines and those who tended them had to stand idle until the surplus was absorbed. At one moment entrepreneurs were scurrying about looking for more workers. The next they were laying off hands by the hundreds and in the process further delaying the emptying of their overstocked warehouses. Periods of hectic expansion thus alternated with periods of business stagnation, heady optimism with black pessimism.

The famines, plagues, and wars of earlier times had often disturbed the balance of supply and demand and caused business activity to grind to a halt. By the nineteenth century, famines and plagues had at least become less catastrophic in Europe.[3] The new industrial disturbances, however, were cyclical in character rather than haphazard. Booms *generated* busts (called panics or crises). Chance events, among which wars were the most common, interacted with and altered the cycles, but the latter were inherent in the system. Mechanization, with its tremendous material advantages, nevertheless caused unemployment. This was the greatest paradox and knottiest problem spawned by the industrial revolution.

Although the demographic expansion, which began about 1750, increased in velocity rapidly in the 1770s, and continued throughout the nineteenth century, has not been adequately explained by historians, it was obviously related to economic expansion, both as effect and as cause. It was not an event, or even, as was the industrial revolution, a series of specific, observable developments. Even more than the industrial revolution, which was actually an evolutionary process, it seems a revolution only in retrospect; from year to year the growth was almost unnoticeable, especially since no government took periodic censuses until the trend was long under way. But like the industrial revolution it exploded the common illusion that there would always be more work to do than people to do it. It provided a different explanation for the prevalance of poverty and unemployment, one easier for ordinary people to accept, and thus drastically altered public policy in these areas.

The French Revolution, on the other hand, had clear-cut immediate effects on attitudes toward unemployment, at least in France itself. A particularly bad harvest in 1788 had caused a typical pre-industrial depression, the soaring cost of bread forcing working people to stop buying practically everything else. In 1789, 120,000 Parisians in a population of about 600,000 were reduced to beggary, and conditions in the provinces were equally bad. Louis XVI's government opened up *ateliers de charité,* but not nearly enough to handle the hordes of indi-

[3] The dreadful Irish potato famine of the 1840s is a major exception to this generalization.

gents seeking work. On July 14, the day the Bastille fell, only 8,600 people in the Paris region were being helped in this way, and in the rest of the country, where local government had broken down following the calling of the Estates General in May and where wild rumors bred fear and panic among the peasants, the suffering was even worse.

During the following two years economic conditions improved somewhat but the political confusion became worse. In Paris the *ateliers* were closed, reopened, closed and opened again. Popular fear that reactionary groups would try to mobilize the relief workers for a counter revolutionary coup mounted. The *ateliers* were dreadfully mismanaged. Women disguised themselves as men to collect the higher rate of pay that male workers received. Laborers employed at the task of demolishing the hated Bastille charged admission to sightseers who flocked to gloat over the ruins. Workers on other projects idled away their time at dice or failed even to appear except to collect their pay; often there were not enough tools for all the hands. Much money was dispensed, little work accomplished. On July 1, 1791, the National Assembly shut the Paris *ateliers* down for good.

Early the next year the newly elected Legislative Assembly instituted a public-works program for the unemployed, but because of the character of the projects no jobs were available for women, and pay, set below the going rate for manual labor, was insufficient to support a family. As the revolution proceeded, conditions deteriorated steadily. Inflation led to price and wage controls, then to food shortages caused by the refusal of peasants to part with their grain. Bad harvests followed. The wars of the revolution strained the government's limited resources. Beginning in 1793 the National Convention authorized the opening of *ateliers* only during the winter "dead season," the assumption being that at other times unemployed artisans could easily find work in agriculture, and by the end of the revolutionary era, under the Directory, poor relief of all sorts had been returned to the vagaries of local control.[4]

But if the revolutionary governments failed to do much about unemployment, the ideologues of the revolution advanced some startling new ideas about the subject, ideas which like so many of their theories eventually had a profound influence all over the world. In the autumn of 1789, the National Assembly abolished taxes in support of religion and confiscated the property of the church. Almsgiving was to cease;

[4] Michel Bouchet, *L'Assistance publique en France pendant la Révolution* (Paris, 1908), pp. 210–42, 383–85, 663–64, 638–39; Yvonne Forado-Cunéo, "Les Ateliers de Charité de Paris pendant la Révolution Française," *La Révolution Française*, 86 (1933), 317–35; 87 (1934), 29–61, 103–16; O. H. Hufton, *Bayeux in the Late Eighteenth Century* (Oxford, 1967), pp. 150–52; George Rudé, *Paris and London in the Eighteenth Century* (New York, 1971), p. 171.

the state assumed sole responsibility for caring for those in need.

Then in January 1790 the Assembly set up a Comité pour l'Extinction de la Mendicité headed by the Duc de La Rochefoucauld-Liancourt (another member was Dr. Joseph Guillotin, soon to become famous for his supposedly humane device for executing traitors). This committee proceeded to enunciate some high-sounding principles about the causes of unemployment and what the state should do about it. Poverty was the result of a "disproportion" between the number of people and the amount of work to be done. Industrial development would help ease the problem, but manufacturing also caused unemployment by putting "whole cities in a continuing cycle of great activity and total inertia." Agricultural output should obviously be stimulated. Tax reform, the removal of restrictions on the movement of workers from place to place, and the repeal of government regulations on business activity would help. Church land should be broken up into small holdings sufficient only to support a family. But whatever the causes of unemployment, the existence of poverty was the government's fault (*"La misère des peuples est un tort des gouvernements"*). Therefore, "every person has a right to subsistence, and society must provide that subsistence to those who lack jobs. . . . Work in abundance for those able to work."[5]

The committee stopped short of advocating that the state should actually provide jobs for all the unemployed, limiting the obligation to "encouraging" and "multiplying" opportunities to work. "The government must take care not of each individual, but all." Guaranteeing the unemployed work, the committee reasoned, would give them "the dangerous idea" that they had no responsibility for finding it for themselves. It took almost as hard a line against idleness as that prevalent during the Old Regime. "If everyone has a right to say to society, 'Give me food (*fais-moi vivre*),' society has equally the right to answer: 'Give me your labor.' If the poor person refuses, society has the right to punish him." Although the committee recommended the abolition of branding, whipping, and other forms of physical punishment for begging, it insisted that those repeatedly caught seeking alms ought to be confined to houses of correction and made to work.[6]

Even with these limitations, the program of the Comité de Mendicité

[5] La Rochefoucauld-Liancourt and probably other members of the committee were much influenced by Rousseau's argument in *The Social Contract* that "everyone has a natural right to what is necessary" and that the rich are entitled to the protection of their wealth only on the condition that no member of society is deprived of these essentials. Bouchet, *Assistance publique en France*, p. 164n.

[6] *Ibid.*, pp. 123–41, 158–65, 191–92; Forado-Cunéo, "Ateliers de Charité," 86: 338–41; R. B. DuBoff, "Economic Thought in Revolutionary France," *French Historical Studies*, 4 (1966), 437–42.

made a sharp break with the past. But its radical objectives were not achieved, despite the passage of legislation based on its recommendations in 1793. On balance the revolution, by its disruption of old patterns, increased the amount of unemployment in France. This was inadvertent. However, by their deliberate seizure of the assets of the church, a major source of funds for public assistance before 1789, the revolutionary leaders made the lot of the unemployed and of all the poor far worse than it had been.[7]

All these late-eighteenth-century upheavals could not fail to alter the thinking of economists. In the broadest terms, however, the underlying cause of the change was their growing awareness of the complexity of economic relationships, complexities which the upheavals both reflected and produced. Industrialization created far more intricate internal business relationships in every country. International trade loomed even more vital to prosperity than it had before; the Americas, Africa, and Asia were supplying raw materials in increasing volume and also becoming ever-larger markets for European products. The English cotton-textile industry, for example, was dependent upon other parts of the world for its raw cotton and sold much of its output overseas.

Earlier thinkers, in the main, had not looked much beyond the ends of their noses when analyzing economic questions. They were coping with specific problems, not trying to construct a system.[8] If the objective was, say, to encourage the manufacture of woolens, they might favor imposing a heavy tax on foreign cloth without thinking through the effects of the tax either on foreign trade or on other domestic activities. They advocated keeping wages low in order to make manufactured goods more competitive in foreign markets without considering the impact of low wages on domestic consumption. The result of this piecemeal approach over time was that every nation had constructed a maze of regulations, subsidies, and prohibitions governing economic activity.

By the middle of the eighteenth century, however, economics had become a scholarly discipline, if not exactly a science. Its practitioners were more eager to make general statements about the subject than to answer particular questions. They were impressed by the interactions of superficially isolated events and policies. In France, a group calling themselves *économistes* (they are now known as physiocrats) formed the first self-conscious school in the field. Disturbed by the indirect effects of Colbert's regulatory policies on French agriculture, these physiocrats stressed the circularity of economic activity. Their

[7] Bouchet, *Assistance publique en France*, pp. 381–97; Hufton, *Bayeux*, pp. 237, 248.
[8] William Letwin, *The Origins of Scientific Economics* (New York, 1964), p. 223.

leader, François Quesnay, a physician at the court of Louis XV, worked out an elaborate chart, the *Tableau économique*, purporting to show by means of a *"ziczac"* of crisscrossing lines, how money circulated through society. "Everything is intertwined," Quesnay explained. An economy is "a general system of expenditure, work, gain, and consumption."[9]

When the existing system was examined from this perspective, it appeared most unsatisfactory. Rules and regulations by their nature assumed consistency of application and implied uniformity of interest among the groups they affected. Yet it became increasingly apparent that when they were enforced unforeseen and undesirable consequences often ensued. A dynamic society put a premium on adaptability, and adaptability required freedom from rigid controls. Awareness of the intricacies of investment, production, commerce, and consumption by which millions of people, scattered over the globe, earned their livelihoods and enjoyed the fruits of their efforts gradually inspired in those who turned their minds to the subject a healthy respect for the limits of the possible. As they achieved some sense of the almost infinite ramifications of every decision and action in the economic sphere, they became at once more intellectually ambitious and more conscious of the practical limitations of what could be done with their knowledge. They sought to view the economy whole, as an integrated system, and to discover the laws governing its functioning. The laws they discerned, however, were general principles (in a sense, conceptions of human psychology) which by definition were not subject to political manipulation. Quesnay drew a distinction between positive laws, enacted by governments, and natural laws, which although hard to pin down were the fundamental principles that positive laws sought to explicate. If, as the first great synthesizer of the new view, the Scottish philosopher Adam Smith, insisted, principles of economics governed the uncountable decisions of millions of independent producers and consumers, it was as though an "invisible hand" were coordinating these decisions, and tampering with the economy in pursuit of any short-range benefit was likely to cause trouble. Such reasoning implied that an essentially benevolent order, a harmony of interests, ruled the universe, a belief typical of the eighteenth century. It made patience a cardinal virtue—not all things, but just rewards would come to those who waited.

The catch phrase for this approach to economics, *laissez faire*, dates from the early eighteenth century, perhaps even from the seventeenth, but except in the minds of certain popular writers, the term did not

[9] Peter Gay, *The Enlightenment* (New York, 1969), II: 349.

mean that nations should never try to regulate economic activity. Although skeptical of its effectiveness, the economists were not primarily concerned with limiting state power. Rather they sought to unshackle the individual, the theory being that since no one could judge a person's interests better than himself, society would profit if all its members were free to do what seemed best for them. The energy driving the economic machine was the individual's desire for gain; freedom to pursue that selfish interest would increase the expenditure of this energy. The mechanism for controlling individual self-interest in the public interest was competition; freedom to struggle for personal profit would produce rewards only for the efficient and at the same time prevent the efficient from extracting too high a price for their skill and talent.

This way of looking at the economy had important effects on attitudes toward labor and the "want" of employment. If, like everything else, wages and the number of jobs were determined by immutable laws, and the general good best achieved by allowing competitive forces to operate freely, efforts to fix wages, control the movement of workers, and force the idle to labor were at best futile, and likely to be counterproductive. In this area, the failure of earlier policies was particularly evident, a fact which added weight to the new argument.

Adam Smith and most of the later economists who looked to him as master were far more humane in their view of working people than their predecessors. In his great and influential book, *The Wealth of Nations* (1776), Smith attacked many conventional assumptions. It was *not* true that most workers were congenitally lazy; "on the contrary, when they are liberally paid by the piece, [they] are apt to over-work themselves, and to ruin their health." It was *not* necessary to hold wages down in order to increase the national wealth; wage earners make up the large majority of society, and "what improves the circumstances of the greater part can never be regarded as an inconveniency to the whole. No society can surely be flourishing and happy, of which the far greater part of the members are poor and miserable."[10]

Smith criticized laws prohibiting the movement of laborers from place to place and restricting their right to practice trades freely. "The patrimony of a poor man lies in the strength and dexterity of his hands; and to hinder him from employing this strength and dexterity in what manner he thinks proper without injury to his neighbour, is a plain violation of this most sacred property." The apprentice system, presumably designed to teach young workers a trade, was actually a device for keeping them in a state of subordination long after its skills had

[10] Adam Smith, *An Inquiry into the Nature and Causes of the Wealth of Nations* (New York, 1937), pp. 78–82.

been mastered. He also pointed out how disadvantaged ordinary workers were in bargaining with employers, the latter having usually the resources to hold out a long time, the former in most cases being unable to survive without wages for a week. "We have no acts of parliament against combining to lower the price of work," he noted, "but many against combining to raise it." He was even sympathetic toward—though he did not condone—the use of force by workers during labor disputes. "They are desperate, and act with the folly and extravagance of desperate men, who must starve, or frighten their masters into an immediate compliance with their demands." And although he was writing in the infancy of the machine age, Smith recognized that the monotonous repetition of simple tasks was mentally debilitating, making the worker "as stupid as it is possible for a human creature to become."[11]

Yet *The Wealth of Nations* had almost nothing to say about unemployment. Smith seems to have assumed that full employment was the normal state of affairs, his reasoning being that high wages and economic growth were sure signs that the demand for labor exceeded the supply. While he made frequent reference to the existence of poor people in Great Britain, he claimed that wages were generally above the level of mere subsistence—if not, how could the population continue to grow? Eschewing "any tedious or doubtful calculation" to prove this point, he employed the curious additional argument that since workers managed to exist when wages were at their lowest they must have a surplus at all other times. In countries where output was declining—he used Bengal as an example—"many would not be able to find employment," but in Britain, where the economy was expanding, this was not the case. To buttress his argument still further, he cited the ease with which 100,000 soldiers and sailors demobilized after the Seven Years' War had found work, suffering no more than "some inconveniency" in the process.[12]

Of course Smith knew that every British worker was not always fully occupied. He recognized the ripple effect of bad harvests and high food prices on industrial activity, writing that "in a year of sudden and extraordinary scarcity . . . a considerable number of people are thrown out of employment." He dealt with this problem, however, only as a way of demonstrating how the law of supply and demand influenced wages. He also noted that "employment is much more constant in some trades than others" and he mentioned the "anxious and desponding moments" that, for example, bricklayers must endure when bad weather or a dearth of "customers" left them without income for

11 *Ibid.*, pp. 122, 135, 140, 67, 734.
12 *Ibid.*, pp. 67–68, 73–74, 437.

protracted periods. But he argued that workers in seasonal trades earned higher daily wages than those whose labor was steady, and that on an annual basis the differences balanced out. Unemployment therefore seemed to him of only marginal significance. "In the greater part of manufactures, a journeyman may be pretty sure of employment almost every day of the year that he is able to work." So long as entrepreneurs earned profits and invested them in productive enterprises, work would be available for all. The most important action a government could take to foster the process was to allow free play— subject to common standards of moral conduct—to the natural acquisitive desires of all citizens, allowing investors to take advantage of opportunity, farmers and manufacturers to produce whatever they wished, workers to sell their services on the best terms they could make.[13]

In the long run everyone would benefit. If in any field supply exceeded demand, whether of goods, labor, or capital, self-interest would push the excess into other activities or competition would redress the balance. If manufacturers produced more cloth than could be sold at a profit, some would turn to making different goods, supplies would shrink, prices rise, and profits for the others would be restored. If an excess of textile workers drove down wages, either some would shift to other trades or (because of the cost of manufacturing cloth would fall) competition among producers would force down prices, causing the demand for cloth to rise and manufacturers to increase output by hiring more hands.

Smith wrote *The Wealth of Nations* before the effects of the new industrial methods had been much felt, before anyone realized how rapidly population was increasing, and before the French Revolution. By the 1790s, his argument—and it must be repeated that his achievement was in synthesizing and persuasively expounding ideas that had been developing for years—was beginning to dominate the thinking of economists and businessmen all over Europe. Therefore, reactions to the hard times of that decade, which these upheavals and a series of bad harvests produced, were influenced by his work.

The mind set of the analysts, in other words, was dominated by the assumption that natural laws governed economic behavior. They focused their attention on trying to understand how these laws functioned and on devising policies that would conform to them. In the area of work and poverty, for example, this resulted in the abandonment in France of the principle that the state was responsible for maintaining every needy citizen. Even while the Comité de Mendicité

[13] *Ibid.*, pp. 86, 103, 319–21.

was proclaiming the right of everyone to work and subsistence, it was recommending that old restrictions on producers and workers be swept away in the name of *liberté* and *égalité*. The Jacobin interval of price fixing and other controls marked a shift in the other direction, but by 1795 a delegate to the National Convention was warning of the dangers of too much government intervention and dismissing the idea that the state could care for all the poor as an "absurdity"—the poor had a *right* only to the "general commiseration" of society. Under the Directory the government abandoned the commitment to finding work for the unemployed, and in 1798 turned the relief problem (along with their old revenues) back to the general hospitals.[14]

In that same year Thomas Malthus published his *Essay on Population.* Malthus's conclusion that population tended to increase geometrically, food supplies only arithmetically, and that the masses were therefore doomed to exist on the edge of starvation, their numbers held in check by "misery and vice," was another illustration of the Smithian view of social dynamics. As Malthus described it, the process was automatic and inexorable; since the number of mouths was ultimately controlled by the amount of food available to fill them, there would always tend to be more people than could be properly nourished and the surplus would die of malnutrition and disease, or, almost equally likely, of one or another of the vices attendant upon poverty. Nothing the state might do could check or reverse the process. The British poor law, especially the Speenhamland system of subsidizing the wages of low-income workers, he claimed, only made the situation worse because it encouraged these workers to have more children than they could support by their own efforts. He recommended that systematic poor relief—"the vain endeavour to attain what in the nature of things is impossible"—be gradually abolished.[15]

Coming at a time when the population of Europe was rapidly increasing, and after a series of bad harvests, Malthus's essay caused a sensation. He was both attacked and praised in extravagant terms. Responding to criticisms, he published a longer (and much duller) version of his *Essay* in 1803 in which he conceded that in addition to vice and misery, growth might be contained if the poor would exercise "moral restraint"; they need only postpone marriage (and of course sexual intercourse) until they had accumulated enough to support the diminished number of children they might "reasonably expect" to produce in their remaining fertile years. Presumably Malthus did not

[14] Bouchet, *Assistance publique en France*, pp. 629, 638–40, 653; DuBoff, "Economic Thought," 434–35.

[15] T. R. Malthus, *First Essay on Population: 1798* (New York, 1965), pp. 14–16, 83–87, 134–35, 98.

consider moral restraint a form of misery.[16] He repeatedly argued—one might almost say with relish—that working people were responsible for their own poverty. "The knowledge and prudence of the poor themselves," he wrote in his *Principles of Political Economy* (1820), "are absolutely the *only* means by which any general and permanent improvement in their condition can be effected. They are really the arbiters of their own destiny."[17]

But, like Adam Smith, Malthus thought that labourers were being exploited, and his intent was to help them if it was possible to do so. His reliance on the frail reed of moral restraint was an indication of his desperate search for a way to avoid his own conclusions. Eventually he came to believe that raising the wages of workers might offer a better solution; if living standards rose (and if workers were better educated) prudence might lead them to limit their families in order to maintain their gains. "The power of commanding a large portion of the necessaries of life" might "generate prudential habits among the lower classes." And to his credit he added that civil and political liberty were even more important than material comfort in fostering these habits because they "teach the lower classes of society to respect themselves by obliging the higher classes to respect them." Thus, in his mature thought, Malthus postulated that what workers considered a subsistence wage might be determined by their psychological rather than their crudely physiological needs alone. It is ironic that while there was little sign of their developing rising expectations in Malthus's day, they eventually did so, whereas the impoverishment of the masses because of overpopulation, which appeared so imminent in the early nineteenth century, did not come to pass. In any case, Malthus never displayed much confidence that the masses would exercise moral restraint, in their own or the national interest.[18]

Yet despite his pessimism, Malthus did not consider unemployment a major problem. Although he could write: "A man who is born into a world already possessed . . . if society do not want his labours, has no claim of *right* to the smallest portion of food, and, in fact, has no business to be where he is," his theory made a kind of social virtue of joblessness. If people could not support children they might exercise

---

[16] His words were: "moral restraint, or the abstaining from marriage till we are in a condition to support a family, with a perfectly moral conduct during that period, is the strict line of duty." However, he opposed any attempt to enforce celibacy by law, and he objected to birth control on moral and religious grounds. *An Essay on the Principle of Population* (Homewood, Ill., 1963), p. 271.

[17] T. R. Malthus, *Principles of Political Economy* (New York, 1951), p. 279.

[18] *Ibid.*, pp. 226–27; Lionel Robbins, *The Theory of Economic Policy in English Classical Economics* (London, 1952), p. 77; A. W. Coats, ed., *The Classical Economists and Economic Policy* (London, 1971), pp. 163–64.

moral restraint and the pressure of population on the food supply would lessen. The central problem, however, was not any lack of work to be done but the ultimate impossibility of producing enough food by any amount of labor. The surplus of people he so feared would make the whole working class poor, but not idle. This aside, he believed that Adam Smith was "quite correct" in his analysis of the role of supply and demand in the labor market, and he accepted Smith's argument that "inconstancy" of employment did not affect annual income. In *Principles of Political Economy* he recognized that under some circumstances a decline in national income would cause "thousands [to be] thrown out of employment," but he saw such unemployment merely as an "almost unavoidable preliminary" to the reduction of wage rates which would "enable the general income of the country to employ the same number of labourers as before." During such periods of transition, the government might even "assist the working classes" by building roads and other public works, which would not compete with products already on the market.[19]

Workers could also be replaced by machinery, but since the efficiency of machines lowers the cost and increases the volume of commodities, demand would soar and "notwithstanding the saving of labour, more hands, instead of fewer," would be employed. Malthus conceded that industrial profits might be saved rather than reinvested (a point seized upon a century later by John Maynard Keynes). In that case, unemployment would result. He believed, however, that "in the actual state of things" this danger was most remote.[20] He was as convinced as Adam Smith that an expanding economy was *ipso facto* a fully employed economy and that the process by which jobs were created was an automatic one. His argument in behalf of moral restraint and prudence further suggests that he thought laborers could ignore the possibility of extended periods without work, since he assumed that at a certain point in life they could raise children without the risk of being unable to care for them properly.

This tendency to pay little heed to unemployment was characteristic also of David Ricardo, whose *Principles of Political Economy and Taxation* was published in 1817. Ricardo was the prototypical economist's economist. The influence of both Smith and Malthus was heightened by their ability to express their thoughts in language that ordinary readers could readily understand. They had been trained in the communication of ideas—Smith had been a professor, Malthus a clergyman—and while they were seeking to discover general principles of human behavior, they were also deeply concerned with explaining how the prin-

[19] Malthus, *Principles*, pp. 220–21, 393, 429–30.
[20] *Ibid.*, 351–52, 360.

ciples operated in everyday life. Ricardo, however, was by profession a stockbroker and by temperament a detached logician. His method was purely deductive; he wished to reduce the jumble of economic activity to its essences. His examples were hypothetical, deliberately simplified, often mathematical. Descriptions of how real people bought and sold goods, contracted to work for wages, lent money, or invested in a business are rare in his pages, for everyday reality had small significance in his intellectual system. "Ricardo offers us," wrote Keynes in his *General Theory of Employment, Interest, and Money,* "the supreme intellectual achievement, unattainable by weaker spirits, of adopting a hypothetical world remote from experience as though it were the world of experience and then living in it consistently."

Although Ricardo had made a fortune in the market, as an economist the marketplace or even the forces that shaped its activity did not particularly interest him. Once, while testifying before a parliamentary committee, he was asked: "Are you aware that there is at present a considerable stagnation of trade?" He replied: "I have heard so but I am not engaged in trade, and it does not come much within my knowledge." After the publication of his *Principles* he was elected to the House of Commons, but he seldom participated in the debates. "I have no hope of conquering the alarm with which I am assailed the moment I hear the sound of my own voice," he explained.[21]

Ricardo accepted Smith's assumptions about individual self-interest and competition, and the Malthusian theory of population growth. Wages were determined, he wrote, by "the natural operation of the proportion of the supply to the demand; labour is dear when it is scarce, and cheap when it is plentiful. . . . In the natural advance of society, the wages of labour have a tendency to fall . . . for the supply of labourers will continue to increase . . . while the demand for them will increase at a slower rate." However, Ricardo went beyond Smith and Malthus in his analysis. Supply and demand set what he called the "market price of labour," but there was also a "natural price," that which will "enable the labourers . . . to subsist and to perpetuate their race, without either increase or diminution." This natural price was determined by the price of food and other necessaries of life. What controlled the standard of living of workers, he reasoned, was the amount of capital invested in productive enterprises, which brought into being the volume of goods (what later economists would call the wages fund) available for workers to consume. The larger the number of people dependent upon this supply, the smaller each individual's

[21] J. M. Keynes, *The General Theory of Employment, Interest, and Money* (New York, 1964), p. 192; B. A. Corry, *Money, Saving and Investment in English Economics* (London, 1962), p. 63n.; Charles Gide and Charles Rist, *A History of Economic Doctrines* (Boston, [n.d., second English edition]), p. 155n.

share. For a time the market price of labor might be above or below the natural price but the tendency of wages was always toward the natural price. If wages fell below subsistence the population would have to shrink. If they rose above it the Malthusian principle would cause the population to grow—as Ricardo put it, an increase in the demand for labor gives "a continued stimulus to an increase of people," and he added: "It is a truth that admits not a doubt, that the comforts and well-being of the poor cannot be permanently secured without some regard on their part, or some effort on the part of the legislature, to regulate the increase of their numbers."[22]

Ricardo's description of the labor market left no room for serious unemployment. He assumed that every potential laborer had to work or starve, and that employers would hire all who applied for jobs. If the supply of capital became larger or if the size of the work force shrank, the market price of labor would go up. If the supply of capital was reduced or if the number of workers increased, the market price of labor would fall. In all instances, all would be employed. Since the natural price of labor was a function of the ratio between already existing supplies of food and other consumer goods and the number of workers and their dependents, it had no relation to employment either; it affected how well people lived (and in the long run how many could survive) but not the number of those living who could find work.

Although he did not say it in so many words, Ricardo believed that the poor laws (which scaled assistance according to family size) encouraged idleness. His main objection, like that of Malthus, was that the laws discouraged working people from limiting the number of their children—"they have rendered restraint superfluous, and have invited imprudence." They therefore drove down the natural wage by increasing the number of people without adding to the supply of capital. Further, the poor rates diverted capital into agriculture that could otherwise be invested in more productive enterprises. Thus the system impoverished the whole society. But the poor laws also destroyed incentive by diverting the poor from looking "to their own exertions" for support. "The principle of gravitation," Ricardo wrote in one of his rare excursions into the area of public policy

is not more certain than the tendency of such laws to change wealth and power into misery and weakness; to call away the exertions of labour from every object, except that of providing mere subsistence; to confound all intellectual distinction; to busy the mind continually in supplying the body's wants; until at last all classes are infected with the plague of universal poverty.[23]

[22] Piero Sraffa, ed., *Works of David Ricardo* (Cambridge, 1962), I: 93–95, 101, 106–107.
[23] *Ibid.*, I: 107–108, 257–61.

Beyond this oblique reference to idleness, Ricardo also admitted that "temporary reverses and contingencies" could cause industrial laborers to be thrown out of work: he mentioned wars, new types of taxes, and "the tastes and caprice" of consumers. Such disruptions forced manufacturers to transfer their capital from one activity to another; while they were doing so, and for some time thereafter, "much fixed capital is unemployed, perhaps wholly lost, and labourers are without full employment." But he reasoned that except where capital had actually been destroyed "after temporary suffering, the nation would again advance in prosperity." He recognized that it was not easy to shift capital that was invested in plant and machinery, but passed over this difficulty as the unavoidable price that an industrial country must pay for its wealth. "It would not be more reasonable to complain of it, than it would be in a rich merchant to lament that his ship was exposed to the dangers of the sea, whilst his poor neighbour's cottage was safe from all such hazard."[24]

In the last edition of his *Principles,* almost as an afterthought, Ricardo mentioned another possible cause of unemployment, the substitution of machinery for human labor. An obscure young economist, John Barton, had drawn a sharp distinction between fixed capital invested in machinery and circulating capital, arguing in effect that only circulating capital contributed to the wages fund that sustained all labor. The distinction was one Ricardo had seldom made—his use of the term "fixed capital" in discussing disruptions of trade was most unusual—and it did not per se undermine his case for full employment, since in his system the size of the wages fund controlled the real income of workers but not their numbers. But apparently Barton's argument (and a careful rereading of the treatment of the subject in Malthus's *Principles*) changed his thinking. He proceeded by means of one of his hypothetical illustrations to show how a manufacturer might, by investing in machinery, earn as much profit from a smaller output as from a larger volume produced by employing more workers. If the manufacturer reduced his circulating capital in order to pay for the machinery—in Ricardo's example, from £13,000 to £5,500—"all the labour which was before employed by £7,500 would become redundant." And Ricardo asked, with typical *sang-froid,* "if the net income be not diminished, of what importance is it to the capitalist, whether the gross income be of the value of £3,000, of £10,000, or of £15,000?" But his whole argument was chiefly a mental exercise. He quickly pointed out that manufacturers usually financed purchases of machinery out of profits, not by "diverting capital from its actual

[24] *Ibid.,* I: 263–66.

employment," that is, from the wages fund. The fear of workers that they could be displaced by machines, he wrote in a passage that perfectly reveals his approach to economics, was "conformable to the correct principles of political economy," but as a practical matter labor would benefit from mechanization because the efficiency of machines would reduce the cost of consumer goods and also, by increasing the capitalists' profits, lead to further investment and to a larger demand for "menial servants." The introduction of machinery "could never be safely discouraged," for in a competitive world any nation that did not mechanize its industry would lose out, and so would its labor force.[25]

With Ricardo what is now called "classical economics" reached maturity. The enormous differences between the classical writers' reasoning and that of their predecessors with regard to labor are obvious. The earlier theorists believed that economic growth required more people, that poverty was a goad to productivity, that idleness represented lost production and that therefore the state should compel people to work. Classical economists believed that plenty of labor already existed, that working-class poverty was caused by overpopulation, that idleness was a personal more than a social problem, and that hunger would compel everyone to work. Yet in a sense nothing had changed. Involuntary idleness remained unimaginable or at most exceptional, since, in the classical system, whatever its size the whole work force would be employed, competition merely reducing real wages when the supply of labor relative to capital increased. If approached the other way round, unemployment caused by overproduction was also inconceivable, since according to a "law" that the French economist Jean-Baptiste Say expounded in his *Traité d'économie politique* (1803), the very existence of goods produces a demand for them. "A product is no sooner created, than it opens up a market for other products of the same value." Apparent oversupplies of anything actually reflect shortages of something else, Say explained, and because "nothing is more favorable to the demand of one product than the supply of another," any "superabundance" is sure to stimulate economic activity. Therefore business slumps can never last long and (more important) they are self-correcting.[26]

In their laudable and it should be remembered brilliantly successful efforts to discover the laws governing economic relationships, the classical writers detached themselves from particularities. Seeking essential principles and ultimate realities, they tended to dismiss as aber-

[25] *Ibid.*, I: 386–89, 395–96; Oswald St. Clair, *A Key to Ricardo* (New York, 1965), pp. 226–46.
[26] J.-B. Say, *Traité d'économie politique* (Paris, 1972), pp. 138–42.

rations the blind irrationalities of day-to-day economic behavior. Both their method and their purpose compelled them to take the long view, to follow, in an illogical world, the implications of their theories to "logical" conclusions. As one close student of Ricardo's mind put it, "he has a habit of belittling or minifying the importance of intervals that interrupt or delay the operation of long-term trends." Ricardo himself boasted: "I put these immediate and temporary effects quite aside, and fix my whole attention on the permanent state of things." All the classical writers suffered from what the Harvard economist Wassily Leontief once called their "theoretical farsightedness." They could "appraise correctly the long-run trends" but had "a singular inability to explain or even describe the short-run changes and fluctuations."[27]

This perspective deflected the classical economists from looking carefully at the problem of unemployment. Consider their treatment of subsistence wages. The logic of their argument was impeccable: If wages fell below subsistence, some people would stop subsisting; then the balance between mouths and resources would be restored. They were aware of the suffering this would entail, for they were not without compassion. But they ignored the fact that no sharp line separated subsistence from extinction, that people who do not have enough to eat do not starve quickly. They recognized the "misery and vice" that substandard conditions produced, but did not understand the ultimate effects—shorter lives and less efficient workers but not necessarily fewer. Malthus's argument in his later years that subsistence was a variable, influenced by what workers were accustomed to, was an accurate explanation of how workers would *feel* about any reduction from this standard, but not (especially in a society that adopted Malthus's and Ricardo's stern views of poor relief) of how they would behave when forced to choose between less pay and none at all.

It is no doubt true that the classical writers exaggerated both the rationality of businessmen and the irrationality of workers; Ricardo's rhetorical question about the central importance of net profits to capitalists and his and Malthus's assumptions about the inability of working people to pursue their own best interests are excellent examples of this generalization. But in a sense the economists were even more committed to a materialist view of history than their most creative student and severest critic, Karl Marx. Nothing reveals this more clearly than their critique of poor relief, as witness Malthus's reasoning that people would not restrain their procreative drives if assured of

[27] St. Clair, *Key to Ricardo*, p. 129; J. M. Keynes, *Essays in Biography* (New York, 1963), p. 116; S. E. Harris, ed., *The New Economics: Keynes's Influence on Theory and Public Policy* (New York, 1963), p. 240.

enough food to feed their children, Ricardo's that giving anything to the average person for nothing would stifle initiative and eventually reduce the whole society to "universal poverty," and, conversely, Say's argument that if society rigidly refused to care for the aged, workers "would put aside each day a small sum against the time when age . . . would deprive them of the ability to labor."[28]

Perhaps the central cause of their cold-blooded approach—it has often been so charged—was their isolation from the masses whose fate they dissected with such detachment. (How they could have reasoned differently, given the attitudes of their times, without losing that detachment is a difficult question; those of their contemporaries who were able to identify with the problems of ordinary workers were seldom capable of dispassionate analysis.) And one further aspect of the period needs to be remembered. Relatively few people, especially in industrial regions, were totally unemployed—life was too hard for that. Almost a decade before Adam Smith published *The Wealth of Nations,* Turgot wrote in his *Réflexions sur la formation et la distribution des richesses:* "The ordinary worker has only his arms and his labor, there is nothing else he can sell to others. *Il ne gagne que sa vie.*"[29] Probably *vie* is best translated "livelihood," but it would not be wrong to translate the sentence: "He gets only his life," in that only by working could a poor person survive. The problem in the late eighteenth century and still more in the early nineteenth was more underemployment than total idleness. Everywhere thousands scrounged for a living as street hawkers, peddlers, porters, laundresses, mountebanks, carters, and scavengers. By the modern definition these marginal types could scarcely be considered workers, but they were far from idle. They could not afford to be unemployed, to look for, much less wait for, a job. This is why the classical economists could see them as evidence that too many people were consuming the wages fund, but not as unemployed.

The key books on political economy, even the difficult work of Ricardo, attracted immediate attention, were swiftly translated, and were disseminated in simplified form by a host of popularizers. *The Wealth of Nations* passed through five editions before Smith's death in 1790 and three more by 1796. Johann Friedrich Schiller translated it into German between 1776 and 1778. French and other translations followed, and soon a host of commentators were expounding Smith's ideas, the most notable being J.-B. Say, whose *Traité* was in large measure an interpretation of the masterwork. Say's book was itself widely translated and frequently reprinted, while Malthus's *Essay on Population* appeared in German in 1807 and Ricardo's *Principles* in

[28] Say, *Traité,* pp. 382–83.
[29] A. R. Turgot, *Oeuvres* (Paris, 1808), V: 7.

French in 1818, the latter with notes by the ubiquitous Say.[30]

The extraordinary success of books that, however engagingly written, dealt with complicated technical issues is not hard to understand. As has been said many times, the economists were telling the manufacturers what they wanted to hear—that their acquisitive urges should be freed from outdated restraints. Political events were further reinforcing the economists' arguments. By its mere eruption, the American Revolution discredited the policy of closely regulating colonial economies, and when British trade with the new United States boomed after the regulations were cast off as a result of American independence, the old system appeared to have been even more absurd. The French Revolution provided a further ideological justification for a libertarian approach to economics; its democratic ideology appealed to individualists and social reformers alike, while the failure of the oppressive regulatory legislation of the Terror strengthened the conviction of conservatives that the state ought not to meddle with private business. Both the Napoleonic wars and the struggle for markets when peace was restored added to the persuasiveness of the laissez-faire position.

The triumph of the new ideas in the political arena, however, took a long time and was never complete. Restrictions on foreign trade, for example, were very difficult to do away with; only in Great Britain and there not until the 1840s were all tariff barriers removed. Changes in the relationships between workers and their employers and in public policies toward unemployment came more swiftly, but were also not of one pattern. In Britain, the restrictions on apprenticeship of the ancient Elizabethan Statute of Artificers were removed in 1813, and the next year the minimum-wage provisions of the statute were repealed. On the other hand the emigration of workers trained in the construction and operation of factory machinery was prohibited until 1825, and the Combination Acts (1799–1800) declared organizations of both workers and employers illegal. In France the law d'Allarde of 1791 abolished guilds, another act passed in that year banned the secret societies of the journeymen *compagnons,* and in 1810 all associations of more than twenty persons were outlawed. In Prussia, reformers led by the Freiherr vom Stein, converts to the new economics (which was called *Smithianismus* in Germany), pushed through similar laws in 1810.[31]

Workers greeted such measures with mixed feelings, for they

---

[30] W. G. Roscher, *Geschichte der National-Ökonomik in Deutschland* (Munich, 1874), pp. 598, 610–15; D. V. Glass, ed., *Introduction to Malthus* (London, 1953), p. 39; Sraffa, *Works of Ricardo,* I: L.

[31] Thompson, *English Working Class,* pp. 544–55; Emile Coornaert, *Les corporations en France* (Paris, 1968), pp. 173–75; Coornaert, *Les compagnonnages en France* (Paris, 1966), pp. 55–56; Roscher, *Geschichte der National-Ökonomik,* p. 598; Friedrich Lütge, *Deutsche Sozial- und Wirtschaftsgeschichte: Ein Überblick* (Berlin, 1960), p. 304.

affected different types of workers in different ways. Some 300,000 English artisans signed petitions protesting the repeal of the Statute of Artificers because they wished to retain control over the admission of apprentices to their trades, whereas workers in textiles, shipbuilding, and other manufacturing industries objected to the old statute because the section forbidding laborers to leave work unfinished was often used to prosecute them when they went on strike.[32] Although laws against unions were widely resented, they were not always enforced. During the Napoleonic period and under the Bourbon restoration after Waterloo, the *compagnnonages* were sometimes tolerated, sometimes repressed. The historian of the movement, Emile Coornaert, calling French policy "paradoxical" and "opportunistic," cites a case against some stone masons that the court settled by declaring that their organization was not legal but that nothing prevented them from making "lawful agreements" *(conventions licites).*[33] The British Combination Acts also failed to stop workers from organizing and were repealed in 1824, but a new law passed the next year imposed harsh penalties on strikers and the use of violence or threats in labor disputes.

To strike a balance in evaluating the impact on workers of the great changes of the late eighteenth and early nineteenth centuries is probably impossible, chiefly because the many kinds of working people were affected in many different ways. If they are lumped together—something only historians and sociologists can do to them—then it is clear that the industrial revolution and the energies released by casting off outdated economic restrictions and releasing the acquisitive drives of entrepreneurs produced material advantages for the work force as a whole. The rapid increase in population that Malthus viewed with such alarm is surely evidence that the system was producing enough to sustain more people.

It is, however, equally clear that industrialization did not do away with the misery and vice that Malthus properly associated with poverty. He and the other classical writers pictured the United States as a land of milk and honey because of its sparse population and huge food-producing capacity.[34] But misery, vice, and poverty existed even there. In 1814 seventeen thousand people in New York City were dependent upon charity.[35] And, if some of the benefits of industrial growth went to wage earners, the benefits were not distributed equally among them,

[32] Thompson, *English Working Class,* pp. 517–18, 507.

[33] Coornaert, *Compagnonnages,* pp. 290–91.

[34] In 1856, Ralph Waldo Emerson wrote: "America is the paradise of the [English] economists; it is the favorite exception invariably quoted to the rules of ruin." Quoted in Alistair Cooke, *The American in England: Emerson to S. J. Perelman* (Cambridge, 1975), p. 24.

[35] R. A. Mohl, *Poverty in New York; 1783–1825* (New York, 1971), p. 20.

even putting aside the subjective question of whether their total share was as large as it should have been. As for the unemployed, the changes of the period apparently had little effect. Those who for one reason or another were outside the labor force remained about as numerous proportionately as in earlier times. For those accustomed to live by their own labor, the problem, as I have said, was more one of sporadic and unproductive labor than of long-term joblessness, at least until cyclical depressions began to become serious after the Napoleonic wars.

Despite the upheavals of the recent past, methods of dealing with the idle were little different in 1815 from what they had been in the eighteenth century. In France the revolutionary experiments had been rejected and the old hospital-workhouses were again functioning, their efforts still buttressed in hard times by *ateliers de charité*. In northern Italy, a relatively humane system of poor relief had been first undermined financially by war and then bureaucratized by Napoleonic administrators during the French occupation. *Dépôts de mendicité* had been set up to put beggars to work, along with *ateliers libres de charité* in agricultural districts designed to provide jobs for farm laborers in slack seasons. These proved no more effective in Tuscany than in France itself, and in the chaos accompanying the liberation they collapsed. Unemployment rose and in 1816–17 famine ravaged the region.[36] In Prussia and in the Hapsburg domains of central Europe the workhouse method of dealing with the problem was losing its charm as problems of administration and of inadequate financing mounted, but no substitute for the workhouse was in sight. The Elizabethan poor law remained in force in Great Britain, and so did the workhouses and the Speenhamland system of subsidizing wages. The practice of shuttling unemployed rural workers from farm to farm, where they received room and board in return for their labor, was another late-eighteenth-century device that continued to be used, both in Britain and throughout northern Europe.

In the new United States (where supposedly labor was in short supply and poverty nonexistent), relief was generally based on the English system. In New York, for example, unemployed rural workers were hired out on contract or "auctioned" to farmers in return for their support. Most of the large towns had workhouses, although, as in Europe, little work was actually done in them. New York City's Bellevue workhouse had 1,563 inmates in 1821, but despite vigorous efforts to make the place self-supporting, only 145 persons were productively employed.[37]

[36] S. J. Woolf, "The Treatment of the Poor in Napoleonic Tuscany," *Annuario dell'Istituto Storico Italiano*, 23–24 (1971–72), 453–74.

[37] Mohl, *Poverty in New York*, pp. 55–59, 86–95.

Dissatisfaction with such methods was everywhere rife, in part because of their ineffectiveness and (in the opinion of critics) high costs, and still more because idleness now seemed more inexcusable. The political economists had *proved*—at least to the satisfaction of those predisposed to believe them—that any person who wanted to work would be hired, and if wages were too low, that too was the workers' fault.

In the prevailing climate of opinion (I refer of course only to the views of those who determined policy) some stiffer deterrent to idleness seemed necessary. There was a reversion to the tough attitudes of the seventeenth century, but with this difference: in that era the unemployed, while resented because of their parasitism, represented primarily unproduced wealth, an unused potential; in the nineteenth century they seemed more a drain on existing resources. But the practical implications were the same—the unemployed must be made to work.

The best example of how this attitude affected policy is provided by the changes made in the English poor law. Throughout the late eighteenth century and especially during the food shortages of the mid-1790s there had been a relaxation of the requirements for receiving relief in most parishes, aid being dispensed without much effort to distinguish between those who worked and those who did not. The policy of supplementing the wages of workers who had many children, either by relating the payments to the price of bread under the Speenhamland system or more haphazardly, reflected a general awareness that agricultural laborers in particular could not earn enough to support large families. With the passage of time, however, the costs of poor relief rose steadily, even during the prosperous years of the Napoleonic wars. Between 1784 and 1813 they more than tripled.[38] The economic depression that followed the end of the wars in 1815 caused expenditures to rise still higher and precipitated a great debate that culminated in the new poor law of 1834.

The financial burden was the primary cause of concern, but discussions of the problem were also influenced by the new economics and by Malthus's theory of population growth. As early as 1797, after a pioneering field study of conditions throughout England, Sir Frederick Morton Eden published *The State of the Poor*. Because of his diligent massing of data on wages, spending patterns, and food prices, Eden's book greatly impressed his contemporaries, and it remains an important historical source, but his conclusion—that the poor law ought gradually to be done away with—was preconditioned by his commitment to Smithian economics. "It seems," he wrote, "very problemati-

[38] Sidney and Beatrice Webb, *English Poor Law History: The Last Hundred Years* (London, 1963), I: 1.

cal whether a government ever attempted directly to regulate the course of industry without producing considerable mischief." Poor relief was based on "the mistaken principle that . . . people must be compelled to follow their own interest. . . . A legal provision for the Poor . . . seems to check that emulative spirit of exertion, which the want of the necessities, or the no less powerful demand for the superfluities, of life gives birth to." Creating jobs for the unemployed would be counterproductive, for "it is impossible to provide work or any species of employment without in some degree injuring those already engaged in similar undertakings."[39]

As for the Malthusians, pegging assistance to family size seemed pure madness—a positive encouragement to irresponsible procreation. Supplementing wages appeared to economists an exercise in futility—bound to reduce the wages of people not on relief and, if pursued to its logical conclusion, likely to reduce the whole nation to poverty. In 1817 Malthus published a new (fifth) edition of his *Essay on Population,* in which he argued that the postwar depression had made it *impossible* for the country to care for the indigent adequately and that it was therefore both unfair and an incitement to disorder to claim to be able to do so. Better to confront the sufferers with the facts; perhaps then they would begin to control their numbers. Wage supplements, called allowances, only force actual wages down and "make the supply of labour exceed the demand."

In that same year a parliamentary committee, while not recommending any major change in the poor law, charged that the system weakened the "natural impulse by which men are instigated to industry and good conduct," increased the "misery it was designed to alleviate," and drained off capital that "would otherwise have been applied more beneficially to the supply of employment." Echoing the reasoning of the economists, the committee added:

> By holding out to the labouring classes that they shall be at all times provided with adequate employment, they are led to believe they have nothing to dread while they are willing to labour. The supply of labour, therefore, which they alone have the power to regulate, is left constantly to increase, without reference to the demand, or to the funds on which it depends.

Two years later a bill was introduced denying all aid to persons who were employed. Relief would consist only of support for those who could not work and jobs for those who could; instead of giving subsidies to workers with large families, the parishes would take over the care and employment of their children directly.[40]

[39] F. M. Eden, *The State of the Poor* (London, 1928), pp. 91–93, 97.
[40] J. R. Poynter, *Society and Pauperism* (London, 1969), pp. 225–26, 246–47, 286–87; Webb, *English Poor Law,* I: 41–42.

The focus of dissatisfaction on allowances was understandable enough, despite the paradox that a method devised to compensate for low wages was now seen as the cause of low wages. The allowance system was probably not as pervasive as its critics thought (although it was and remains difficult to know its extent because of the extreme decentralization of poor relief at that time). Even when ordered to pay allowances by the magistrates, local officials often used their own judgment about doing so. Nevertheless, it seemed immoral or counterproductive not only to economists and Malthusians, but also to employers, who preferred that labor be dependent on them; to recipients of allowances, who saw them as a poor substitute for decent wages; and to radicals, who objected both to public contributions that in effect subsidized employers and to the eroding effects of the allowances on the independence of workers. The bill was rejected by the House of Lords, not out of any sympathy for wage supplements but because of the fear that the cost of maintaining and training the children of the poor would be even greater.[41]

It was a tribute to the persuasiveness of post-Smithian economics that even those who disapproved of the proposed "reform" of the poor laws accepted most of its precepts. The old poor law survived chiefly because, despite the arguments of Malthus, Ricardo, and their followers, the thought of how those receiving its benefits would suffer if it were abolished made the most hard-hearted pause. The fear of what the poor might do if deprived of assistance was another stumbling block to drastic change. Doing away with all relief, one member of Parliament pointed out, "would give to popular commotion the colour of necessary resistance against wanton oppression."

The problem as seen by reformers in the 1820s was the same problem that had confronted Juan Luis Vives and other municipal reformers three hundred years earlier: how to care for the helpless but compel the able to work. Telling the deserving from the undeserving, wrote Josiah Quincy of Massachusetts in a report to the state legislature in 1821, was impossible because of "the minute shades of difference between the pauper who . . . can do absolutely nothing, and the pauper who is able to do something." The government, Quincy added, "is absolutely incapable to fix any standard . . . by which the claim of right to the benefit of the public provision shall absolutely be determined."

Quincy's view was similar to that of the dominant opinion among British experts, whose writings he had studied in detail. Gradually sentiment was developing for going back to something like the workhouse test, for creating what J. R. McCulloch, one of Ricardo's most

[41] Poynter, *Society and Pauperism*, pp. 280–81; Thompson, *English Working Class*, p. 223.

influential disciples, called *"some very powerful counteracting circumstances"* that would prevent those who could work from taking advantage of society's compassion for those who could not. Although as a Malthusian he had opposed poor relief on theoretical grounds, by the late 1820s McCulloch had come to believe that since the institution had existed for over two hundred years without destroying society it would be a mistake to abolish it. A really tough workhouse "such . . . as will not be resorted to except by those who have no other resource" would be, he thought, a more effective check on family size than moral restraint.[42]

Matters came to a head in the early 1830s. A rural insurrection in 1830, although primarily a protest against labor-displacing threshing machines, was seen in retrospect by critics of the poor law as a further argument against the allowance system, since the outbreak had been most violent in districts where allowances were most widely paid. In 1832 Parliament created a royal commission which put a large staff to work visiting parishes and towns all over England and Wales. Two years later, the commission published its report, which was largely the work of Nassau Senior, professor of political economy at Oxford and one of the leading English economists of the post-Ricardian generation.

The commission's recommendations, which were swiftly enacted into law with only minor alterations by large parliamentary majorities, produced two important changes in the poor law. One was to centralize the administration of all relief under a powerful national board. The other was to forbid all public assistance to the able-bodied poor except in "well-regulated workhouses," these to be run on the principle that the "situation" of an inmate "shall not be made really or apparently so eligible as the situation of the independent labourer of the lowest class." The assumption behind this principle of less eligibility, as it came to be called, was that the indolent, dispirited, and feckless, when faced with a choice between working harder and living in what amounted to a prison, would become industrious, alert, and responsible. The law was expected to achieve miracles. "New life, new energy is infused into the constitution of the pauper," one of the commission's investigators insisted. "He is aroused like one from sleep . . . he surveys his former employers with new eyes. He begs a job—he will not take a denial—he discovers that every one wants something to be done. . . . He is ready to turn his hand to anything."[43]

The new law appealed to humanitarians because it acknowledged public responsibility for aiding anyone who sought help and continued

[42] Poynter, *Society and Pauperism*, pp. 297–98, 305. [Josiah Quincy], *Report of the Committee on the Pauper Laws of the Commonwealth* [Boston, 1821], p. 5.
[43] Webb, *English Poor Law*, I: 45–57, 60–62.

support in their own homes for persons whom everyone recognized as incompetent. Uniform rules and standards of assistance appeared to be another major improvement. To those concerned about loafers and dissolute types feeding at the public trough, less eligibility promised lower taxes and much moral satisfaction, while employers could look forward to receiving a new army of petitioners, marvelously purged of bad habits, eager, even desperate, for a chance to earn their daily bread. And, although central supervision was imposed on local authorities, thus rousing considerable opposition, it was done without eliminating all their functions or meddling with their methods of handling the impotent poor. At least this powerful vested interest was not threatened with extinction by the change. And the system of supplementing wages was promptly terminated, something that pleased taxpayers and the political economists mightily.

As for the former recipients of these allowances, who were not consulted, they promptly dubbed the new workhouses "Bastilles." Less eligibility was surely an effective means of goading the lethargic to greater effort, but what if their efforts proved fruitless? The new law, like the economics that inspired it, made no allowance for involuntary unemployment or for the far-more-prevalent contemporary problems of underemployment and seasonal unemployment. In good times, when work was plentiful and food cheap, the system worked reasonably well. But during depressions it caused almost unbearable hardships. The principle of less eligibility offered no incentive at all when there was no work to be had. Furthermore, if it was true, as the economists claimed, that wages tended toward subsistence, it would be possible to make workhouse life less attractive only by starving the inmates or by exerting inhuman psychological pressures upon them. Thus willing workers who could not find jobs or who for whatever reason could not survive on the wages they could earn were condemned to a terrible existence. Cut off from public aid yet unable to maintain their families, they had no alternative but to go—and by law their families had to accompany them—to the workhouse.

It took many years for the poor law commissioners appointed under the law to organize the thousands of parishes into manageable units, called unions, and to set up the necessary workhouses. Although disabused of any expectation that even a "well-regulated" workhouse could be self-supporting, these administrators soon abandoned the plan of the original commission for maintaining able-bodied inmates separate from orphans, old people, and others who needed institutional care. Instead they constructed in each district a union workhouse where all welfare recipients were confined.

These places became houses of horror rather than of either work or custodial care. They could scarcely have been otherwise, as the mixed workhouses of the previous century should have demonstrated, but the new system positively insured this result. In the older institutions the objective—admittedly seldom achieved—was to train, inspire, or force those presumed to be capable of labor to work; in the new the objective was to make the environment so unpleasant that anyone who could possibly do so would shun them like the plague, or, if driven by circumstances to enter, leave at the first glimmer of a chance to get by outside. This objective was only too easily achieved; poor people were known to sell the shirts off their backs to avoid the workhouse. But it guaranteed that those whom everyone considered the helpless wards of society, whose lot the law of 1834 had not intended to make more painful, would be immeasurably worse off.

Several pressures combined to bring about this disastrous development. Union workhouses were easier to administer from London and cost less to run than separate units, and as one assistant commissioner pointed out, a single imposing structure "would give dignity to the whole arrangement, while the pauper would feel it was utterly impossible to contend against it." Most important, however, was the policy of less eligibility, which could only be effectuated by compelling those seeking "shelter" to enter and leave the houses in family units. (If a poor man could escape his responsibilities by putting his children in an institution or leave the workhouse without taking them with him, one might as well continue paying allowances.) This policy made separate units impractical. The commissioners recognized the need to keep different types of inmates apart—indeed, they saw separating the sexes and parents from children as major deterrents to seeking public assistance. They defined no fewer than seven categories of inmates, each to be isolated from the others in the workhouse complex. In practice, of course, this could never be done. Children and sick people had to be cared for and the buildings maintained, and no money was provided to have these tasks performed by outsiders. Everyone ate in common halls, the mad, the doddering, the dissolute along with the rest.

Under such conditions both the strong and the weak had to suffer terribly. To criticism that the helpless poor deserved better treatment, the commissioners replied: "If the condition of the inmates of a Workhouse were to be so regulated as to invite the aged and infirm . . . to take refuge in it, it would immediately be useless as a test." Furthermore, "the frugality and forethought of a young labourer would be useless if he foresaw the certainty of a better asylum for his old age than he could possibly provide by his own exertions." The first explanation was inhumane but possibly accurate, the second merely specious.[44]

[44] *Ibid.*, I: 276, 158–59.

5

The "English Industrial System"

As time passed and the pace of industrialization quickened, in Great Britain and elsewhere, the persistence of poverty and of surplus labor despite the expansion of wealth and output that industrialization made possible became the subject of increasing concern. Both the British example and the theories of the British classical economists affected other industrializing nations mightily. "England," the French economist and historian Jérôme Adolphe Blanqui wrote in 1837, "has become an immense factory." Its economists have treated their subject like algebra, employing "inexorable logic" and "giving to the language of economics a precision that has contributed greatly to the progress of ideas."[1] The French, Germans, and others sought to copy British manufacturing techniques, and first in France and then elsewhere they made remarkable advances, although not matching the rate of British growth. But the social problems resulting from industrialization also seemed to be of British origin, and these caused misgivings. Few French theorists, for example, accepted without reservation the abstractions of Ricardo and his school, which in Blanqui's words "separated the well being of workers from questions of production and mechanization" and were "insensitive to the suffering of the working classes."[2] Thus, what was called "the English industrial system" had become the wonder of the Western world, but it was viewed, like all awe-inspiring phenomena, with a mixture of respect and fear.

Much of the fear was related to what was happening in cities. Industrialization was an urbanizing development; Lowell in Massachusetts, Manchester in England, the urban agglomerations of the Rhineland were created by the factory system. Industrialization also attracted hordes of rural people to every major city of western Europe and the

[1] J. A. Blanqui, *Histoire de l'économie politique en Europe* (Paris, 1945), II: 311–12.
[2] *Ibid.*, p. 311.

Americas. Living conditions in the cities deteriorated, for water and sewage systems, housing, and other facilities failed to keep pace with population growth. Slums proliferated. Death rates rose, as did those of crime, prostitution, and other social evils. After a long period without a major plague, in 1832 a cholera epidemic swept across Europe and on to Quebec, Montreal, Boston and New York, all the way to New Orleans, killing tens of thousands, the poorest supplying a disproportionate share of the victims.

Methods of dealing with poverty and unemployment devised for pre-industrial societies broke down under the new conditions. The reformed English poor law, for example, was designed with rural poverty chiefly in mind. However harsh, it dealt realistically with the problem of demoralized and underemployed agricultural workers who had grown accustomed to depending on allowances. When some of these laborers entered the workhouses and when others drifted off to the cities in hopes of escaping them, the wages of the rest rose enough so that they could usually survive without public aid. But in industrial regions, especially in those where the factory system of making cloth was developing, it was ill suited to conditions and bitterly resisted.

Output in the textile towns was expanding rapidly and the chronic unemployment and underemployment characteristic of rural districts did not exist. Unemployment took a different form: cyclical "trade depressions" caused manufacturers to lay off masses of workers suddenly, a situation superficially similar to what had happened in past centuries when crop failures had caused food prices to soar and the demand for everything else to collapse. "Circumstances occasionally occurred," a member of Parliament from the industrial town of Leeds explained, "which threw 400 or 500 persons in a single parish out of employment." To threaten such people with the workhouse in an attempt to make them work harder would be senseless.

Furthermore, in the villages around the factory towns there were thousands of families who lived by weaving machine-spun yarn into cloth on hand looms in their own homes. Competition, particularly after the invention of the power loom, drove the weavers' wages down relentlessly. They were desperately poor, even when work was available. Since they were paid by the piece, under the old poor law local relief administrators could determine their incomes quite accurately and thus force them to work to the limit of their endurance before doling out aid. Therefore, the allowance system did not seem so wasteful to taxpayers in these districts. The weavers clung desperately to their independence—it was all they had. To devise a "less eligible" workhouse for hand-loom weavers was not only impossible but un-necessary.[3]

In short, a law intended to make labor more competitive by ending wage subsidies could only cause harm in places where labor was already too competitive, and during times when mass unemployment had deprived workers of any alternative "more eligible" than a work-house. In 1841, a year of severe depression in the textile districts, one manufacturer commented: "When we who live amongst it, see a thousand families . . . brought to poverty by mere want of employment . . . or pining in want who never asked for relief before, we cannot stand silently by or stamp them all imposters." And he added ruefully: "I wish we could."[4] The logic of the situation was so compelling that by the early 1850s the authorities had abandoned their attempts to force the able-bodied unemployed into institutions during depressions and slack seasons. The idea of less eligibility, however, was not abandoned; in return for assistance, the victims of cyclical depressions were compelled to perform the most disagreeable and meaningless labor conceivable, such as breaking up rocks, shredding hemp, or chopping wood in Labour Yards, often isolated from one another in small stalls. The poverty of these poor workers, which was exposed by a parliamentary investigation in 1838–41, added plausibility to Malthus's argument about the dangers of overpopulation. So did the growth of cities, which was everywhere enormous in the 1830s and 1840s. As early as the 1820s, journals of opinion in Paris were devoting much space to Malthusian theory, and local officials and medical men were collecting and publishing census data and health statistics that buttressed the theory with hard data. The early novels of Balzac reflected a similar concern, as did many of the essays submitted in prize contests sponsored by the Académie Française in 1827 and 1829 on the subject: "Charity in relation to the moral state and well being of the lower classes of society."[5]

Out of this interest in the effects of industrialization came some remarkable early examples of sociological research. The collection of social data in the field began in the late seventeenth century with the work of Gregory King in England and Marshal Vauban in France, and took a long step forward with Eden's *State of the Poor* in 1797. The legislatures of Massachusetts in 1821 and New York in 1824 commissioned studies of poverty and relief methods, the investigators query-

[3] J. L. and Barbara Hammond, *The Bleak Age* (London, 1947), p. 99; Cecil Driver, *Tory Radical: The Life of Richard Orstler* (New York, 1946), pp. 280–81; S. E. Finer, *Life and Times of Sir Edwin Chadwick* (London, 1952), p. 128.

[4] Finer, *Chadwick*, p. 182.

[5] Louis Chevalier, *Classes laborieuses et classes dangereuses à Paris pendant la première moitié du XIXe siècle* (Paris, 1958), pp. 28–34, 63–64, 152.

ing overseers of the poor and collecting statistical data.[6] In 1829, Alban de Villeneuve-Bargemont, a prefect in the textile region of northern France, made a study that revealed that 163,000 of his department's population of slightly less than a million people were dependent upon public assistance, and that 44,000 of these were destitute because of unemployment. The publication of the twenty-six volumes of reports of the investigators dispatched by the English Poor Law commissioners in 1834–35, by far the largest field survey ever made up to that time, had a powerful impact. The idea (in Eden's words) of looking "into many minute circumstances, which have been generally overlooked by theoretical reasoners," from which has grown all modern empirical social research, came into its own in the late 1830s.[7]

French investigators were particularly active, in part because of their awareness of troubling developments in Great Britain, whose industrial course France was so obviously following. Villeneuve-Bargemont, for example, became convinced that the *"système anglais"* was the prime cause of the poverty he had discovered. Publication of the reports of the English poor law commissioners provided a model and lent a sense of urgency to their work. One of the most important of the French field studies was Louis René Villermé's *Tableau de l'état physique et moral des ouvriers.* Villermé was a physician and statistician and a member of the Académie des Sciences Morales et Politiques, which sponsored his work. In 1835–37, he visited the major cotton, wool, and silk manufacturing cities of France and, for purposes of comparison, Zurich, collecting data on wages, income, housing conditions, and family expenditures, along with health and other vital statistics. He talked with workers on the job, observed them in their homes, shared meals with them, and he also interviewed manufacturers, doctors, and local officials, his object being "to see everything, to hear everything, to understand everything." The two volumes of his *Tableau* were packed with tables and statistics, but also with harrowing first-hand descriptions of poverty and "profound degradation." After quoting Villeneuve-Bargemont's stark account of life in the slums of Lille, he demonstrated that conditions there were even worse than the prefect had in-

[6] The reports of these commissions recommended doing away with outdoor relief as tending "to encourage the sturdy beggar and the profligate vagrant" and to "relax individual exertion by unnerving the arm of industry." A decade and more before the revision of the English poor law these and other American authorities were advocating the use of workhouses as a means of saving money and compelling idlers to work. D. J. Rothman, *The Discovery of the Asylum* (Boston, 1971), pp. 157, 166, 188–89, 194–95.

[7] J. B. Durouselle, *Les débuts du catholicisme social en France jusqu'en 1870* (Paris, 1951), p. 699; Albert Aftalion, *L'oeuvre économique de Simonde de Sismondi* (Paris, 1899), pp. 239–41; F. M. Eden, *The State of the Poor* (London, 1928), p. 2.

dicated. He described cellars nine feet on a side and only five feet four inches from floor to ceiling, where whole families, rank with filth, slept unclothed in a single bed. Local doctors and the police commissioner told him that under such conditions incest was common.[8]

Villermé, who was touched deeply by the plight of the workers, recognized the relationship between poverty and the crime and vice that accompany it. He pointed out that in Reims, for example, where the illegitimate birth rate was four times as high as in the Department of the Marne as a whole, so many poorly paid women textile workers became streetwalkers after work that a local expression had developed to describe their moonlighting—*"faire son cinquième quart de journée."* He scathingly denounced the heavy drinking prevalent among French workers, which he insisted destroyed families, undermined the health and character of the drinker, and was the principal cause of criminal and riotous behavior. But he insisted that the underlying causes of such evils were environmental. "The virtues and the vices of workers are mainly . . . the results of their surroundings, in a word, of the circumstances in which they live, and especially in which they are brought up."[9]

Villermé was also well aware of the existence of industrial unemployment and of its effects on the working class. New methods of production reduced costs, thus increasing demand. To expand, manufacturers employed more labor. But expansion always led to competition and then to an economic crisis, what one of Villermé's sources called "a dreadful *mêlée*, a death struggle between manufacturers." During these crises, Villermé wrote, competition shatters the work force. "Hordes of laborers fall into horrible distress, which crushes mostly the weakest and lowest paid. . . . In lacking work, they lack everything." He also recognized the periodic character of these new industrial depressions, which he calculated were occurring every six or seven years. "Too often," he warned, "when everyone is employed, unemployment is around the corner."[10]

But Villermé was so impressed by the terrible state of working people that he did not devote much attention to unemployment. His laboriously collected data on wages and living costs convinced him that low wages were the principal material cause of poverty. Nearly all industrial workers were living so close to the edge of destitution that ten centimes a day could make the difference between "a kind of ease" and "great trouble" *(une grande gêne)*. Anything could push them over the edge—a rise in the price of bread, a slight decline of wages, illness,

[8] L. R. Villermé, *Tableau de l'état physique et moral des ouvriers* (Paris, 1840), I: vi, 82–83.
[9] *Ibid.,* I: 226–27, II: 37, 50.
[10] *Ibid.,* II: 322, 310, 318.

a bout of drunkenness, another child. Unemployment seemed to Villermé only one of many possible catastrophes. Moreover, he was thoroughly conditioned by the prevailing economic orthodoxy. Industrialization had enormously increased wealth. Textile workers were very poor, but overall the laboring class was better off than ever before. To limit the hours of labor or fix minimum wages "would not result in any improvement in the condition of workers." Municipal public works projects would help during depressions, but if the jobless were put to work producing goods, they would be competing with other workers and thus delaying recovery. "Nothing is more difficult than to do good," he noted in this connection, "and measures designed to do good often result in a new and unexpected evil."[11]

Indeed, in summing up his investigation, Villermé appeared to ignore both much of what he had seen and the masses of statistical data he had collected. Man is certainly fated to earn his bread by the sweat of his brow, he admitted, but factory work is no harder than agricultural and is usually better paid. The trouble was that "industrial workers are commonly lacking in sobriety, thriftiness, foresight, and good habits, and too often they are responsible for their own poverty."[12]

A similar point of view infuses the pages of Honoré Antoine Frégier's study of Paris, *Des classes dangereuses de la population,* written about the same time as Villermé's *Tableau.* Frégier was a police official; his book was, as the title indicates, mainly concerned with criminality and vice, but much of what he wrote involved laboring people. One of his principal themes was the way poverty and bad influences turned honest workers into lawbreakers. Frégier well understood the hardships faced by Paris workers during what he called *"époques de chômage,"* those "frightening convulsions in the manufacturing industries" which "shake the foundations of society." In every Paris industry, he wrote, there was a more or less permanent cadre of foremen and skilled workers, and "a mobile and floating" mass, "hired irregularly, according to the activity of the business," whose numbers were quickly discharged and rendered destitute during depressions.[13]

The *"élite"* among the unemployed were those who had connections in rural areas—they could retire to the farm when they lost their jobs and return to the city when business picked up. For the rest, the government could alleviate some of their suffering by adjusting its public-works expenditures to the ups and downs of economic activity. Manufacturers could help by adopting a more paternalistic attitude toward their workers—Frégier mentioned a dyer in Paris who rotated

[11] *Ibid.,* II: 19, 342–43, 193–95, 201–202, I: 148–49.
[12] *Ibid.,* II: 350–51.
[13] H. A. Frégier, *Des classes dangereuses de la population* (Paris 1840), pp. 361, 294, 304.

his men in bad times, and a house painter who paid his workers more than they actually earned in slack seasons, reimbursing himself when business improved. The government ought to encourage such benevolence by exhortation and by awarding decorations and medals to manufacturers who made sacrifices to help the unemployed. But since "the simplest laws of economics" fixed "permanently and decisively" both the number of jobs and the levels of wages, the workers' best hope was to "employ their modest resources usefully," to be frugal, sober, and loyal to their employers. Life in the industrial age was hard and uncertain, but "the principle of competition comes closest to the idea of justice and is most favorable to the progress of a great people."[14]

In Great Britain, royal commissions and parliamentary committees conducted field research on a broad scale in the 1830s, the investigations of the Poor Law Commission being an early example. The most revealing of these governmental studies was the massive inquiry into the condition of the hand-loom weavers. This commission gathered data on unemployment as well as wage rates, an indication that the investigators recognized that the amount of work as well as the rate of pay affected the way the weavers lived. But, while the commission deplored the terrible state of the weavers when wages fell or when there was "a slack demand for labour," its report, which was written by the same economist who had drafted the poor law study, Nassau Senior, had little to say about how that state could be improved beyond urging the weavers to "flee from the trade."

> If we are right in believing that the low rate of the wages of the hand-loom weavers arises principally from a disproportion between the supply of their labour and the demand for it, it must follow that no measures can effectually raise their wages except by getting rid of that disproportion.

This was almost tantamount to saying, as a French critic pointed out, "let them die philanthropically for the greater glory of the principles of Malthus."[15]

In addition to these government investigations, a number of the private statistical societies that were springing up in most of the principal British industrial centers in the thirties made door-to-door surveys of working-class families to collect data. However, since their interest was in the "moral and intellectual condition" of the lower orders, the statisticians concentrated on such matters as church attendance, edu-

[14] *Ibid.*, pp. 282, 285, 300–302, 363–65, 371–75.
[15] Marian Bowley, *Nassau Senior and Classical Economics* (London, 1937), pp. 258–59; Eugène Buret, *De la misère des classes laborieuses en Angleterre et en France* (Paris, 1840), II: 29; E. P. Thompson, *The Making of the English Working Class* (New York, 1963), p. 301.

cation and literacy, and the condition of the workers' homes. The prevailing view was that expressed in a report of the Bristol Statistical Society in 1839: bad living conditions were the result of bad morals; primarily, what was needed to improve slum conditions was for the poor to develop a "reasonable sense of decency and cleanliness." All of these researchers were alarmed by what was happening to people and to society in the new industrial regions, but as historian Eileen Yeo has put it, they paid little attention to unemployment because they were "blinkered by the political economy maxim that the adult male worker must be left free from legislative 'interference' to the mercies of the free market."[16]

The political economists themselves were well aware of how industrialization had evolved since the appearance of the seminal works of Malthus and Ricardo, and not unmoved by its effects on so large a proportion of the working population. Most of them came to see the need for government regulation of child labor, for example, although they tended to accept particular legislation only after the fact. Even Senior, who was perhaps more devoted to economic abstractions than Ricardo and who confessed his "reverence for the principle of non-interference," thought that the state should do something about slum housing, which, he said, was "not one of the matters which can be safely abandoned to the parties immediately concerned." Unemployment and wage rates, however, remained in the opinion of the classical economists beyond human control. John Stuart Mill stated their position firmly in his *Principles of Political Economy* in 1848, and in later editions of this monumental work. During periods of business "stagnation," he wrote, "a manufacturer, finding a slack demand for his commodity, forbears to employ labourers." When "the labour market is overstocked," however, competition for jobs causes wages to fall, reducing costs and prices and thus stimulating consumption. Therefore, after these "temporary fluctuations," all will find work. "The rate of wages which results from competition distributes the whole existing wages-fund among the whole labouring population."[17]

Not every economist of the period, however, accepted the classical analysis. Of those who did not, the most interesting for our purposes was Simonde de Sismondi, a Swiss, who attacked it as early as 1819 in his *New Principles of Political Economy*. Sismondi admired Adam Smith, but he believed that later classical writers, especially Ricardo and Say, had indulged too heavily in abstract theorizing. "Let us examine things

[16] Eileen Yeo and E. P. Thompson, eds., *The Unknown Mayhew* (New York, 1972), pp. 52–54.

[17] Bowley, *Senior*, p. 260; J. S. Mill, *Principles of Political Economy* (London, 1925), pp. 344–45, 362.

as they really are," Sismondi wrote. "Let us desist from our habit of making abstractions of time and place." The proper purpose of economics was not cold-blooded analysis but human betterment, the theory of doing good (*bienfaisance*).

To do good, one must know what is bad, and Sismondi excelled at pointing out the evil consequences of laissez-faire capitalism that the classical economists were ignoring, minimizing, or accepting as inevitable. The harmony of interests that the individual pursuit of material profit was supposed to produce did not exist. Human beings did not always behave in economically rational ways. The accumulation of wealth was not the only purpose of life; leisure (*repos*) was equally important—"man works so that he can rest." Industrialization, whatever its benefits, had vastly increased human suffering. More specifically, even if it was true that business cycles were inherently self-correcting and unemployment a temporary phenomenon, their short-run effects were devastating. Fixed capital cannot easily be shifted from place to place, and working people do not pull up roots and move merely because opportunities are better elsewhere. Unrestricted competition leads to mindless concentration on producing goods in advance of any demand, and thus to unsalable surpluses, wage cutting, and unemployment. Mechanization—Sismondi's *bête noire*—further encourages overproduction and both displaces adult workers and fosters the use of child labor. Machines also debilitate, brutalize, and depress those who tend them. Most important of all, the goods produced by machinery are unfairly distributed:

> I direct my objections not against machines, not against new discoveries, but against the present organization of society. . . . Today it is not the new techniques that are evil, it is the unjust distribution that is made of their fruits.

Since he believed that state action was the only way to eradicate these evils, Sismondi rejected laissez faire out of hand. Ideally, he favored a simple economy based on artisan and peasant labor; this being impossible to achieve, governments ought to try to check "the social chariot which, in its accelerated course, seems to be on the point of plunging us in the abyss." But he was vague about what the state should actually do and, despite his condemnation of the practices of industrialists, placed his hopes on a kind of benevolent paternalism in which employers would be permanently responsible for their workers, in sickness and old age as well as during periods of unemployment.

Sismondi, in other words, was a trenchant critic of capitalism, but as incapable of suggesting solutions to its problems as the system's apologists. "I admit," he wrote, "that having indicated where in my opinion principle and justice lie, I do not feel competent to devise means of effecting [reform]. The distribution of the fruits of labor among those who have worked together to produce them seems to me defective, but I also feel that it is almost beyond human power to conceive of a system absolutely different from what we now have."[18]

Sismondi's impact on the classical economists was negligible, however, not because he failed to provide answers—after all, in this respect they were in the same boat—but because he was in the technical sense a very poor economist. His distrust of abstract reasoning may well have resulted from his own incapacity in this difficult field. Although many of the great classical thinkers knew him well and admired him as a person, they could and did refute his theoretical propositions without, so to speak, raising their voices. In arguing for a stable rather than an expanding economy, for example, Sismondi had written, "one can only exchange the total product of one year for the total of the previous year." To which Malthus replied: "If this were really the case, it would be difficult to say how the value of the national product could ever be increased." Similarly, John Stuart Mill disposed of his claim that depressions were caused by "general overproduction" in a chapter, commenting that "the doctrine appears to me to involve so much inconsistency in its very conception, that I feel considerable difficulty in giving any statement of it." Ricardo demolished Sismondi's explanation of the supposed effect of taxation on prices in a paragraph.[19]

Yet Sismondi had an enormous influence. If he sometimes appeared confused, perhaps it was because he recognized and tried to account for complexities that Ricardo, for example, did not even try to understand. Exposing the technical flaws in his economics did not detract from the importance of his insights, or eliminate the economic conditions that had inspired his *New Principles of Political Economy,* or persuade other critics to accept the status quo with equanimity. Most of these critics had no patience for logical niceties; they were unimpressed by descriptions of immutable laws that made doing anything about wages and unemployment impossible. It is not difficult to imagine, for example, how they reacted to this "advice" to the unemployed, offered in 1831 by Charles Knight, an Englishman interested in the spread of "useful knowledge" among the poor:

> When there is too much labour in the market, and wages are too low . . .
> do not combine with the vain hope of compelling the employer to pay more

[18] J. C. L. Simonde de Sismondi, *Nouveaux principes d'économie politique* (Paris, 1971), pp. 250, 274–78, 356; Charles Gide and Charles Rist, *A History of Economic Doctrines* (Boston, [n. d.]), pp. 184–211; Blanqui, *Histoire de l'économie politique,* II: 234–35.

[19] T. R. Malthus, *Principles of Political Economy* (New York, 1951), p. 366; Mill, *Principles,* pp. 556–57; Piero Sraffa, ed., *Works of David Ricardo* (Cambridge, 1962), I: 380–81.

for labour than there are funds for the maintenance of labour. . . . When there is a glut of labour go at once out of the market; become yourselves capitalists.[20]

Working people, unemployed or not, obviously rejected such advice, some of them reacting in exactly the opposite manner. Especially in England, skilled workers were beginning to organize, and this trade-union movement was giving birth to some bold new ideas. To the Malthusian argument that the working class could improve itself only by restricting its numbers, John Gast, an early English labor organizer, responded that wage rates were not negotiated "between Mechanics and their sweethearts and wives" but "between the employed and their employers." To the classical theorists' insistence that the wages fund could not be increased without diverting capital from investment and thus causing employment to decline, a writer in the radical paper *Gorgon* retorted:

> The circumstances of the workmen do not in the least depend on the prosperity or profits of the masters, but on the power of the workmen to *command* —nay to *extort* a high price for their labour."[21]

To a degree such statements were mere bombast; to a degree they represented only hopes or expectations. But in part they were based on actual experience, for labor unions were beginning to win significant gains in some of the skilled trades. Whether real or fanciful, the statements reflected a growing tendency to reject the classical economists' model of a self-regulating system and their focus on long-run results.

The new unions also, however, focused on wage rates and working conditions rather than on jobs themselves, as the quotation from *Gorgon* shows. One could reject the teachings of the economists or, as happened more often, ignore them, but to insist that employers could afford or could be compelled to pay labor more was far from suggesting that if they did so they would be able—or could be forced—to hire additional hands. It is not a very great exaggeration to say that the labor militants were as bankrupt as the economists when it came to devising ways of reducing unemployment. In the main, British unions represented skilled laborers who, under the pressure of mechanization, were closing ranks against threats both from above and from below. They had failed to prevent the repeal of the Statute of Apprentices in 1813, but by the 1840s they had, in the words of E. P. Thompson, a particularly sympathetic and perceptive student of the English

20 R. K. Webb, *The British Working Class Reader, 1790–1848: Literacy and Social Tension* (London, 1955), p. 119.
21 Thompson, *British Working Class*, pp. 777, 773.

working class, "closed the doors against the mass of unapprenticed and semi-skilled labour clamouring without."[22] In the language of the London artisans, their trades were divided into "honourable" and "dishonourable" sectors, the former served by unionized "society men" who formed "the aristocracy of the trade," the latter by "competitive men," also known as "cheap men" and "slop workers." The societies were committed, as a statement by the London Chairmakers' Society put it, "to relieve their members when unemployed or in sickness." But they comprised only a small fraction of the labor force in each trade and they barred their doors to outsiders as firmly as had the medieval guilds. They had little to offer the bulk of the casual workers in the cities and factory hands everywhere, and these were the people who suffered most from inadequate wages and irregular work. They were not really challenging either free-enterprise capitalism or the classical writers' analysis of how capitalism functioned. John Stuart Mill, for example, conceded that unions could increase the wages of their members. But if the whole labor force were organized for this purpose, he added, "this could only be accomplished by keeping a part of their number permanently out of employment."[23]

There were, however, thinkers who agreed with Sismondi's argument that capitalism was "defective," but who, unlike him, *could* conceive of a different system. The ideas of these critics varied one from another, but all began by rejecting competition as the mainspring driving the social clockwork. For competition they would substitute cooperation. Substituting conscious planning for the "invisible hand" was thus also inherent in their thinking about the economy, although who would direct the cooperators was not always clear. They did not deny that individuals were motivated by self-interest, but rather assumed that people could learn to recognize that their interests would better be served by cooperating with one another than by seeking to best one another. In this respect they were as committed to taking the long view as Malthus and Ricardo. In another sense, however, they saw cooperation as leading to order and efficiency directly, whereas the classical economists believed that only after infinitely complex adjustments would competition produce these results. Allowing capital a

[22] *Ibid.*, p. 252. This situation persisted throughout the century. "From [the] world of the radical artisan, the unskilled and casual poor were almost wholly cut off, not only by the social exclusiveness of those above them, but also by their poverty, their hours of work, their physical exhaustion, and their lack of education." G. S. Jones, *Outcast London: A Study in the Relationship Between Classes in Victorian Society* (Oxford, 1971), p. 341.

[23] Yeo and Thompson, *Unknown Mayhew*, pp. 372, 376–79; Mill, *Principles*, p. 934n. In the 1871 edition of his *Principles*, Mill admitted that a "limited" general increase was possible without unemployment, the addition coming from the profits of the capitalists. P. 934.

share of the rewards of enterprise was not necessarily excluded by the cooperationists' proposals. The elimination of exploitation—not equal shares but fair shares—was the goal, the assumption being that when the fruits were distributed equitably everyone would have enough. Cooperation would also reduce confusion and waste—eliminating the capitalist-as-middleman was a common objective.

This essentially utopian attitude precluded much direct concern with involuntary unemployment. Indeed, these reformers' approach to idleness more resembled that of the seventeenth and eighteenth centuries than that of the nineteenth, albeit without the overtones of authoritarian compulsion associated with the earlier period. The Comte de Saint-Simon, progenitor of a French school that found a great deal wrong with capitalism but was short on practical plans for improving it, dreamed of a new order in which the state would organize production in the general interest but in which "everyone will be obliged to do some work." An English cooperationist, William Thompson, author of *An Inquiry into the Principles of the Distribution of Wealth* (1824), *Labour Rewarded* (1827), and *Practical Directions for the Speedy and Economical Establishment of Communities* (1830), put it this way: Under competition, unemployment was "the master-evil of society." Members of cooperative communities, however, would "not be liable to be discharged" because they would have no masters. "Instead of working for you know not whom," he urged, "work for each other." Another English cooperationist, the manufacturer Robert Owen, devised a plan for decentralizing production in small cooperative communities. Like some of the more benevolent workhouse plans of the eighteenth century, Owen's idea entailed locating factories in rural areas so that agriculture and manufacturing could be coordinated on a human scale; in such an environment all would live well because, since no one but those who produced would share in the rewards of the common effort, all would be inspired to produce. The ideal community would thus give birth to the ideal worker, and both voluntary and involuntary idleness would simply disappear.[24]

The most immediately influential of the theorists of this stripe was the French writer and historian Louis Blanc, whose *L'organisation du travail*, published in 1839, went through five editions by the end of the next decade. Blanc confronted the precepts of "heartless" classical political economy *(l'économie politique sans entrailles)* head on. Competition was ruining the bourgeoisie and exterminating the working people. To get rid of it the government must become "the supreme regu-

[24] Gide and Rist, *Economic Doctrines*, p. 218n; R. K. P. Pankhurst, *William Thompson (1775–1833): Britain's Pioneer Socialist, Feminist, and Co-operator* (London, 1954), pp. 55–57, 143.

lator of production." Blanc insisted that the competitive system could be done away with peacefully. First the state should create a limited number of "social workshops" *(ateliers sociaux)* in key industries, borrowing the necessary capital and recruiting workers of good character to conduct the experiment. For the first year, while the workers were getting to know one another and learning to understand the virtues of cooperation, the government would manage each enterprise. Thereafter, the shops would be run by the workers themselves. At the end of each year profits would be divided into three equal parts, one distributed share and share alike among the workers, another devoted to the support of their aged and infirm fellows, the third invested in tools and equipment so that the workshops could expand and take in more workers. In the beginning the social workshops would have to compete with private industry but they would win out easily, for the state would prevent the latter from using cutthroat methods. Capital and labor alike would soon recognize the advantages of cooperation and the system would become universal. Private capital invested in the workshops would earn interest, but the capitalists would share in the profits only if they actually worked. "In our system," Blanc claimed, "the state will become the master of industry little by little, and we will destroy competition not through monopoly but by association."[25]

Blanc saw his workshops as a way of reeducating both laborers and capitalists; the experience of cooperation would, so to speak, change human nature, bring about "a profound moral revolution." This argument gave him an easy answer to those who claimed his system was impractical, and provided the basis of his counterattack on classical economics. When critics insisted that if the possibility of private gain were eliminated workers would become lazy and economic growth cease, he replied that while self-interest was indeed a powerful motivating force, the classical economists had defined it too narrowly. Once workers realized that they would gain more individually by cooperating with one another, they would "without exception" work hard and efficiently, and collective self-interest in economic affairs would be as common as loyalty to flag and country, or to church, which millions shared. When no longer cheated by capitalists of so large a share of the fruits of their labor, "they would do zealously, carefully, and quickly what they now do slowly and unwillingly."[26]

Thus Blanc proved, at least to his own satisfaction, that the "complacent premises" of Ricardo and the "horrible conclusions" of the cold-blooded Malthus were invalid. Competition was not necessary for prosperity and progress, and by doing away with it, the evils it engen-

[25] Louis Blanc, *L'organisation du travail* (Paris, 1839), pp. 28–84, 88, 102–107.
[26] *Ibid.*, pp. 105, 115, 138–39, 199.

dered, including the cyclical crises that caused unemployment, would be snuffed out. Instead of depriving men of work, new mechanical inventions would make their work easier and give them more leisure "to exercise their intelligence."[27]

Louis Blanc was a thoroughgoing democrat, but there was an element of paternalism in the thinking of many of the cooperationists. Few students of the contemporary industrial scene were more hostile to competition and laissez faire than Eugène Buret, a young follower of Sismondi, whose book, *De la misère des classes laborieuses en Angleterre et en France* (1840), a synthesis of the ideas of Sismondi and the Saint-Simonians and of the social research that had been conducted in England and France in the 1830s, was the most impressive work in this genre.[28] Buret described competition as "the blind force that controls the workers' share of the fruits of their labor." The classical economists made it a kind of god, both "the master and the fate of nations."[29] Because of competition, he wrote, production had been "abandoned without direction to the influence of individual self-interest, and "perpetual warfare" had become the only means of seeking stability and order. The result had been "disastrous"—poverty and all its consequent vices, which Buret spelled out in vivid detail, drawing upon his own investigations and those of Villeneuve-Bargemont, Villermé, the British report on the condition of the hand-loom weavers, and other studies. Individual liberty was a fine thing, he admitted, but must it be accompanied by "this frightful laisser-faire, which provides an excuse for workers to use violence against employers, employers to resort to trickery and to be indifferent to workers?"[30]

Buret also saw more clearly than earlier observers the causal connection between poverty and crime and vice. While generally admiring of Villermé's work, he called attention to its inconsistencies. Villermé, he wrote, "floats indecisively between optimism . . . and the horrible facts that industry puts before his eyes."[31] He understood the effects of cyclical depressions and of chance events, stock-market rumors, political upheavals, and developments in far-distant parts of the world, all matters beyond the control of working people, on the level of employment in the industrial countries. He recognized the existence of what Karl Marx was to call "the industrial reserve army," in Buret's words

[27] *Ibid.*, pp. 110, 112.

[28] Buret had won a contest sponsored by the Académie for a manuscript on the causes of poverty and its manifestations in various countries. He used his 2,500-franc prize to conduct further research in England. *De la misère* is an expanded version of his prize manuscript.

[29] Buret, *De la misère*, II: 176.

[30] *Ibid.*, I: 23–25, II: 56–57.

[31] *Ibid.*, II: 199.

"this floating population in the great cities, this mass of men that industry collects but cannot occupy steadily, that it holds always in reserve." He wrote the following condemnation of the system:

> To be conducted successfully industrial warfare requires large armies that can be concentrated in one place and decimated. And it is neither devotion nor a sense of duty that leads the soldiers of this army to endure the hardships that are imposed upon them; they do so only to escape the harsh necessity of hunger. They have neither affection nor gratitude for their chiefs, and the chiefs are bound to them by no feeling of good will—they know them not as men but as instruments of production who must bring in much and consume as little as possible. . . . The industry which calls the workers up only supports them when it needs them and as soon as it can do without them it abandons them without the slightest hesitation.[32]

Yet Buret was no revolutionary. Reform could be achieved by intelligence and good will. Violence was unnecessary; "to destroy property or to reduce the poor to servitude would be to end social discord the way death ends disease." He had nothing but praise for workers' mutual-benefit societies that aided their ill and aged members, but he insisted that when workers formed trade unions *(coalitions)* they "furnished new forces for social warfare" and acted "in direct opposition to the rest of society." The ideal mutual-benefit society would include employers as well as workers, the former contributing guidance and moral support along with gifts of money.[33] He suggested a number of specific reforms—restrictions on inheritances, taxation according to ability to pay, elimination of protective tariffs, the decentralization of manufacturing[34]—but his main emphasis was on making capital and labor cooperate. Association was "the magic word" that would do away with poverty and social strife. The economy must be organized, "the anarchy of production" ended. Every healthy citizen must be guaranteed a steady job at a wage adequate to support a family. Since, under existing competitive conditions, industry could not hope to organize itself, the state must "do for all what each cannot do alone."

By law, every local industry should be required to create a "family council," its members elected by employers and workers. These councils would set wage rates and regulate working conditions. No employee was to be discharged, nor might he quit, without giving the council two weeks' notice. Ultimately, through their savings, workers might be expected to acquire shares in the business, further strengthening the cooperative spirit. These family councils were to send repre-

[32] *Ibid.,* II: 165, 196, 243, I: 68–69.
[33] *Ibid.,* I: 84, II: 301–303.
[34] *Ibid.,* II: 358–59, 377–414, 420–21.

sentatives to regional councils, which would compile statistics and settle conflicts between trades. Above the regional councils would sit departmental councils, and, at the apex of the pyramid, the Supreme Council of National Production, charged with determining the country's economic policy and "regulating output in accordance with needs." This system would substitute reason and order for mindless competion; it would therefore do away with waste and confusion, eliminate cyclical economic fluctuations, and put an end to the brutal conflict raging between capital and labor. Under such a system, "no one would be without a job." For any able-bodied person who willfully avoided work under the new dispensation, Buret suggested "a workhouse on the English model."[35]

Alas, the cooperationists quickly discovered that putting their marvelously rational schemes into practice was as difficult as making a workhouse earn a profit. Many experimental communities were founded, Owen's American venture, New Harmony, being one of the best known, but none succeeded in demonstrating much more than that small groups of dedicated, like-minded persons could sometimes work together effectively. Nevertheless, the idea of substituting social and economic planning for competition had a powerful appeal. Eugène Buret died in 1842, still in his early thirties, but his work provided an early statement of the theory of the corporative state, which was to have a long and checkered history. Others, despairing of or rejecting the support of capitalists, turned to more radical approaches. Robert Owen lost interest in cooperative communities after the failure of New Harmony in 1829 and, along with other cooperationists, some far more profound thinkers than he, became deeply involved in urging workers to organize in order to do away with the capitalist system, which Owen began to call "the most anti-social, impolitic, and irrational that can be devised," and to substitute for it state ownership of the means of production.[36]

These early socialists, however, offered no intellectually satisfying theory explaining the functioning of an economy without competition and private property. Their diagnosis of the diseases of laissez-faire capitalism was penetrating, but their prescriptions for curing them were even less persuasive than, say, Louis Blanc's. Their estimation of the adaptability of institutions and of human nature was to say the least overoptimistic; that individuals, rich or poor, would not easily abandon the pursuit of self-interest and work for the common good escaped them. And as logicians they were imprecise—closer in style to the writers of the seventeenth century than to the classical masters.

---

[35] *Ibid.*, II: 296, 337, 416, 427–30, 467.
[36] Thompson, *British Working Class*, p. 804.

John Stuart Mill, who in his mature thought did not reject socialism out of hand, exposed both these weaknesses as early as 1852 in the third edition of his *Principles*. People in general, and especially the working classes, he wrote, were not yet ready "for any order of things, which would make any considerable demand on either their intellect or their virtues." More important, the way wealth was owned and controlled did not affect the fundamental laws governing its production. These laws, Mill insisted—and the full weight of the classical tradition was behind his words—"partake of the character of physical truths." Like it or not, production depended upon "previous accumulation" (capital) and on the energy and skill with which labor was applied to the manipulation of this capital. The early socialists, in other words, were only suggesting a different way of distributing wealth, which Mill somewhat rashly conceded was totally subject to human control.[37] But, except for arguing that under state ownership workers would be more highly motivated and production more efficient, they simply assumed that their system would increase the world's wealth. They neither refuted nor even challenged the classical analysis of production. Since, doubts about the capacity of human beings to subordinate personal gain in the general interest aside, the world's wealth did not seem adequate to support everyone at a decent standard, the socialist position attracted few converts.

[37] Mill, *Principles*, pp. xxix, 199. "The things once there, mankind, individually or collectively, can do with them as they like. They can place them at the disposal of whomsoever they please, and on whatever terms." (p. 200).

6

The Discovery
of Unemployment

In the second half of the nineteenth century free-enterprise industrial capitalism was everywhere in the ascendant, dominant in Britain and America, of growing strength on the European continent. The age of the railroad had begun, further stimulating economic growth and ushering in a period of general improvement of living standards for wage earners. The population of the industrial nations was growing as rapidly as Malthus had predicted, but contrary to his expectations the food supply was keeping pace as new lands were brought beneath the plow and as improved methods of cultivation were increasing yields. Although masses of people might still go hungry, Europeans now very rarely faced the threat of general food shortages. The era of the bread riot was ending at last, and along with it the economic disruptions that famine and soaring food prices had always caused.

General prosperity and security did not eliminate poverty or provide all who wished it with steady work. There were beggars in the streets and vagrants on the highways in the best of times, and during cyclical industrial downturns, which struck repeatedly, tens of thousands lost their jobs. But the expanding economy, with its steady bounty of new technological wonders, encouraged complacency among the comfortably off and posed a formidable problem for social critics. When opportunity appeared to beckon from so many quarters, it was less plausible to blame poverty on the system. The persistence of idleness, ignorance, crime, and corruption under such conditions made it possible for those who did not examine the problem too closely to hold the downtrodden and the dissolute responsible for their own degradation.

Material abundance also added to the prestige of classical political economy, which purported to explain both how the system functioned and why so little could be done to improve the lot of the laborer.

Although theorists were finding the classical tradition less and less satisfactory and were therefore beginning to move in new directions, the influence of the classical school on the larger society was at its height. Economic growth and rising living standards seemed, as it were, to flesh out the Ricardian abstractions, giving readers who lacked the patience or the intellectual capacity to follow the economists' arguments confidence in their conclusions. Thus, from any of several perspectives unemployment did not seem to be an issue of great practical importance: it was only a temporary, if recurring, phenomenon; its victims were in large measure responsible for their own condition; state efforts to eliminate it were sure to fail.

Even the economists who sought to move beyond the classical analysis had little that was constructive to say about unemployment. On the one hand, there were the new academic economists, most of them trained in mathematics, who made the so-called marginal revolution. Men like Léon Walras of the University of Lausanne, Karl Menger of the University of Vienna, and W. Stanley Jevons of Manchester and London tried to determine the best possible use of given resources; they displayed little interest—at least as practitioners of their science —in the merits of capitalism or in possible ways of improving the distribution of resources in society. Such matters as the business cycle and the impact of machinery on the labor market simply did not concern them. Indeed, the strength of these and other neoclassical economists for half a century after 1870 lay in micro-economics, which, as the economic historian Mark Blaug has put it, "was ill suited to the discussion of remedies for general unemployment."[1]

On the other hand, Karl Marx, who certainly did concern himself with unemployment in *Das Kapital* (1867), treated the subject in such a way as to discourage efforts to understand how it might be reduced or eliminated. There were according to Marx two kinds of capital: constant capital, consisting of raw materials, tools and machinery, and other "means of production"; and variable capital, which he defined as "that part of capital represented by labour power." The capitalist system caused unemployment in the following way: Any expansion of output increased the demand for labor. In response to this demand, wages rose. But then manufacturers shifted capital from wages (variable) to machines (constant) and discharged some of their workers, who became what Marx called "a disposable industrial reserve army" *(eine disponible industrielle Reservearmee)*.[2] Marx argued that the system

[1] Mark Blaug, *Economic Theory in Retrospect* (Homewood, Ill., 1962), p. 601.

[2] It was one of the internal contradictions of capitalism, Marx said, that while all the capitalists' profits were extracted from labor, the system drove them inexorably to reduce the proportion of their capital invested in labor. See David McLellan, *The Thought of Karl Marx: An Introduction* (New York, 1974), pp. 73–74.

produced and indeed could not exist without this reserve army, a labor force that could find work only in boom periods.

> Capitalistic accumulation . . . constantly produces . . . a relatively redundant population of labourers. . . . The increase in the variable part of capital, and therefore of the number of labourers employed by it, is always connected with violent fluctuations and transitory production of surplus-population.[3]

The unemployed made up "a mass of human material always ready for exploitation." When demand increased or when a new form of economic activity was developed (Marx used the example of the railroad) it was thus possible to throw "great masses of men suddenly on the decisive points without injury to the scale of production in other spheres." The economy grows by "fits and starts"; each boom is followed by a sharp contraction.

> But the former is impossible without disposable human material, without an increase in the number of labourers. . . . This increase is effected by the simple process that constantly "sets free" a part of the labourers; by methods which lessen the number of labourers employed in proportion to the increased population. The whole form of the movement of modern industry depends, therefore, upon the constant transformation of a part of the labouring population into unemployed or half employed hands.

Not the workers' lack of "moral restraint" but technological unemployment produced the excess supply of labor that depressed living standards and made possible capitalist exploitation. In ordinary times the existence of the reserve army kept wages from rising; in boom periods its employment reduced the pressure for increases and thus kept labor's "pretensions" in check.[4]

Marx did not himself devise the reserve army theory. In 1807 John Weyland, an English justice of the peace, defended the English poor law against the criticisms of Malthus by arguing that the excess of labor that the poor law encouraged was necessary if the economy was to grow. The term itself was used by English radicals as early as 1838, and Marx's friend and associate Friedrich Engels wrote in 1844 in his *Condition of the Working Class in England:* "Industry must always have a reserve of unemployed workers. . . . The existence of such a reserve is essential in order that labour may be available . . . when the business boom reaches its climax."[5] But the classical economists, while sometimes, as in Nassau Senior's report on the hand-loom weavers, recog-

---

[3] Karl Marx, *Capital: A Critique of Political Economy* (Chicago, 1906), I: 690.

[4] *Ibid.,* I: 694–95, 701.

[5] John Weyland, *A Short Inquiry into the Policy, Humanity and Past Effects of the Poor Laws* (London, 1807), pp. 33–42; Friedrich Engels, *The Condition of the Working Class in England* (Stanford, 1973), pp. 97–98.

nizing this function of idle labor, normally dismissed unemployment as a transitory, self-correcting condition of only minor social importance despite its catastrophic effects on individuals. They insisted that whatever the immediate effects of mechanization, in the long run every willing worker would find a place.

By the 1870s, however, decades of experience had demonstrated that the adjustment process was slower and less smooth than these classical economists had thought. Machines, after all, did displace large numbers of laborers, and no argument about how the machines ultimately would create more new jobs than they destroyed could disguise the fact that the actual workers who were displaced often did not easily find new employment. Moreover, the classical reasoning that prosperity generated an increased labor supply by enabling workers to support more children did not square with the rapid changes in the demand for labor in recurrent cycles of growth and stagnation. As Marx put it, "before, in consequence of the rise of wages, any positive increase of the population really fit for work could occur, the time would have been passed again and again."[6]

Above all, with his reserve army thesis, Marx put the question of unemployment in a new context. Whether they blamed joblessness on the laziness or incompetence of the idle, or on society, or on fate, earlier writers had treated the problem as an aberration. Marx saw unemployment as an entirely normal and necessary aspect of capitalism, and once examined, his view of the role of the industrial reserve army during booms seemed self-evidently correct. How else could an economy grow? Indeed, the modern thesis that growth is essential for the maintenance of full employment is really only Marx's argument put the other way round.

For Marx, the inevitability of the reserve army under capitalism was a reason for doing away with the system, but relatively few people among those who found his explanation of unemployment convincing were prepared to demobilize the reserve army by such drastic means. The broad effect of his argument, therefore, was to increase the willingness of people to tolerate unemployment, or better, the effect was to channel the efforts of those troubled by the human and social costs of unemployment into trying to lessen its effects rather than into attempting the apparently impossible task of eliminating it.

Marx was a classical economist who rejected capitalism in part because of his conviction that capitalism made mass unemployment inevitable. The American Henry George, another radical thinker of the period who merits our consideration, was a believer in capitalism who

[6] Marx, *Capital,* I: 699.

rejected classical economics because it justified a system of land ownership that he believed made unemployment inevitable. George was much influenced by the experience of living in California during the hectic expansion following the discovery of gold. He was struck by the presence of poverty even amidst such prosperity and growth, and gradually came to the conclusion that "where the conditions to which material progress everywhere tends are most fully realized . . . we find the deepest poverty, the sharpest struggle for existence, and the most of enforced idleness." What caused this paradox, he decided, was the monopolization of land by rich speculators. Control of land enabled these speculators to exact unearned profits in the form of rent, which properly belonged to society; in economic terms, of the factors of production, too much profit was going to land, not enough to capital and labor.

Speculation in land, George wrote in *Progress and Poverty* (1879), was "the true cause of industrial depression" because it drove up rent and thus stifled production by adding billions to "the price of being allowed to go to work and produce wealth." This "lock-out of labor and capital by land owners" threw the economy "out of gear" and resulted in the "strange and unnatural spectacle of large numbers of willing men who cannot find employment." According to George, the monopolization of land by speculators explained why so many rural people were flocking into the cities.

> It is because men cannot find employment in the country that there are so many unemployed in the city. . . . If these now unemployed men were producing wealth from the land, they would not only be employing themselves, but would be employing all the mechanics of the city . . . creating effective demand that would be felt in New England and Old England, and . . . throughout the world.[7]

The way to end poverty and "give remunerative employment to whoever wishes it" was to confiscate not land—"that would involve a needless shock to present customs and habits of thought"—but rent. Part of all rents already went to the government in the form of taxes. Now the state should take it all. With the imposition of what was later to be called the "single tax," no other levy would be necessary and, with its vast income spent for the public's benefit instead of the landlords', society would be more equitable as well as more prosperous.[8]

George was much more than a concocter of panaceas. *Progress and Poverty* mounted a powerful attack on classical political economy—on

[7] Henry George, *Progress and Poverty* (New York, 1887), pp. 6, 241, 243, 246–48.
[8] *Ibid.*, pp. 362–65.

the wages fund, on Malthusian population theory, and on the law of diminishing returns. It was widely read, translated into many languages. George became an international celebrity. But, despite his argument that his reform would injure no class and cause no social disruption, no government dared to enact the single tax. Like Marx, George went too far for his times. Nevertheless, the continuing co-existence of "progress and poverty" and the recurrence of puzzling sharp fluctuations in the volume of economic activity deeply worried many of their contemporaries.

This concern stimulated a great deal of empirical social research. By the 1870s and 1880s field work was being conducted in Germany and the United States as well as in Great Britain, France, and Belgium. This work varied in quality and in objectivity, but in its totality it brought to light masses of facts about the suffering of the poor and developed valuable new ways of examining social conditions. Much of it, however, reflected in its conclusions and recommendations the preconceptions of researchers who were concerned with preserving institutions rather than with breaking them down. Consciously or unconsciously, such investigators tended either to minimize the extent of unemployment or to deal with the phenomenon as an aspect of something else—poverty, education, alcoholism, and so on.

In 1878 the chief of the Massachusetts Bureau of the Statistics of Labor, Carroll D. Wright, made a pioneering effort to count the unemployed. Broad concern about the jobless had developed in the United States for the first time during the depression of the middle 1870s. America had always had a large population of rootless persons without specific occupation, but whereas previously they were known by such names as "pioneers" or "backwoodsmen," now, with the frontier disappearing and the economy depressed, they began to be called "vagrants" or, more popularly, "tramps." Attempts to determine the size of the tramp population and of the number of unemployed generally led to exaggerated estimates, 3 million being the most widely quoted total. As early as 1877 Wright had polled Massachusetts employers on the subject, concluding from their responses that except for the unskilled and perhaps also workers in the building trades "no large bodies of men were found out of employment" in the state.[9] Recognizing that such estimates lacked specificity, the next year Wright sent letters to all the Massachusetts town assessors asking them to estimate the number of local workers who were unemployed. When the 2,000-odd responses were tabulated, the total came to less than 22,000, which led Wright to conclude that the national total was only about

[9] Massachusetts Bureau of the Statistics of Labor, *Tenth Report* (Boston, 1879), pp. 3–13.

570,000. The figure 3 million, he declared, was an "absurdity."

In this last he was no doubt correct; his own estimate was almost surely closer to the reality. But he was a far from dispassionate investigator. He bewailed the "industrial hypochondria" of the times, which made economic conditions seem worse than they actually were. In his instructions to the assessors he asked them to count only "able-bodied males over 18" and of that group "those only who really want employment," the former restriction eliminating many jobless children and female textile workers, the latter (while reasonable in itself) likely to encourage the assessors to reduce their estimates. "The testimony of officials in very many cases was," Wright reported, "that a large percentage of those out of employment would not work if they could."[10]

Carroll Wright was by no means anti-labor; in the same report that contained his estimates of unemployment he published excerpts from responses to a questionnaire he had circulated among workers, a questionnaire that included such items as "Do you consider yourself overworked?" and "In what way, if any, do you consider your employer profits unfairly by your labor?" as well as one dealing with unemployment.[11] But he was convinced that the American economy was healthy, and predisposed to believe that unemployment was not a serious problem. "Courage, patience, and faith in hard work," he stated, "will reward the worker in the near future with continued occupation."[12]

In Germany social research developed more slowly than in Britain and France, but by the 1870s a beginning had been made. The Reichstag authorized a study of factory labor in 1875 which combined the British device of holding hearings in industrial centers with the technique of field investigations developed by Villermé and other French social scientists. The Verein für Sozialpolitik, founded in 1872 and dominated by academicians, conducted a number of investigations beginning in the 1880s, but in this period it avoided controversial issues and collected evidence mainly through questionnaires, gener-

[10] *Ibid.*, pp. 7–8.

[11] Wright discovered to his chagrin that despite the wide publicity given his questionnaire few workers bothered to fill it out. Only 230 usable answers were sent in. Of these, incidentally, 155 claimed to have been unemployed an average of 94 days during the year ending August 1, 1878. *Ibid.*, pp. 99–139.

[12] *Ibid.*, p. 13. In 1887 Wright published the results of an elaborate investigation of unemployment in Massachusetts based on evidence collected in the 1885 state census. The study revealed that about 30 percent of the labor force had been unemployed during part of the twelve months before May 1885. About a third of the unemployed had been out of work for more than four months. Wright's analysis was devoid of the moralizing tone of his earlier work on unemployment. This report contains the earliest use of the word "unemployment" that I have found. It is, indeed, the source of the first usage cited in the *Oxford English Dictionary*, an 1888 article in *Science* summarizing Wright's findings. Massachusetts Bureau of the Statistics of Labor, *Eighteenth Annual Report* (Boston, 1887).

ally sent to third-party "experts" whose views tended to reflect middle-class social attitudes. Similarly in France Frédéric Le Play, who pioneered in the social-survey method by gathering data on how working-class families all over Europe spent their incomes, and whose influence on later social research was enormous, allowed his own conservative, one might say protofascist, opinions to color his supposedly objective analyses. None of these researchers dealt directly with unemployment.[13]

Although the best English investigators were more open-minded than, say, Le Play, they too were limited by what a modern sociologist has called their "professional middle-class anxieties to maintain the stability of institutions."[14] The work of Charles Booth illustrates this generalization. Booth was a well-to-do commission merchant and ship-owner who undertook in the mid-1880s to discover the extent of poverty in London. A socialist organization had made a survey purporting to show that a quarter of the workers of the city were not earning enough to support their families at a minimum standard; Booth was sure this was an exaggeration, and to prove the point he hit upon an ingenious technique. In 1886, he and a few assistants set out to interview all the London School Board Visitors, officials whose job it was to visit periodically the homes of every family with school-age children. The Visitors had, therefore, an intimate knowledge of the occupations and family life of a very large section of the London population. By interviewing them at length and studying their records of every such family, Booth collected data which enabled him to classify the entire population into eight groups (A to H on a rising scale of affluence). Later he checked this information against the 1891 census returns, and he interviewed ministers, social workers, and other informed persons. He and his staff tramped up and down the streets of the city; he took lodgings in working-class homes; he prepared minutely detailed maps showing the degree of wealth and poverty of every London street. By the time his great study was completed in 1913 it filled seventeen volumes.[15]

Booth made every effort to be fair. "The facts," he boasted, "have been gathered and stated with no bias nor distorting aim and with no

[13] Anthony Oberschall, *Empirical Social Research in Germany: 1846–1914* (The Hague, 1965), pp. 4, 21–26; Maurice Halbwachs, *La classe ouvrière et les niveaux de vie* (Paris, 1912), p. 163; P. F. Lazarsfeld, "Quantification in Sociology," in Harry Woolf, ed., *Quantification* (Indianapolis, 1961), pp. 181–87, 196–200.

[14] O. R. McGregor, "Social Research and Social Policy in the Nineteenth Century," *British Journal of Sociology,* 8 (1957), 154.

[15] T. S. and M. B. Simey, *Charles Booth: Social Scientist* (Oxford, 1960), pp. 64–70, 87–90; Charles Booth, *Life and Labour of the People in London* (London, 1902), I: 3–7, 24–27, 33; H. W. Pfautz, ed., *Charles Booth on the City* (Chicago, 1967) pp. 21–22.

foregone conclusions." He sought only to show "how things are." In this he succeeded to a remarkable degree, the best evidence of his objectivity being the fact that, despite his preconceptions, he concluded that not 25 but more than 30 percent of all Londoners were living below what he called the poverty line.

But he could not escape from his preconceptions. There were, he said, three basic causes of poverty: "questions of employment," "questions of habit," and "questions of circumstance." By "questions of employment" he meant lack of work and low pay. "Questions of habit" included drunkenness and improvidence, "questions of circumstance," illness and other infirmities, and too many children.[16] By far the most important of these (it explained over 2,500 cases of 4,000 of the poorest families studied) was the first, and while Booth did not distinguish statistically between low wages and insufficient work as causes of poverty, his discussion made it clear that irregularity of income was a major cause of privation. But he found no reason, either in his statistical summaries or in his description of individual families, to blame unemployment on the prevailing economic system. Although apparently unfamiliar with the writings of Marx—in his one known reference he spelled the name "Marks"[17]—he subscribed to the reserve army thesis as a matter of course. "The modern system of industry will not work without some unemployed margin—some reserve of labour," he declared, in what was to become probably the most-quoted sentence in his entire work. That margin was much too large, he insisted, but responsibility for the excess rested primarily on the shoulders of the idle themselves. "The unemployed are, as a class, a selection of the unfit."[18]

Booth's reasoning grew out of his classification system. Having divided the people into eight socioeconomic groups, he proceeded to generalize about the characteristics of each, always reminding his readers that the lines between classes were blurred. The lowest (class A) he dismissed as antisocial and beyond redemption, "a savage, semi-criminal class" of casual laborers and derelicts, "battered figures who slouch through the streets, and play the beggar or the bully." Fortunately class A was small—probably not many more than 37,000 people in a London population of over 4 million. Its members do little work but rather "foul the record of the unemployed."[19]

Those in class B, "the very poor," while also relatively few in number, about 317,000, were according to Booth the "crux of the social

[16] Booth, *Life and Labour*, I: 4, 172, 146–47.
[17] Simey, *Booth*, p. 58
[18] Booth, *Life and Labour*, I: 149–52.
[19] *Ibid.*, I: 37–38; II: 21.

problem." Men in this group tended to work only irregularly—in other words they were frequently unemployed. But Booth believed most of them neither sought nor were capable of steady labor. The class was a "deposit of those who from mental, moral, and physical reasons are incapable of better work," or as he put it in another place, "lack of work is not really the disease with them, and the mere provision of it is therefore useless as a cure." Classes C and D also lived below Booth's poverty line and there were nearly a million Londoners in these two categories. Some were poor because of frequent unemployment, some because, while they worked steadily, their wages were very low. The former tended to be "shiftless and improvident," the work the latter did required little skill or intelligence, but to Booth these groups were the real victims of the system, "hard-working struggling people," and "decent steady men, paying their way and bringing up their children respectably."[20]

Seen from this perspective, the poor of London were being oppressed not by their capitalist employers but (unwittingly) by the very poor. "The disease from which society suffers is the unrestricted competition in industry of the needy and the helpless. . . . The competition of B drags down C and D." Put differently, most of the London poor were underemployed (in Booth's terminology, "insufficiently employed"). "Some are superfluous," he wrote, "though each individual may be doing a share of the work." Booth realized that good workers were sometimes thrown out of work by depressions, but for one so committed to helping the deserving poor he was curiously complacent about them. "I do not doubt that many good enough men are now walking about idle," he wrote. The number of these "*definitely* unemployed" was "said to be large" and "may be greater than can be faced with complacency." But he did not trouble to count them. At another place he mentioned that even those in his relatively well-off class E were "cursed by insecurity against which it is not easy for any prudence to guard."

The solution to the problem of poverty was to get class B out of the labor market. Booth proposed to accomplish this exclusion by what he called "a limited form of Socialism."

> To effectually deal with the whole of Class B—for the State . . . to provide for those who are not competent to provide for themselves—may seem an impossible undertaking, but nothing less than this will enable self-respecting labour to obtain its full remuneration and the nation its raised standard of life.[21]

[20] *Ibid.*, I: 176, 44, 48–50, 149; II, 21.
[21] *Ibid.*, I: 149, 151, 161, 165.

But what he actually had in mind was little more than a refinement of eighteenth-century ideas about the perfect workhouse. The Bs should be settled in "industrial groups" outside the cities. Family life should be preserved, and the children carefully educated, since "incompetence need not be hereditary." Inmates would have to work hard "from morning to night," building their houses, cultivating the land, and making their own clothes and furniture. Unlike the earlier reformers, Booth was not so naïve as to believe that these government-run communities could be made to pay their own way. "It would be merely that the State, having these people on its hands, obtained whatever value it could out of their work." Those who failed to reach some minimum standard of efficiency, however, would be consigned to the poorhouse.

With class B removed from the scene, "class A, no longer confounded with 'the unemployed,' could be gradually harried out of existence," while classes C and D could easily perform the work previously done by class B. The value of this labor, in itself insufficient to support anyone decently, when added to their wages would raise them above the poverty line. Many indirect benefits would follow. Trade unions would cease to represent only the aristocracy of labor; mutual-aid societies would flourish; the morale of all workers would improve and with it their efficiency, thus the profits of employers, too.[22]

In other words, Booth attributed the unemployment he observed to a surfeit of people not to a shortage of jobs. The problem could, of course, be stated either way, but Booth's choice obscured the fact that London, while the center of British culture and wealth, was becoming more and more an *industrial* backwater. Rising land values were driving heavy industry out of the city. Much of what manufacturing remained was run on a very small scale employing simple machinery and unskilled labor. Booth also, despite his evident sympathy for the London poor, thought that the lower classes ought to be held responsible for their own behavior and that indiscriminate relief during bad times would "unnerve the suffering poor" and "habituate" the unemployed to idleness. He also believed that a certain amount of unemployment and material privation strengthened character. In these attitudes he was close to the point of view of persons who lacked his concern for (to say nothing of his intimate knowledge of) the condition of the lower orders of society.[23]

Blaming the unemployed for their idleness was not a late-nineteenth-century invention, but the persistence of this attitude in the

---

[22] *Ibid.*, I: 167–69.

[23] *Ibid., Industrial Series,* V: 73–74, 230–31; G. S. Jones, *Outcast London: A Study of the Relationship between Classes in Victorian England* (Oxford, 1971), pp. 20–32; J. A. Hobson, *Problems of Poverty* (London, 1891), pp. 92–93.

face of mounting evidence of the cyclical character of unemployment is not easily explained. Some middle-class criticism of the idle poor merely reflected the preconceptions of the critics. Some, however, was based on accurate observation. Especially among craftsmen, the habit of celebrating Saint Monday did not disappear; absenteeism, often associated with drunkenness, is described so frequently and in such detail that it cannot be passed off as inconsequential. The tendency of persons receiving charitable assistance in bad times to cease looking for work and to accept a dependent status is also mentioned by too many careful English, French, American, and other commentators of the period to be dismissed as no more than a figment of middle-class imaginations. Probably the fact that there was so little difference between what the under class could earn when work was available and what even the most niggardly charitable assistance provided had much to do with this deplorable situation. Seen from this perspective, the strenuous efforts of so many Victorian reformers to inspire the down-trodden to greater effort by religious exhortation appears less fatuous and impractical than at first glance.

In any case, concern about the work habits and moral condition of laborers was everywhere very great. The most circumstantial discussion of the related problems of drunkenness and absenteeism was surely that of Denis Poulot, a French manufacturer of machine tools. In *Le Sublime,* subtitled "The worker as he is in 1870 and as he could be," Poulot classified Parisian wage earners according to eight types —types that he claimed to know intimately since he had himself been for many years a laborer and foreman. These ranged from "the real worker" *(l'ouvrier vrai),* who possessed all the conventional virtues, down through *l'ouvrier mixte* (well meaning, but easily led astray because ignorant and impressionable), to various forms of what he sarcastically called *sublimisme—le sublime simple, le sublime descendu,* and *le vrai sublime*—all characterized as "dirty, disgusting, brutal, boorish, ignorant, mindless *(instinctif),* and bestial."[24]

Unwillingness to work steadily was the chief outward sign that an individual was a *sublime.* "The number of days a year laborers work is an almost certain criterion of their type," Poulot claimed. Most *ouvriers* worked 300 days a year or more, that is, they took off only Sundays and the major national and religious holidays. A *sublime simple,* on the other hand, averaged only 200 or 225 days a year; he tended to devote Sunday to his family but then spent Monday in a café with his friends. This *chômage du lundi* and time lost because of frequent changes of jobs accounted for the idleness of the class. As for the *vrai sublime,* he put

[24] Denis Poulot, *Le sublime: ou le travailleur comme il est en 1870 et ce qu'il peut être* (Paris, 1872), pp. 20–21.

in at most 170 days a year. He was an alcoholic who drank a powerful raw *eau de vie* instead of wine; if deprived of this *ration de vitriol* for any length of time he suffered gnawing stomach pains and acted like a madman. Poulot believed that many real and ordinary *ouvriers* were slipping into the *ouvrier mixte* class, and that *sublimisme* was on the increase in France. Among the iron workers he knew most about, he estimated that only one in ten was an *ouvrier vrai,* while 60 percent were *sublimes.* "The *sublime simple* descends little by little, with the help of the wine merchant, laziness and drunkenness lending him a hand."[25]

All this might suggest that Poulot was merely giving vent to feelings typical of many employers in every generation. This was by no means the case. Poulot believed, for example, that workers had a right to organize and that employers would do well to help them do so. Employers need not concern themselves about unions being dominated by radicals because radicals only have influence when they are persecuted. Allow laborers to organize freely and they would laugh at the communists' impractical ideas. Moreover, Poulot was quite conscious of the "terrible calamity" of unemployment, at the mere thought of which an honest worker "feels strangled, shakes, trembles with emotion." The "unmerited despair" of unemployment, he admitted, was the sort of thing that led men to become socialists. He also wrote, apparently without any awareness of his inconsistency, that unemployment was a cause of the growth of *sublimisme.* Here is part of Poulot's highly colored description of how a worker reacts to losing his job:

> He trembles, grows pale, gets gooseflesh. . . . When he collects his last pay he cannot speak, his teeth are clenched, he holds back a torrent of tears. . . . In the street his legs give way, he totters like a drunk. When he arrives home . . . his wife senses what has happened from his manner; she cries, throws herself in his arms; it is too much—the accumulated tears burst out. . . . He falls into his chair, his head in his hands, and through his tears, cries out "What have I done to deserve this misery?"[26]

Poulot's system of classification was much less precise than Charles Booth's, but allowing for national cultural differences their types were essentially the same. Poulot's *vrais sublimes* corresponded roughly to Booth's class A, his *sublimes simples* to class B, the *ouvriers mixtes* to class C, and so on. Booth and Poulot were far from agreeing, however, about what could be done to improve the condition of the working classes. Although the *sublimes* seemed both responsible for their own terrible state and incorrigible, and despite what seemed to him their

[25] *Ibid.,* pp. 67, 73, 91–92, 157, 168, 229–30.
[26] *Ibid.,* pp. 221–23, 294–312, 226–27.

growing numbers, Poulot believed that the type was fated to die out. He placed his hopes for improvement on labor organizing, on political action, and especially on increasing production by means of intense mechanization. *"Des machines, encore des machines, toujours des machines,"* he wrote.[27] The idea of a necessary reserve army of idle workers found no place in his thought.

However, the burden of Poulot's argument even more than Booth's was on the weaknesses and faults of a large segment of the wage-earning population. Both these well-meaning, knowledgeable, and eminently practical-minded men understood that idleness could be involuntary as well as willful, but they focused on the latter variety, which provided a more comprehensible villain, was more easily explained, and (most important) did not so directly challenge the morality and justice of the existing economic system. If idlers were merely lazy, they could be either exhorted or compelled to work, or left to their own miserable devices. If ignorance or a bad environment explained idleness, then moral guidance, or more education, better housing, and other improved social services might be expected to solve the problem. But if the system itself caused unemployment any more extensive and long-lasting than the experts had explained was inevitable in a self-adjusting economy. . . . Little wonder that most persons who prospered in such an economy preferred other explanations, and that even people like Booth and Poulot who were deeply concerned about poverty and its attendant social problems tended to confuse the different causes of unemployment.

In the late nineteenth century, cyclical depressions associated with industrialization were making unemployment more severe. At the same time, slum conditions, the lack of steady work, the regimentation incidental to machine methods of production, and other social pressures were dashing the hopes and undermining the sense of loyalty to the community of many people, making them poor workers and worse citizens. As Marx (whose view was not clouded by sentimental or selfish attachments to existing economic institutions) had stressed, capitalism *did* have a tendency to alienate labor, although, as Marx and countless others noted, it also raised the hopes and expectations of workers by greatly increasing material output.

Those who looked closely into the lives of wage earners encountered many examples of both involuntary and voluntary idleness, but often found it difficult to distinguish one from the other. Close association, interacting with prejudices growing out of class differences, made most

[27] *Ibid.*, pp. 268–69, 373–76. Poulot admitted that new machines could cause "a certain disturbance" in the labor market, but insisted that on balance machines always created more jobs than they eliminated.

of them keenly aware of the failings of many poor people. They tended to give up on at least the worst of these, even though their study of the lives of the poor made them recognize the social causes of the failings and the blurred line that separated the disreputable and undeserving from the "respectable" poor. Thus the revived concern about beggars in western Europe; the emergence of the "tramp problem" in the United States (as I have pointed out, before the 1870s Americans without jobs or fixed abode who moved about in search of a better life without knowing exactly where they were going were usually called "pioneers"); the flood of literature and oratory describing the horrors of working-class alcoholism, and bemoaning the decline of industriousness, thriftiness, and initiative in the lower orders.

More intimate knowledge of the problems faced by the urban poor but also of their often-reprehensible behavior only compounded middle-class confusion. Anyone who had spent time in a slum district became aware of the influence of the environment on the inhabitants. This awareness, however, did not necessarily give birth to more benevolent attitudes. For example, the idea that giving money to an unemployed person risked making him dependent and lazy was an environmentalist concept; indiscriminate public relief, the Philadelphia Society for Organized Charity announced during the 1870s, "encourages the idle, the shiftless and degraded to live at the public charge rather than earn their own bread." In its more extreme forms this led to the reasoning that urban crowding was caused by generous urban public-assistance programs and that giving shoes to poor children so that they could go to school encouraged parents to keep their children out of school in order to get them free shoes.[28]

These attitudes produced a great deal of well-intentioned but often meddlesome investigation and supervision of the poor. In Great Britain, the Charity Organisation Society, founded in 1869, committed itself to the close examination of applicants for aid in order to restore some sense of personal commitment among the givers of help and to provide guidance and moral uplift to the recipients, but also to weed out the undeserving loafers among the applicants. In Germany, where industrialization came with a rush in mid-century, the so-called Elberfeld system, first developed in the industrial town of that name in the 1850s, carried supervision of relief to a point where each Guardian of the Poor (*Pfleger*) had no more than four families to deal with.[29] Public

[28] L. H. Feder, *Unemployment Relief in Periods of Depression: A Study of Measures Adopted in Certain American Cities, 1857 through 1922* (New York, 1936), p. 47; Jones, *Outcast London*, pp. 267–71.

[29] Elberfeld had a population of about 70,000 in the 1870s. It was divided into 18 districts, each in turn split into 14 neighborhoods. There were thus 252 neighborhoods, each with its own *Pfleger*.

assistance, furthermore, was doled out for only two weeks at a time. This kind of close control, an admiring commentator on the Elberfeld system wrote, "is the only bar against the reckless indifference or thoughtless soft-heartedness that feed misery instead of combatting it and rooting it out." (A less sympathetic English observer described the control as "so close and searching, so absolutely inquisitorial, that no man who could possibly escape from it would submit to it.") The Elberfeld system attracted much favorable attention, mostly because it reduced the cost of poor relief substantially. Cologne, Dresden, Dusseldorf, Vienna, and numerous other cities adopted the plan. The attitudes of private American charitable organizations were influenced by the Elberfeld system as well as by the theories of the British Charity Organisation Society.[30]

The time-honored technique for exposing fakers was to require work in return for aid, and this approach fitted well with the environmentalism of late-nineteenth-century social workers. Public-works programs also seemed a natural way to aid those of the unemployed who were willing and able to work. However, the social workers and reformers of the period viewed work relief with mixed feelings. It was one thing to agree that work relief was preferable to direct assistance, quite another to provide suitable tasks for thousands of jobless people with widely varied abilities on short notice, and to do so without competing with private business, especially during cyclical depressions.

The futility of trying to create work on a mass scale had apparently been demonstrated by the experience of the French during the Revolution of 1848. With the overthrow of King Louis Philippe and the establishment of a republic, Louis Blanc, author of *L'organisation du travail,* became a power in the government. At his urging a "right to work" decree was issued and National Workshops were created to hire anyone who wanted a job. These workshops did not resemble the Social Workshops Blanc had advocated in his book; they were more nearly replicas of the eighteenth-century *ateliers de charité,* although financed entirely by the state. The result was what the contemporary economist Blanqui, no reactionary, described as an "economic saturnalia." In Paris and in the provinces, applicants by the thousands flooded the workshops, so many that it proved impossible to keep

---

[30] August Lemmers, "Elberfeld," in A. Emminghaus, ed., *Das Armenwesen und die Armengesetzgebung in Europäischen Staaten* (Berlin, 1870), pp. 89–97, esp. p. 94; Emil Münsterberg, *Die deutsche Armengesetzgebung und das Material zu ihre Reform* (Leipzig, 1887), pp. 504–505; H. St. Marc, "Le système d'Elberfeld," *Revue d'économie politique,* 1 (1887), 441–77; W. Chance, "The Elberfeld and English Poor Law Systems," *Economic Journal* 7 (1897), 332; Emil Münsterberg, *Die Armenpflege* (Berlin, 1897), pp. 42–48; Feder, *Unemployment Relief,* pp. 60–61.

more than a fraction of them occupied. Manual labor on public projects was the only work offered and many of the unemployed found the tasks beyond their strength. Yet in the confusion, some who were capable of hard labor managed to collect their two francs a day while doing nothing. A few useful projects were undertaken, but the general record of the workshops was by any standard dismal. Different political factions tried to mobilize the relief workers for their own ends, raising fears of a coup. Then, when a newly elected National Assembly dominated by moderate republicans decided to dissolve the workshops, a bloody insurrection, "the June Days," followed. By the time order was restored the National Workshops had become an "object of almost universal odium."[31]

The work-relief idea, however, remained appealing, humanitarians seeing it as educative, sterner types as punitive. Especially when depressions caused the numbers in need of relief to soar, tying assistance to some kind of work seemed essential both to bolster the morale of those in need and to prevent fraud. At such times most cities were compelled to create emergency "distress" committees and to call upon the citizenry to contribute money for relief. Large sums were often raised, but the distribution was much criticized on the grounds that loafers and cheats got much of what was given and that indiscriminate handouts encouraged idleness. But efforts to create work for unemployed people in return for this "emergency" aid were seldom effective; as one reporter put it, the work was more often than not only "charity with a quasi work test attached." Moreover, whether supervised by charitable organizations or by government agencies, work relief seemed to demoralize recipients rather than to sustain them; the crude tasks, such as chopping wood and breaking up rocks, were hard, but making dispirited workers exert themselves was still harder. "The standard of accomplishment," one investigating committee concluded, "is practically fixed by the unwilling worker." Still worse, experience demonstrated that many down-and-outers preferred this type of labor to better-paying but more-demanding work for private employers.

Municipal governments tried to help during depressions by speeding up their public-works programs, but the results were nearly always disappointing. An early effort occurred in Great Britain during the Lancashire cotton "famine" that resulted from the cutting off of American supplies during the Civil War. The prolonged mass unemployment caused by the closing of the textile factories attracted world-

[31] J. A. Blanqui, *Des classes ouvrières en France, pendant l'année 1848* (Paris, 1849), p. 30; D. C. McKay, *The National Workshops: A Study in the French Revolution of 1848* (Cambridge, Mass., 1933), pp. 10–29, 50–51, 77–79, 107.

wide sympathy and support. Local authorities, drawing upon loans from the central government, spent over 1.8 million in 1863–65 on roads, sewers, and other public improvements. But only a relative handful—never more than four thousand at a time—of the half million textile workers were employed on these projects. Nevertheless, the public-works approach received a thorough trial in Britain.[32]

Joseph Chamberlain pushed the idea hard when he became president of the Local Government Board in 1886; his efforts attracted a great deal of attention, but produced few significant results. American, German, French, and other city emergency works projects fared little better. It was always expensive and often completely impossible to do outdoor work in winter when the need for relief was greatest, and especially with the inefficient and physically inadequate people who made up the bulk of the applicants.[33]

Another device for making work for the jobless that was developed during the period was the labor colony; Charles Booth's plan for settling his class B in rural "industrial camps" was only one of many such proposals. Germany was the leader in this field; the first camp, at Wilhelmsdorf in Westphalia, was founded in 1882, and by 1886 fifteen camps, housing over 5,000 inmates, had been set up. By the 1890s there were also labor camps in Great Britain, France, Switzerland, Belgium, the Netherlands, and the United States. Although there were a few urban camps, most were located in the country and concentrated on agriculture and forestry. Some were little more than prison camps, populated by ex-convicts and shiftless types who, in the words of a German commentator, "have only themselves to thank" for their condition. Others were almost utopian efforts to rehabilitate down-and-outers; General William Booth of the Salvation Army set up two camps in England that were intended to be way stations where "the abject and apparently hopeless may be . . . trained to industry, total abstinence, and godliness" before being sent off to settle in the colonies.[34]

[32] *Report of the Massachusetts Board to Investigate the Subject of the Unemployed* (Boston, 1895), Part I, p. 24; W. H. Beveridge, *Unemployment: A Problem of Industry* (London, 1909), pp. 152–53; W. O. Henderson, *The Lancashire Cotton Famine; 1861–1865* (New York, 1969), pp. 61–67, 78–86; José Harris, *Unemployment and Politics: A Study in English Social Policy* (Oxford, 1972), pp. 73–90.

[33] *Massachusetts Report*, Part I, pp. xxvii–xxviii, 58–107; Geoffrey Drage, *The Unemployed* (London, 1894), pp. 82–94; Ernst Bernhard, "Die Vergebung der öffentlichen Arbeitern in Deutschland," *Kampf gegen die Arbeitslosigkeit* (Berlin, 1913), pp. 35–37, 46–49; Bureau de Travail, *Statistique des traveaux de secours en cas de chômage* (Paris, 1899), pp. 96–98.

[34] G. Berthold, *Die Entwicklung der deutschen Arbeiterkolonien* (Leipzig, 1887); P. T. Ringenbach, *Tramps and Reformers, 1873–1916: The Discovery of Unemployment in New York* (Westport, Conn., 1973), pp. 119–20; *Massachusetts Report*, Part V, pp. xxi–xxvii; D. F. Schloss, "Unemployment in Foreign Countries," *Report to the [British] Board of Trade on Agencies and Methods for dealing with Unemployment in Certain Countries* (London, 1904), p. 47. Harris, *Unemployment and Politics*, pp. 117–27.

Few labor camps provided work for the direct victims of depressions. At best critics found the idea promising; most economists and social workers were skeptical about the possibility of dealing with large numbers of unemployed people in this manner. One not-unsympathetic writer called the camps "receptacles for social wreckage"; another, who stressed the many variant types, concluded that none offered much help for "the genuinely unemployed workman."[35]

Even in failure, however, the work-relief idea affected how involuntary idleness was conceived of and confronted. The idea that unemployment was a special social problem, distinct from the larger problem of poverty, and that it could not be explained entirely in terms of personal inadequacy, was by the late 1880s swiftly winning acceptance, as is seen by the coining of the word at that time. When Alfred Marshall published his influential *Principles of Economics* in 1890,[36] he still used the expression "inconstancy of employment" and said relatively little about the phenomenon, since he treated full employment as the economic norm. Marshall believed that unemployment only *appeared* to be more severe than in earlier times, the reason being that factories were larger and that layoffs therefore attracted more attention.[37] But the great depression of the 1890s, the worst experienced by the industrial world up to that time, put an end to this kind of complacency. Typical was the reaction of leading citizens of Boston when the mayor called a meeting in December 1893 to decide what to do about the soaring number of destitute people seeking relief: "The problem was of a different sort from that which was normally dealt with by the charitable agencies of the city, for the existing distress was . . . due chiefly to non-employment, and not to the ordinary causes of poverty."[38]

In 1894 an English civil servant, Geoffrey Drage, prefaced his study of *The Unemployed* with the sentence: "As far as I am aware no attempt has yet been made in any country to deal comprehensively with the question of the unemployed." At almost the same moment a German economist published a book on the subject in which he berated his colleagues for having treated unemployment in a "stepmotherly" fashion. Suddenly unemployment had become a burning issue; books and articles and the reports of government investigations began to come out in ever-larger numbers. Professor Georg Adler of the University of Basel published a thesis on unemployment insurance in 1894, and

[35] Schloss, "Unemployment in Foreign Countries," p. vii; Drage, *Unemployed*, pp. 45–73; J. A. Hobson, *The Problem of the Unemployed* (London, 1896), pp. 132–43, 156–58; Percy Alton, *The Unemployed: A National Question* (London, 1905), pp. 122–36.

[36] Marshall's path-breaking economics was actually worked out in the 1870s and early 1880s; for various reasons, some sensible, some not, he delayed publishing his work for many years. J. M. Keynes, *Essays in Biography* (New York, 1963), pp. 148–49, 170–77.

[37] Alfred Marshall, *Principles of Economics* (London, 1890), I: 733n.

[38] *Massachusetts Report*, Part I, p. 12.

followed this work with articles on various aspects of the subject, including a brief survey of "Unemployment in History" in which he traced the phenomenon back to the time of Periander of Corinth in the sixth century B.C.[39] In England, Germany, the United States, and to a lesser extent in France and other western European countries, economists, journalists, and social workers filled the periodical press with essays on the causes of and proposed cures for unemployment. The French Bureau of Labor circulated a questionnaire on job placement among unions in 1892, the 267 replies providing some interesting comments on the causes of unemployment.

The next year the Dutch government made a survey of unemployment. Seven American states made sample surveys of the jobless in 1893 and 1894. In the latter year, the Spanish ministry of the interior queried provincial governors about possible public-works projects for the idle, Switzerland held a plebiscite on a constitutional amendment guaranteeing every unemployed person a job (the amendment was overwhelmingly defeated), and the French government began an investigation of the possibility of "alleviating the effects of industrial crises by creating a capital reserve for works that could be started and stopped according to the severity of unemployment." An American researcher sent 1,200 circulars of enquiry to municipal officials and charity societies asking for information on how they were handling unemployment relief.[40] In 1895 a parliamentary committee issued a series of reports on "Distress from Want of Employment."[41] That same year the German government published a study of unemployment based on census data, and a board appointed by the Massachusetts legislature released a massive *Report* discussing the causes of unemployment, relief measures, the tramp problem, and the efficacy of public works as a way of assisting the jobless. In 1896 the French Bureau of Labor published its report on the public-works question. Having examined earlier French experiments, the practices of foreign governments, and the current activities of some 150 French towns and cities, the report had high praise for Turgot's *ateliers de charité* of the 1770s and denounced the "calamitous" National Workshops of 1848.

[39] Drage, *Unemployed*, p. vii; John Schikowski *Über Arbeitslosigkeit und Arbeitslosenstatistik* (Leipzig, 1894), p. 1; Georg Adler, *Über die Aufgaben des Stadts angesichts der Arbeitslosigkeit* (Tübingen, 1894); Adler, "Die Arbeitslosigkeit in der Geschichte," *Die Zukunft*, 13 (1895), 312–17.

[40] D. R. Dewey, "Irregularity of Employment," American Economic Association *Publications*, 9 (1894), 526; Samuel Rezneck, "Unemployment, Unrest, and Relief in the United States during the Depression of 1893–97," *Journal of Political Economy*, 61 (1953), 328–29.

[41] Harris, *Unemployment and Politics*, pp. 90–95. The neologism "unemployment" did not catch on as swiftly as the subject itself. The earliest use of the word in the *Bulletin* of the U.S. Department of Labor occurred in 1913.

It recommended that local communities should continue to decide when to institute special make-work projects, but insisted that those in charge must display "firm discipline and great vigilance to prevent the abuses that insinuate themselves so easily into projects of this type."[42]

The most original of the new students of unemployment was the English economist John A. Hobson. Although he acknowledged their intellectual achievements, Hobson considered the classical economists apologists for vested interests and lacking in any real concern for the welfare of wage earners. The narrow type of analysis fashionable in his own day, "aiming," he later said, "more and more at quantitative exactitude," did not appeal to him either. Temperamentally he was more a social reformer than an economist, and when he turned his mind and the tools of his trade to practical social issues, he came up with a number of startling insights both about the nature of unemployment and about how the problem should be attacked. He recognized the ambiguity of the new term and the fact that its use implied that the problem was a social more than a merely personal one. "Unemployment" meant not only "all forms of involuntary leisure suffered by the working classes" but also "waste of labour-power regarded from the social point of view." A bricklayer idle on a rainy day or even a person who worked very hard for four or five days in order to have the rest of the week for rest and recreation was not wasting labor, whereas all the idle rich were. On the other hand, seasonal and all casual and part-time workers were wasting much potential labor and to that extent were unemployed. So were the able-bodied paupers, for although they were incapable of efficient labor, their incompetence was social in origin, their potential ability wasted.[43]

Hobson was properly respectful of Charles Booth's great work but unwilling to accept Booth's complacency about the "unemployed margin." He was of course familiar with the reserve army theory from his reading of Marx as well as of Booth, and in general he accepted its validity. But, while he was not a revolutionary, he insisted that "the fact that under existing conditions the unemployed seem inevitable should afford the strongest motive for a change in these conditions." And with the argument that surplus unskilled laborers were mostly incompetent or unwilling to work he had no patience. Rudimentary statistics showed that whereas over 13 percent of the British work force had been unemployed in 1886, fewer than 2 percent had been idle during

[42] F. I. Taylor, *A Bibliography of Unemployment and the Unemployed* (London, 1909); *Massachusetts Report;* Kaiserliches Statistisches Amt, *Die beschäftigunslosen Arbeitnehmer im deutschen Reich* (Berlin, 1896); Conseil Supérieur du Travail, *Rapport sur la question du chômage* (Paris, 1896), pp. 127–34.

[43] J. A. Hobson, *Confessions of an Economic Heretic* (New York, 1938), pp. 24–25; Hobson, *Problem of the Unemployed,* pp. 2, 5–10, 30–31.

the boom of 1890. "That in 1890 the mass of unemployed was almost absorbed, disposes once for all of the allegation that the unemployed in times of depression consist of idlers who do not choose to work."

Unfortunately, periods of full employment were rare; most of the time too many unskilled people were seeking too few unskilled jobs. Hobson was not sanguine about the effectiveness of most of the suggestions his contemporaries were making for attacking this problem. Emigration was impractical; the unskilled were not very mobile and the countries that needed additional people did not want them. Labor camps merited consideration but were unlikely to have much effect. Unionization of the unskilled would not create any jobs; to the extent that some members obtained more work or higher wages, they must do so at the expense of others.

Nor could the state easily take up the slack through public-works programs. Socially useful projects would be, or at least ought to be, undertaken by the government "independently of the consideration of providing work for unemployed." If they were not useful, the projects were only charity in disguise, the work done merely pro forma, a kind of grim charade. As for the idea of speeding up ordinary public-works programs during periods of high unemployment, that would either mean taking advantage of depressed wage rates (a form of sweating) or, if "fair" wages were paid, removing the "natural check" on unemployment that wage cuts during business depressions effected.[44]

Finally there was the possibility of the state as what would later be called employer of last resort, the concept behind Louis Blanc's ill-fated National Workshops. Hobson's doubts about this idea were not the usual ones. He admitted that "if the State . . . were to undertake to provide work and wages for an indefinite number of men who failed to obtain work in the competition market, the effect would be to offer a premium upon 'unemployment.' " However, if the state hired all the unemployed, wages would rise, "greater regularity of employment would be secured, and the general improvement of industrial conditions would check the tendency of workers to flow towards the public workshops." Yet if these workshops produced anything, the goods would enter into competition with private industry, probably exacerbating unemployment. This result could be avoided only by utterly useless labor—the example Hobson used was having the men dig holes and then fill them up again. As with his discussion of labor camps, he did not argue that the public-works approach was without merit; he was concerned, rather, with stressing the complexity of the unemployment problem.[45]

[44] Hobson, *Confessions*, pp. 28–29, 35; Hobson, *Poverty*, pp. 15–17, 91, 135–48, 117–20.
[45] *Ibid.*, 122–23.

Hobson's own solution challenged some of the basic postulates of classical economics. The prime cause of unemployment, he insisted, was underconsumption, a shortage of what Malthus had called "effective demand." And the reason why demand could be inadequate was that rich people often did not consume enough—they saved too much of their income. Hobson first advanced these views in *The Physiology of Industry*, a book he wrote with a businessman named A. F. Mummery[46] in 1889; he put the matter succinctly in *The Problem of the Unemployed* (1896). Unemployment was "a natural and necessary result of a maldistribution of consuming-power." These ideas were, of course, economic heresy at the time Hobson advanced them. Ever since Adam Smith had written that "parsimony, and not industry, is the immediate cause of the increase of capital," it had been understood that saving was but a form of investment and thus a stimulus to the economy. Furthermore, Say's law—that supply creates its own demand—and the glosses upon it of most of the major economists from Ricardo to John Stuart Mill had apparently proved that anything that was produced would be consumed. Should the supply of any product increase beyond current demand, production would be cut back, competition would drive its price down, and demand would then rise, restoring the balance.[47]

Hobson dismissed this classical argument as "loose deductive reasoning" and "thoroughly fallacious." Both the *power* and the *desire* to consume everything produced might well exist, but they did not necessarily exist in the same person. Too frequently, those with the power preferred to save rather than spend. Up to a point, Hobson admitted, saving did not inhibit consumption. Parsimony did create capital, as Smith had said, and when the capital was used, say, to build a new factory, an equivalent amount of consuming power was created. But when the new factory began to produce, demand for its goods might not arise. If it did not, trade would be depressed, and workers would lose their jobs. On Crusoe's island or in a simple society overproduc-

[46] The original insight was Mummery's; Hobson became involved in trying to refute the argument and was instead converted. According to Hobson, Mummery, who was a well-known mountain climber in his spare time (and who died in 1895 while attempting to scale Nanga Parbat in the Himalayas), "was a mental climber as well, with a natural zest for a path of his own finding and a sublime disregard of intellectual authority." *Confessions*, p. 30. An American writer, Uriel H. Crocker, had developed the same basic argument in the 1870s. "Savings . . . may be carried to such an extent as to overfill the possible limits of the field of profitable investments. . . . If the great army of savers . . . had employed more of that surplus in the purchase of products to be consumed [they] would have prevented entirely the occurrence of any hard times." *The Cause of Hard Times* (1895), pp. 44–5.

[47] J. A. Hobson and A. F. Mummery, *The Physiology of Industry*, (London, 1889); Hobson, *Problem of the Unemployed*, p. x; Adam Smith, *The Wealth of Nations* (New York, 1937), p. 321.

tion and underconsumption might be impossible; not so in the complex modern world, where rich savers tend to invest too often in already crowded fields.

> That portion of new savings which embodies itself in forms of capital that satisfy new wants is both morally and economically justified: that portion which embodies itself in the socially useless multiplication of existing forms of capital is harmless as regards employment so long as it continues to embody itself thus, but when by clogging the wheels of industry it stops the machinery and checks the investment of new "savings," it contributes to that state of under-employment and under-production which we call "trade depression."[48]

Hobson, it should be emphasized, was not challenging most of the reasoning of the classical economists. Rather he was saying that their reasoning did not reflect current economic reality. Instead of supposedly eternal principles, he was concerned with the practical situation. "If we find labour and capital unemployed," he wrote, "it can only mean an undue diminution of consumption," a sign that too much consuming power has been tied up in capital by the "over-saving" of the rich. He blamed unemployment not on saving, but on too much saving.

Hobson was neither the first nor the last economist to approach the subject in this manner. Indeed, no less a classical authority than Thomas Malthus had said in 1817: "I certainly am disposed to refer frequently to things as they are. . . . A writer may, to be sure, make any hypothesis he pleases; but if he supposes what is not at all true practically, he precludes himself from drawing any practical inferences from his hypotheses." Malthus, incidentally, was almost alone among the writers of the classical era in questioning the tenets of the school that Hobson was attacking; in 1821 he told Ricardo (who disagreed vehemently): "Saving too much, may be really prejudicial to a country. . . . A great temporary saving . . . might occasion such a division of the produce as would leave no motive to a further increase of production," a situation that "must inevitably throw the rising generation out of employment."[49]

Malthus had recommended that to avoid this condition, the rich must engage in a great deal of "unproductive consumption," by which

[48] Hobson, *Problem of the Unemployed*, pp. 72–73, 77–80; Hobson and Mummery, *Physiology of Industry*, pp. 102–104, 132. Forty years later Hobson was still struggling to explain that he was not attacking the idea of saving. "I hope that the later statement of my over-saving heresy has made the right distinction between over-saving and over-investment. . . . It is only when some of the current savings cannot find a profitable investment . . . that depression and unemployment set in." *Confessions*, pp. 192–93n.

[49] Quoted in J. M. Keynes, *Essays in Biography* (New York, 1963), pp. 116–17, 119–20.

he meant specifically, spending on luxurious living and the employment of "menial servants," more broadly, any consumption as distinct from investment in the production of more goods. Hobson's solution, in a more democratic age, was "a reformed distribution of consuming power." The excess savings of the wealthy should be taxed away and devoted to social purposes. Enterprises benefiting from natural or legal monopolies might be either taken over by the state or heavily taxed, as should inheritances and excessive dividends. A progressive income tax was another device for transferring consuming power to hands that would exercise it. Higher wages and shorter hours would also have this effect. Hobson insisted that these policies would not be punitive; they would stimulate the economy and thus increase the incomes of the very people who paid the taxes.

> If the principle be once firmly grasped that a demand for commodities is the only ultimate demand . . . then the existence of 'unemployed' producing power, is proof that increased consumption is possible without a reduction in the present income of any class of the community.[50]

Despite his reassurances, Hobson's explanation of the cause of unemployment, much less his proposals for reducing it, had little effect on how the subject was understood at the time. In part because of his "heretical" attitude toward saving (to the casual reader he appeared to be questioning that bulwark of Victorian orthodoxy, the virtue of thrift) but still more because he was disputing the relevance of the great classical economists, professionals rejected his work. After his *Physiology of Industry* came out, his promising academic career was ruined; invitations to teach and lecture were withdrawn and he was even turned down for membership in the Political Economy Club. Professor Edwin Cannan of the University of London, an authority on Adam Smith, wrote a sharply critical and demeaning review of his *Problem of the Unemployed*. Isolation from academic economics probably accentuated his tendency toward a popular rather than a scholarly style; he became a person of considerable influence in leftish intellectual circles. But even a modern economist seeking to rehabilitate him confessed that "the formulation of his theory was rather crude," his proofs lacking in "rigour." Late in life Hobson himself admitted that he might have developed his argument "in a more orderly way."[51]

In any case, economic activity in the industrial nations picked up in the last years of the century and unemployment became for the mo-

---

50 Hobson, *Problem of the Unemployed*, pp. 98–111.
51 Hobson, *Confessions*, pp. 30–31, 83–84; *Economic Journal*, 7 (1897), 87–89; D. J. Coppock, "A Reconsideration of Hobson's Theory of Unemployment," *The Manchester School* (January 1953), 20, 7.

ment less alarming. In 1899 B. Seebohm Rowntree, the son of a wealthy English chocolate manufacturer, made a remarkable study of his native city of York, inspired by the work of Charles Booth in London. Aided by a single paid assistant and a few part-time volunteers, he visited every working-class home in York, 11,560 residences housing 46,754 persons. He discovered that even by the spartan definition of poverty that he established, 28 percent of these people did not have a decent standard of living. But, when it came to attributing causes to this poverty, he concluded that only 5 percent of the poor were unemployed and that a majority even of these suffered from "irregularity" of work rather than total unemployment.[52]

But most commentators, wherever positioned on the political spectrum, continued to look upon joblessness as a necessary evil under capitalism, the jobless as a necessary reserve. As for the people who made up the reserve, observers in most instances described them according to their own preconceptions, sometimes as victims of society, sometimes as themselves responsible for their unfortunate condition. The popular term in the 1890s was "residuum"—the unemployed were what was left over. If one envisages the labor force as a quart bottle, the actual working population as a pint of water within it, and the unused space as the unemployed, one approaches the common point of view. For the bottle to serve its function it must be larger than the water. The remaining space is an essential but useless element in the relationship between the bottle and its contents.

[52] B. S. Rowntree, *Poverty: A Study of Town Life* (London, 1902), pp. xiii–x, 119–21.

7

A Problem of Industry

Recognition that unemployment was a kind of disease of capitalism did not clarify the ambiguities inherent in the condition. Understanding that cyclical fluctuations in business activity idled thousands of industrious and perfectly capable workers only made separating these "victims" from loafers and incompetents more difficult, and awareness that they merited help did not eliminate concern lest that help undermine their independence and render them incapable of caring for themselves and their families when economic conditions improved. Knowledge of the existence of "unemployment" also stimulated discussions of its causes, without, however, producing any consensus among economists, businessmen, political leaders, or workers. And the debates about how to prevent unemployment and how best to deal with its victims proved equally inconclusive. Certainly the new insights into the workings of the economic system that had given birth to the concept "unemployment" gained favor only very slowly.

As for the causes of unemployment, well after the turn of the century writers were still devoting inordinate amounts of space to quarrels between workers and their employers, the desire of workers to improve themselves by seeking new jobs, inadequate vocational education, age, illness, and many other matters that had little to do with sharp *changes* in the total amount of unemployment over time. The problem of the work-shy *(die Arbeitsscheue, les paresseux)* remained a major focus of attention. Particularly in the United States, immigration was seen as an important cause of joblessness, a point of view that ignored the fact that unemployment tended to increase and decrease on both sides of the Atlantic at the same time. A French historian, writing in 1908, ticked off a long list of causes of unemployment and finally, perhaps in despair, concluded: "The whole society is the cause of unemployment."[1]

When it came to dealing with the unemployed at the practical level, similar confusions existed. As late as 1906, James Stewart Davy, Chief Inspector of the Local Government Board, which administered the British Poor Law, insisted in testimony before a royal commission that any aid more palatable than the workhouse, even for people rendered destitute by cyclical unemployment, would be a temptation to "unthrift" and therefore counterproductive. "The unemployed man must stand by his accidents; he must suffer for the general good of the body politic." Davy's was a minority opinion by 1906, old-fashioned and indeed literally reactionary. Even the British and American charity organization societies, while still claiming that indiscriminate assistance did more harm than good, were coming to recognize that some general protections against unemployment must be developed. What form the protection should assume, however, remained controversial.[2]

Gradually two ways of looking at the problem emerged, one oriented around the idea of preventing or at least reducing unemployment, the other seeking merely to provide support of one kind or another for the unemployed. Preventionists (actually the line between one "school" and the other was only vaguely drawn at this time) thought in terms of establishing networks of employment offices, called labor exchanges, where jobless persons could be brought into contact with prospective employers; of relocating "surplus" labor; of devising means of reducing seasonal fluctuations in certain industries or coordinating ("dovetailing") the peaks and valleys of these cycles of activity in different industries so that workers could shift from one trade to another in slack periods; and of adjusting the pace of government purchases and construction projects so as to increase employment in bad times. The other stressed the idea of making work for the unemployed, and ultimately of compulsory unemployment insurance, financed by workers, employers, and the state.

Both approaches were tried out in various forms in many nations around the turn of the century. The public labor exchange was most fully developed in Germany; as early as 1887 a student of the subject concluded his analysis with the principle, "The improvement of the care of the unemployed demands a comprehensive organization of

1. Max Lazard, *Le chômage et la profession* (Paris, 1909), pp. 345–50; S. J. Chapman and H. M. Hallsworth, *Unemployment: The Result of an Investigation Made in Lancashire* (Manchester, 1909), pp. 93–94; Michel Bouchet, *L'assistance publique en France pendant la Révolution* (Paris, 1908), p. 657.

2. Sidney and Beatrice Webb, *English Poor Law History* (London, 1963), II: 480; John Brown, "Social Judgements and Social Policy," *Economic History Review*, 24 (1971), 111–12; P. T. Ringenbach, *Tramps and Reformers* (Westport, Conn., 1973), pp. xv, 176–77.

employment offices," and during the 1890s most of the major German cities established job registries called *Arbeitsnachweise*. These were organized into the *Verband deutscher Arbeitsnachweise* in 1898, and by the middle of the next decade some 150 agencies were finding jobs for tens of thousands of workers each year—the Berlin exchange alone placing almost 100,000. The French also had an extensive network of exchanges, some private, some run by labor unions, some by the government; in 1904 an estimated million jobs were filled through these offices. By that date there were also government exchanges in Switzerland, Austria, Belgium, and Norway, as well as a few privately operated free exchanges in England. The earliest public exchanges in the United States date from about 1907.[3]

Aside from bringing jobs to the attention of job seekers, labor exchanges served as a check on malingerers and loafers. If registry at an exchange was a prerequisite of unemployment relief, then aid could be cut off instantly when a recipient refused a job. The chief limitation of the exchange idea was that during depressions there were far fewer jobs than applicants. Effective organization of the labor market might reduce "frictional" unemployment, but it did not create new jobs, and to the extent that exchanges succeeded in keeping some unskilled laborers and workers in seasonal industries more occupied—a major objective of enthusiasts—they probably increased the number of totally unemployed workers among the rest. As for what would later be called countercyclical public-works policies, they were almost impossible to implement; government building and maintenance projects could not easily be postponed or speeded up to accord with changes in the state of the economy, and many of the people who lost their jobs during depressions did not have the skills and physical strength these projects called for.

The other concept, unemployment insurance, raised a different set of problems. Far back into the nineteenth century a number of trade unions had developed benefit funds to sustain unemployed members, and in the 1890s municipal governments began to subsidize some of these with public funds. Ghent in Belgium became the model of this technique, the "Ghent system" being adopted by many cities in the Low Countries and also by some in Germany, Switzerland, and Italy. In 1905 the French government began contributing to trade-union insurance plans on a national basis, and over the next few years Nor-

3. Freiherr von Reitzenstein, "Über Beschäftigung arbeitsloser Armer und Arbeitsnachweis," *Schriften des deutschen Vereins für Armenpflege und Wohltätigkeit*, 4 (1887), 74; Paul Berndt, *Die Arbeitslosigkeit: ihre Bekämpfung und Statistik* (Halle, 1899), p. 33; W. H. Beveridge, *Unemployment: A Problem of Industry* (London, 1909), pp. 239–41, 261; Daniel Nelson, *Unemployment Insurance: The American Experience, 1915–1935* (Madison, 1969), pp. 10, 21.

way, Belgium, and Denmark did likewise. These insurance plans were all voluntary; they covered relatively few workers and provided only modest benefits. In 1908 the French *Académie des Sciences Morales et Politiques,* seven decades after sponsoring Villermé's pioneering investigation of industrial workers, offered a prize for the best essay on unemployment insurance. The winning manuscript, a detailed analysis of existing and proposed systems, came down in the end, cautiously it is true, in favor of the Ghent system. It was clear, however, that more comprehensive schemes could be worked out and that compulsory insurance, financed by employers as well as by workers and the state, had much to recommend it.[4]

But the insurance idea was not without its critics. Aside from the objection of libertarians that no one should be forced to contribute, there was the argument that insurance would undermine incentive. The unemployed might cease looking for work if protected by insurance, and the employed might become lazy and inefficient once the fear of being discharged was lessened in this way. Government subsidization of job insurance—important if the payments were to be meaningful—seemed to critics no different from indiscriminate relief: to give the unemployed something for nothing was to invite them to become pensioners; it made the term "insurance" a misnomer, for once actuarial principles were abandoned, political pressures were likely to make the word a euphemism for public charity.

The questions about unemployment that dominated early twentieth-century discussion were most thoroughly thrashed out in Great Britain. Over the years the tough less-eligibility principles of the Poor Law Reform Act of 1834 had been substantially modified. Various make-work schemes as well as outdoor relief had been attempted, with at best indifferent results. The most interesting experiment, financed privately in 1904, involved sending selected unemployed men to rural work camps, their wives and children being supported at home by charitable grants. The intention was to steer a middle course—to provide help that was without stigma but inconvenient enough to encourage the recipient to get back in the labor market on his own at the first opportunity. The same objective characterized the Unemployed Workmen Act of 1905, which attempted to separate workers unemployed because of business recessions from less deserving types. The act authorized make-work programs, the financing of emigration to the colonies and of migration within Britain, and the establishment of employment exchanges. These activities were to be locally planned and administered, however, and little was attempted beyond the con-

4. Beveridge, *Unemployment,* p. 225; A. de Lavergne and L. P. Henry, *Le chômage: causes—conséquences—remèdes* (Paris, 1910), pp. 1, 223–395, 405–409.

ventional municipal work-relief type of program. In practice it proved almost impossible to distinguish between the "elite" unemployed the law was supposed to help and the common run of applicants. In the opinion of most contemporary experts, work-relief efforts under the act of 1905 were an expensive exercise in futility, almost comparable, said one, to the debacle of the French National Workshops of 1848. This did not prevent the Labour party from introducing a new unemployed-workmen bill in 1908 that would have obligated the government to provide work for anyone who applied for it.[5]

In December 1905, before the inadequacies of the Unemployed Workmen Act had become apparent, the government had appointed a Royal Commission on the Poor Law and the Relief of Distress through Unemployment to study the unemployment problem. The commissioners were both informed and of many viewpoints. Charles Booth was a member, as was one of his principal former assistants, Beatrice Potter (Mrs. Sidney Webb); others included prominent officials of the Charity Organisation Society, several poor law administrators, and a number of important religious leaders. After more than three years of study the commission published fifty volumes of reports, testimony, and special staff studies. Besides recommending that the Board of Guardians be replaced by a new administrative system, it called for doing away with the workhouses and the principle of less eligibility, for old-age pensions and free medical treatment for the poor, for improved care for orphans and the mentally incompetent. The able-bodied unemployed should be given "Home Assistance" (a new name for outdoor relief), but only as a back-up to the aid provided by private charities, an indication of the predominant influence of the Charity Organisation Society in the commission. Make-work projects were pronounced "a complete failure," but persons who *refused* to work should be confined in institutions. In addition, a network of labor exchanges should be set up, trade-union unemployment-insurance plans given government subsidies, vocational training provided for unskilled youths, and a countercyclical public-works program adopted. This last suggestion was more fully worked out in a minority report of the commission, which reflected the ideas of Beatrice Webb and her husband. The Webbs did not originate the idea—in 1908, for example, the French government created a commission to study "measures for lessening cyclical unemployment, notably those relating to public works"—but their exposition of the concept was the most detailed and persuasive to that date. They proposed that over a ten-year period government public works be held back when the economy was pros-

5. Beveridge, *Unemployment,* pp. 160–63, 185–91, 195; Webb, *English Poor Law,* II: 652–57. José Harris, *Unemployment and Politics* (Oxford, 1972), pp. 145–87, 241–44..

pering and then speeded up during downswings of the business cycle. In *The Prevention of Destitution* (1911) they developed the idea at great length. By using government orders as "a counterpoise to the uncontrollable fluctuations in [private] orders" and "doing all the Government work in bad years" unemployment could be vastly reduced. The idea was "poles asunder" from the usual make-work relief projects, which the Webbs agreed were counterproductive.[6]

Although the current British government was unready to cast aside the ancient poor law as the commissioners desired, it did make major changes in the treatment of the poor in general and the unemployed in particular at least partly as a result of their recommendations. In 1909, the National Labour Exchange Act established a network of employment offices which were soon regularly filling over a million jobs a year. Two years later the National Insurance Act provided for health insurance for all wage earners and unemployment insurance for those in certain trades, both financed by worker and employer contributions, buttressed by state subsidies.

The unemployment-insurance system was the world's first; the much-admired German social-welfare legislation of the 1880s had not dealt with unemployment. The person most responsible for the measure was Winston Churchill, president of the Board of Trade and then Home Secretary in the cabinet of Prime Minister Herbert Asquith. Churchill knew relatively little about the technicalities of either insurance or the unemployment problem, but he recognized unemployment (the "Achilles heel" of British labor) as an important political and social issue. He quickly availed himself of the most advanced thinking on the subject—his mentors were Sidney and Beatrice Webb, who recognized Churchill's "capacity for the quick appreciation and rapid execution of ideas," and William H. Beveridge, an authority on labor exchanges, whom he met through the Webbs.[7] Like many other English social reformers of the period, Churchill was also impressed by German welfare programs; before entering the cabinet he wrote an important article proposing "a sort of Germanized network of state intervention and regulation" for the protection of the jobless.[8]

6. Webb, *English Poor Law*, II: 474–76, 530–38, 543–44; Beveridge, *Unemployment*, pp. 254–62; Sidney and Beatrice Webb, *The Prevention of Destitution* (London, 1911), pp. 110–24.

7. B. B. Gilbert, *The Evolution of National Insurance in Great Britain: The Origins of the Welfare State* (London, 1966), pp. 246–51, 257–58; Gilbert, "Winston Churchill *versus* the Webbs: The Origins of British Unemployment Insurance," *American Historical Review*, 71 (1966), 846–62; W. H. Beveridge, *Power and Influence* (London, 1953), pp. 66–68.

8. Gilbert, *Insurance in Great Britain*, p. 253; Gilbert, "Churchill *versus* the Webbs," pp. 851–52. In 1907 and 1908, Beveridge, Chancellor of the Exchequer David Lloyd George, and a committee of British trade union leaders all made trips to Germany to examine that nation's social-welfare programs in action.

Churchill did not, however, merely assimilate the ideas of others. The Webbs in particular, being ardent preventionists, were wary of compulsory unemployment insurance, which might seem "an easy alternative to complicated measures of prevention," but which they believed would encourage malingering and be extremely expensive. Under a compulsory system, Beatrice Webb wrote in 1909, "the state gets nothing for its money in the way of conduct." The Webbs favored instead a voluntary insurance program of the Ghent type, which, they argued, would encourage workers to develop thrift, foresight, independence, and "the willingness to subordinate the present to the future," and also free the government from the need to administer a complex system. Insurance was, in any case, only a palliative; the true task was to get rid of unemployment. The Webbs conceded that some people would probably always be out of work, but they were convinced that unemployment as a social problem could be eliminated.

> We can now see before us [they wrote in *The Prevention of Destitution*] a national policy dealing with every aspect of the problem, which, if deliberately pursued and experimentally developed, will progressively operate so as more and more to prevent the very occurrence of involuntary Unemployment.[9]

For various reasons, Churchill did not follow the Webbs's advice. Preventing unemployment might, as they said, be possible, but it would take longer than the politician in Churchill could afford to wait. Moreover, he rejected the argument of the Webbs and so many other social workers and reformers that programs of relief ought to aim at improving the character and morals of recipients. Getting something from the unemployed "in the way of conduct" did not appeal to him. "I do not like mixing up moralities and mathematics," he wrote in 1909. "Our concern is with the evil, not with the causes. With the fact of unemployment, not with the character of the unemployed." Even a worker discharged because of drunkenness should be entitled to unemployment benefits if he had paid insurance premiums. Conversely, where the Webbs favored compulsory labor exchanges, seeing them as a way to organize the labor market and prevent the malingering they believed an inherent danger in any insurance system, Churchill considered such a restriction on individuals unjust. Compulsory insurance, on the other hand, did not restrict anyone's freedom. Furthermore—in this he was following Beveridge—it would create "a motive for the voluntary support of Labour Exchanges," a point which

9. Beatrice Webb, *Our Partnership* (New York, 1948), p. 430; Webb, *Prevention of Destitution*, pp. 107, 168, 205–12.

the Webbs eventually conceded. Churchill and the Asquith government went ahead with compulsory insurance[10] and, after linking it with a health-insurance measure devised by Lloyd George, pushed it through Parliament in December 1911. The scheme covered about two and a quarter million workers and provided modest benefits, roughly equivalent to a third of the wage of a low-paid worker, for up to fifteen weeks of joblessness.[11]

The passage of this insurance act and that creating the labor-exchange network was accompanied by much debate and the writing of many articles and books. Of the latter, the most significant was William H. Beveridge's *Unemployment: A Problem of Industry,* published in 1909. Beveridge had become interested in unemployment while working at the famous London settlement house Toynbee Hall. During the winter of 1903–1904 he interviewed applicants for a Salvation Army relief program, a rural work camp. Later he took the trouble to investigate what had happened to these people. He discovered that most of them were neither better nor worse for the experience; they were again living from hand to mouth, finding occasional menial jobs, barely managing to exist. Soon thereafter he began to give lectures on unemployment. In 1905 he was elected to the Central Unemployed Body of London set up under the new Unemployed Workmen Act. This service further convinced him of the futility of make-work projects; he became committed to the labor-exchange and insurance approach to the problem.

By this time Beveridge had become a professional expert on unemployment—probably the world's first. He had a large influence on Sidney and Beatrice Webb, and with their connivance became a major witness before the Royal Commission on the Poor Law. He traveled to Berlin in 1907 to consult with officials of the Imperial Insurance Office, labor-exchange and trade-union leaders, and other specialists. The next year Churchill appointed him to a post in the Board of Trade, and after the passage of the National Labour Exchange Act of 1909, he became director of the exchanges.[12]

In his book, Beveridge had nothing original to say about the economics of unemployment. He discussed current theories of the business cycle in an even-handed way, ticking off the strengths and weak-

10. The actual system was drafted by Beveridge and Hubert Llewellyn Smith, his superior at the Board of Trade.

11. Gilbert, *Insurance in Great Britain,* pp. 259–60, 271–72; Gilbert, "Churchill *versus* the Webbs," pp. 859n; B. B. Gilbert, *British Social Policy (1914–1939)* (Ithaca, 1970), pp. 52–53; Beveridge, *Power and Influence,* p. 60; W. H. Beveridge, *Unemployment: A Problem of Industry* (London, 1930), pp. 266–69.

12. Beveridge, *Power and Influence,* pp. 23–24, 31–32, 39, 43–48, 56–57, 62–68, 71; Beveridge, *Unemployment,* p. 160.

nesses of each. For example, of Hobson, whom he treated at considerable length and more respectfully than most critics, he wrote:

> There is some reason for saying that cyclical fluctuation of trade . . . repre-
> sents, in fact, the incessantly renewed attempt and partial failure to put into
> operation productive forces normally in excess of the existing demand.

But Hobson's theory, Beveridge also said, did not explain why all
branches of industry were depressed at the same time. Furthermore,
to state that saving caused unemployment was misleading—"it gives,
as a cause of unemployment, that which is simply the cause of the
industrial growth to which unemployment is incident." Beveridge concluded that unemployment was caused by change ("fluctuations"),
principally by unorderly growth that was the inevitable and in his
opinion desirable result of competition between producers. Within
"the range of practical politics" no cure was possible. "The aim must
be palliation."

Beveridge also held quite conventional attitudes on most of the
hotly debated aspects of his subject. He believed that some people—
not many—"were born with an invincible distaste or incapacity for
regular exertion," that "the less tolerable the lot of the idler, the
greater the incentive to industry," that "the selective influence of
personal character" had a great deal to do with determining who kept
a job in bad times and who was let go. He was as vigorously opposed
to dispensing relief indiscriminately as any member of the Charity
Organisation Society; failing to distinguish between the unemployed
and those still working was "to run the risk of demoralising the people
by taking from inefficiency its punishment and from assiduity its reward." He took a dim view of the value of make-work programs.[13]

What was original about *Unemployment* was Beveridge's sharp focus
on the social nature of the problem and his buttressing of his conclusions with masses of facts. Unemployment was, as his title indicated,
"a problem of industry," not of individuals—"the inquiry must be one
into unemployment rather than into the unemployed." It was more
important to discover why so many were jobless than to devise methods of aiding those who were. But, unlike many writers on the subject,
Beveridge did not claim to have found a way to do away with unemployment; indeed, he agreed with those who claimed that some unemployment was necessary for economic growth. Close examination of
trade-union statistics led him to the conclusion that even when business was booming there was an "irreducible minimum" of unemployment—about 2 percent in the skilled trades, more among the un-

[13] Beveridge, *Unemployment,* pp. 58–64, 67, 101, 136, 142, 148, 190.

skilled. "Whatever the demand for labour, the supply tends always and everywhere, not to coincide with it, but to exceed it." The explanation of this "central paradox of the unemployed problem" lay in the need for a "reserve of labour" which (although Beveridge did not mention him) was essentially Marx's "disposable industrial reserve army," made up of people needed only during periods of peak production.[14]

Beveridge, however, argued that the reserve was always *larger* than the maximum number employed. His reasoning was based upon his study of trade-union data, which showed that in good times and bad the number of members filing claims under union unemployment-insurance plans did not vary very much. Among the London compositors, for example, over a ten-year period the figure ranged only between 18 percent and 26 percent—roughly eight out of ten members were almost never out of work. What varied sharply was the amount of time unemployed members were idle—this figure rose in depressions and fell in prosperous periods. In 1890 an average of 2.1 percent of the members of the Amalgamated Society of Engineers were unemployed at any one time; in 1893 the corresponding percentage was 10.2, about five times as high. The percentage of the membership that suffered any loss of work during the two years hardly varied at all—it was 21.4 percent in 1890 and 26.4 percent in 1893. But the unemployed group lost about 30 days per man in 1890 and 118 days in 1893. In good years and bad, however, there were always some engineers collecting benefits. The reason, Beveridge decided, was that the pool of irregularly employed labor (those attracted to a trade by the possibility of work) was larger than the maximum ever needed. The same group always supplied those who were let go when business was slack, but the same individuals were not always discharged. All were sustained by hope and none disappointed often enough to drop out of the competition for jobs.

> The general formula . . . in an industry appears then to be this: for work requiring . . . at most ninety-eight men, there will actually be eighty in regular employment and twenty in irregular employment; there will be a hundred in all, so that at all times two at least are out of work. . . . The idleness, now of some, now of others, of the reserve is mainly responsible for the irreducible minimum of unemployment. The figures here given are only an illustrative value . . . [but] the principle is of the greatest generality.[15]

It was this explanation of the "reserve of labour" that led Beveridge to rely so heavily on labor exchanges, which he saw as far more than

[14] *Ibid.,*, pp. 3, 69–70.
[15] *Ibid.,* pp. 73, 76.

devices for reducing frictional unemployment by putting prospective employers and applicants in touch with one another. Since unemployment was "as necessary to [the industrial] system as are capital and labour," the task was to hold it to the "irreducible" minimum. For the thousands of separate pools of labor, each clustered around a single business establishment, each slightly larger than the maximum ever employed, the exchange system would substitute a single pool, "a compact mobile reserve" replacing "the enormous stagnant reserve which drifts about the streets to-day." The exchanges should deliberately concentrate available work so as to keep the best people fully occupied, "squeezing out" the inefficient entirely. This "sheer surplus (a fundamentally different thing from a reserve)" could then be retrained for work in "newly created industries" in Britain or in the colonies. Thereafter the unavoidable fluctuations of the business cycle could be dealt with "up to a certain point" by adjusting the length of the working day and beyond that point by unemployment insurance. "Unemployment," Beveridge concluded, is "part of the price of industrial competition," but "there may be worse things in a community than unemployment. The practical reply is to be found in reducing the pain."[16]

"Reducing the pain"—that the new social problem, "unemployment," would not yield to any easy solution was the heart of Beveridge's message and the part of his message that most impressed his contemporaries. The preventionists were having difficult times; even the Webbs, while continuing to insist that unemployment could be eradicated, found *Unemployment: A Problem of Industry* persuasive, at least to the extent that they accepted with (for them) remarkable complacency the government's decisions not to control the labor market and to institute compulsory unemployment insurance.[17]

So did most other readers; *Unemployment* and the British legislation of 1909–11 established the context for discussions of the problem for many years. In 1910, even before the insurance bill had become law, its merits, as contrasted with the voluntary Ghent system, were debated at the first International Conference on Unemployment in Paris. In the United States reformers and economists began to publish large numbers of articles and books on insurance and employment exchanges. William M. Leiserson, a young economist, was one of the first Americans to make a specialty of unemployment; his position was

---

[16] *Ibid.*, 103, 203–206, 219–20, 235.

[17] Sidney Webb, ed. *Seasonal Trades* (London, 1912), pp. viii, x. However, as late as 1929 the Webbs wrote: "Though the State scheme has averted a social catastrophe and has not yet done all the harm we feared, it still seems to us that its effect upon mind and conduct must become quite seriously bad in those cases in which Unemployment in long-continued." *English Poor Law History, II: 834.*

almost a carbon copy of Beveridge's. In a report drafted for the New York legislature in 1911 he stressed the need for state employment bureaus to compensate for "the failure of idle workmen to connect with employers." Unemployment was "a permanent feature of industrial life." Beveridge's analysis of the employment of casual labor, Leiserson wrote a few years later, was the most important contribution to an understanding of unemployment since *Das Kapital.* A French economist, although carefully avoiding committing himself too enthusiastically to any explanation, surmised that there was a positive correlation between unemployment and "the number of establishments in an industry."[18]

There was, however, an ironic aspect to Beveridge's influence. His emphasis on unemployment as distinct from the unemployed, on the "problem of industry" rather than of individuals, was modern and indeed forward looking. His system of "palliation," principally through labor exchanges, was practical enough if not particularly imaginative. But his analysis of the causes of unemployment—supposedly his prime purpose[19]—was rooted in the past. Indeed, the similarity between Beveridge's view and that of Charles Booth, whom he quoted approvingly and at length in *Unemployment,* is striking and not merely coincidental. Both believed that a surplus of labor was inevitable and necessary, but that the surplus was currently too large. To reduce it, both proposed forcing the most inefficient and degenerate elements in the work force out of the labor market. (Where Booth wanted class A "harried out of existence" and Class B herded off to labor camps, Beveridge was for "squeezing out the very lowest class of men" and providing "some form of training or convalescent institution where they could be dieted and disciplined into other ways.")

This is not to say that Beveridge merely copied Booth or that he was unfamiliar with the changing character of unemployment. Nothing could be further from the truth. But, like Booth, Beveridge was greatly influenced by his observation of the jobless of that industrial backwater London, where hordes of unskilled casual laborers, especially the dock workers, provided a classic example of a decentralized, inefficient, and overpopulated labor market. Despite his up-to-date, even avant-garde perspective, the particular problem that most attracted his attention

---

[18] Nelson, *Unemployment Insurance,* pp. 10–12; W. M. Leiserson, "The Problem of Unemployment Today," *Political Science Quarterly,* 31 (1916), 8–9, 17–19; Lazard, *Chômage,* p. 351.

[19] "The inquiry must be essentially an economic one. The object in view is not the framing of palliatives for present distress, but the discovery of causes and the suggestion, if possible, of preventive measures and final remedies. . . . The first question must be, not what is to be done with the unemployed individual, but why he is thus unemployed." P. 3.

was an ancient one. Throughout history London and every large city, in Europe and elsewhere, had been host to this type of underemployed laborer—carters, message bearers, and other hired hands, as well as ragpickers, peddlers of every sort, and the like. Their condition was deplorable, Beveridge's proposal for aiding them by centralizing hiring was a good one, but neither they nor the proposal had much connection with the mass unemployment resulting from cyclical depressions that comprised the real "problem of industry" in the twentieth century.[20]

If Beveridge was somewhat confused about his subject, so were his contemporaries and not merely because of his influence upon them. Most economists still tended to look at depressions as deviations from normality.[21] Yet at the same time most of them adhered to the idea that some unemployment was necessary so that expansion could take place during booms—evidently prosperity was also abnormal. In 1903 Alfred Marshall, then at the height of his prestige as professor of political economy at Cambridge, drew a distinction between unemployment caused by cyclical depressions (which he called "occasional"), and "systematic" unemployment, the joblessness of persons "who will not or can not work steadily or strongly enough to make it possible that they should be employed regularly." The former type was becoming less common, Marshall opined. It would further diminish as more was discovered about "trade fluctuations," as world markets expanded, and as people learned to save money in good times instead of spending all they had without thought of the future. Systematic unemployment he thought a far more serious problem, a "disease" that society should spare no expense to cure by such methods as "de-urbanizing life" and applying "kindly but severe discipline" to its victims.[22]

The now-classic eleventh edition of the *Encyclopedia Britannica*, published in 1911, was the first to contain an article on unemployment. The author, Thomas Allan Ingram of Trinity College, Dublin, called it "a modern term for the state of being unemployed among the working classes." Ingram described unemployment as "a social question" caused at least in part by matters "over which the worker has no control." But he viewed the problem chiefly as one of surplus labor—the old reserve army—rather than as one stemming from structural flaws in the economic system. Full employment was the exception; under "normal" circumstances, large numbers of laborers tended to

[20] Beveridge, *Unemployment*, pp. 206, 77–95.

[21] "When good times and normal times prevail . . . there will . . . be no unemployment . . . but in bad times, unemployment will exist." A. C. Pigou, *Unemployment* (London, 1913), p. 98.

[22] A. C. Pigou, ed., *Memorials of Alfred Marshall* (London, 1925), pp. 446–47.

be without jobs. And he implied that there was nothing unusual about the current situation. Unemployment had only become a "specially insistent" problem in the twentieth century, he wrote, because it was getting more publicity, because workers had achieved political power, because economics had become more scientific, and because of the "humanitarian spirit of the times."[23]

Such muddled thinking could not stand close scrutiny. The more attention economists paid to cyclical changes the more the connection between the cycles and industrial unemployment became apparent. Observers had been aware of patterns in the ebb and flow of economic activity since at least the eighteenth century, but there had been much confusion between the rhythms of the seasons, which caused unemployment to rise in the winter, the impact of natural and man-made calamities, such as floods and wars, and the long-term trends that appeared to be products of the system itself. In his introduction to the first English edition of Marx's *Capital*, written in 1886, Friedrich Engels spoke of the "decennial cycle of stagnation, prosperity, overproduction and crisis," but two sentences later remarked that "each succeeding *winter* brings up afresh the great question, 'what to do with the unemployed.' " A less radical economist, writing in the *Economic Journal* in 1896, noted that "variations in employment may exist during periods of either increasing or diminishing prosperity," a statement that was correct but not calculated to throw much light on the nature of cycles.[24]

By the second decade of the twentieth century, however, more precise reasoning predominated. For example, Arthur Cecil Pigou, successor to Alfred Marshall as professor of political economy at Cambridge and in most instances a devoted (critics said slavish) follower of Marshall, made a far more sophisticated analysis of unemployment than his mentor. In *Wealth and Welfare* (1912) and in *Unemployment* (1913) Pigou argued that the prime cause of unemployment was the failure of wage rates to adjust to changes in the price level. If wage rates in one field went up as a result, say, of union pressures, more people would "attach themselves to the industry" and some of them would be unemployed. Theoretically, according to Pigou, unemployment could be eliminated by lowering wages, because when wages go down so do the costs of employers, who can then cut prices causing demand to increase, thus output, thus employment.

Pigou's work bore a superficial resemblance to that of the classical writers; he spoke of an "aggregate wage-fund" and was fond of explaining how the long-run and indirect results of seemingly sensible

[23] *Encyclopedia Britannica* (11th edition) 27: 578–80.
[24] Karl Marx, *Capital* (Chicago, 1906), I: 31; *Economic Journal*, 6 (1896), 146.

policies could make the policies wrong-headed. But he was trying to grapple with modern conditions, in particular the sharp fluctuations of economic activity associated with industrial depressions. If real wages could be stabilized by making wage rates "perfectly plastic," unemployment could be avoided even if the demand for labor fluctuated. Pigou recognized that such perfect plasticity of wages could not be achieved and he was prepared to see the state adopt many techniques for reducing unemployment and for easing the suffering of the jobless, not only labor exchanges, special educational programs, and subsidized compulsory insurance, but also countercyclical public-works programs, for which he made a particularly persuasive case. He also favored (on scientific as well as humane grounds) distributing the burdens of unemployment more widely by shortening the work week in slack times instead of discharging part of the labor force.

However, Pigou was aware that reducing the frequency and intensity of cyclical depressions would be the most practical way to deal with unemployment. "Whatever . . . tends to diminish industrial fluctuations tends also, in the end, to lessen the volume of unemployment." He believed that some manipulation of the value of money with the objective of stabilizing prices might be the best way to check cyclical swings.[25]

The efforts of economists to discover the dynamics of business cycles dated back at least to Clément Juglar's *Des crises commerciales et de leur retour périodique*, first published in 1860, and to W. Stanley Jevons's startling theory, announced in 1875, that periodic changes in the intensity of sun-spot activity were responsible for the cycles through their effects on climate and thus on agricultural output.[26] This concern mounted with each new cycle of boom and bust. Around the turn of the century, beginning with the Russian Michael Tugan-Baranowski's analysis of English "industrial crises" in 1894 and Eugen von Bergmann's *Die Wirtschaftskrisen (Economic Crises)*, which was published in 1895, economists began to write histories of cycle theories and of the cycles themselves. In 1907 Jean Lescure, a French economist, published an elaborate study of cyclical changes in economic activity in Europe and the United States from 1810 to 1906, along with an attempt to extract from this mass of "facts always the same" an explanation of "the development of modern economies."

[25] A. C. Pigou, *Unemployment* (London, 1913), pp. 55, 114, 75–76, 124–28, 175–81, 191–95, 244.

[26] Jevons's theory was admittedly based on sketchy sources and was pretty thoroughly exploded by evidence gathered by economists and astronomers. It is revelatory of the early twentieth-century concern with cycles that in 1909 Jevons's son, who was also an economist, attempted to revive the sun-spot theory. H. S. Jevons, "The Causes of Unemployment," *Contemporary Review*, 96 (1909), 167–89.

These pioneering works made groping efforts to understand the social effects of cycles. Tugan-Baranowski, for example, argued on the sketchiest of evidence that "an industrial crisis kills more people than an epidemic." He concluded that cycles "were rooted in the very essence of the capitalist economic system" and could only be eradicated by destroying the system. Until that was accomplished, he added, "the unemployment question is insoluble." Lescure suggested (citing Emile Durkheim rather than his own researches) that suicides increased in hard times. But most importantly, these writers called attention to the complexity of the subject. Tugan-Baranowski described three types of explanations of cycles, one focusing on production, another on money and credit, the third on the distribution of goods. Bergmann claimed to have discovered 230 different theories of cycles, which he lumped into eight types. Lescure, while finding Bergmann's system too complicated, described the subject as a "labyrinth" and a "mosaic"; his own classification was only less elaborate. Lescure believed, however, that the fluctuations could be greatly moderated if not totally eliminated—by better statistical information, by government regulation of speculators and of interest rates, by countercyclical public-works policies and tariffs, and by industrial self-regulation on the pattern of American trusts like U.S. Steel, which he greatly admired.[27]

Interest in the study of business cycles rose to a peak just before World War I. The Austrian economist Joseph Schumpeter's *Theorie der wirtschaftlichen Entwicklung* (*Theory of Economic Development*, 1912) contained an important chapter on cycles. Then in 1913 came the French economist Albert Aftalion's *Les crises périodiques de surproduction*, the Englishman Ralph G. Hawtrey's *Good and Bad Trade: An Inquiry into the Causes of Trade Fluctuations*, a revised and expanded version of Tugan-Baranowski's study, published in a French translation, and Wesley Clair Mitchell's *Business Cycles*, a book that had an impact comparable to Beveridge's *Unemployment*.

Mitchell was an American economist, when he wrote *Business Cycles* a professor at the University of California. His approach to the subject was pragmatic: taking the explanations of the cycle phenomenon that had been advanced by various writers, he attempted to validate them "by putting them to the practical test of accounting for actual experience," that is, by checking them against what had happened in the industrial nations between 1890 and 1911. For example, he found the theory that depressions were caused by the lack of consumer demand

[27] Michel Tougan-Baranowsky, *Les crises industrielles en Angleterre* (Paris, 1913), pp. 303, 463, 467; Jean Lescure, *Des crises générales et périodiques de surproduction* (Paris, 1907), pp. 431, 13, 411, 433, 456, 533–51, 283–88, 592, 603–604; W. C. Mitchell, *Business Cycles: The Problem and Its Setting* (New York, 1927), pp. 7–13.

unconvincing because in 1907 producers' goods had fallen in price earlier than consumers' goods, the opposite of what the underconsumption theory predicted. Mitchell had a theory of his own which he modestly said was based on "borrowed ideas" modified as a result of his "elaborate statistical inquiry." But his most important contribution was his insistence that the ebb and flow of economic activity called the business cycle was an "unceasing process," without a beginning or an end.

> With whatever phase of the business cycle analysis begins, it must take for granted the conditions brought about by the preceding phase, postponing explanation of these assumptions until it has worked around the cycle and come again to its starting point.

Since no phase was more typical or atypical than any other, a depression was not a deviation from normality.[28]

Mitchell naturally discussed unemployment in his book, although, because his prime concern was with the dynamics of cycles, he tended to see unemployment as one of many forces in ever-changing interaction. Depressions caused the jobless to suffer privations but they also stimulated technological advances and the elimination of waste, processes that produced gains for labor in the long run. Most important in this connection, his book added weight to Beveridge's contention that unemployment was a problem of industry, a built-in element in the functioning of the modern economy. And both Mitchell's argument and his statistical data tended to turn discussion away from the labor-reserve view of unemployment. He admitted that a "reserve army of labor" existed, but instead of stressing its role in making possible economic growth, he argued that because the reserve was "relatively inefficient" it served as a brake on expansion by raising costs. In general, Mitchell focused his attention on prices and profits, on investments and credits, on "the money surface of things" rather than on production or the satisfaction of wants. "Modern economic activity," he wrote, "is immediately animated and guided, not by the quest of satisfactions, but by the quest of profits." This was the direction that twentieth-century economics was taking.[29]

[28] W. C. Mitchell, *Business Cycles and Their Causes* (Berkeley, 1963), pp. ix–xii, 59–60, 149–50, 163. Other writers, of course, had recognized the relationship of different aspects of the cycle to one another. Lescure, for example, wrote: "To situate the crisis of overproduction in time one must understand the evolution. . . . The depression [comes] after the expansion. It is therefore necessary to go back to history and to the evolution of the expansion to be able to understand the depression." Nevertheless, Lescure called the "crisis of overproduction" a "pathological phenomenon." *Crises de surproduction,* pp. 7, 12.

[29] Mitchell, *Cycles and Their Causes,* pp. 32, 187–90.

8

Learning to Live
with Unemployment

The Great War of 1914–18, after a brief period of adjustments, brought unemployment down sharply, conclusively demonstrating, as Sidney and Beatrice Webb pointed out rather smugly some years later, that there was no " 'surplus' population for which neither occupation nor wages could possibly be found," and that most of the people usually classified as unemployable on mental, moral, or physical grounds could be "usefully and even profitably" put to work.[1] But the very conditions that produced full employment—all-out war production and the mobilization of millions for service in the armed forces —brought the unemployment problem again to the fore after the restoration of peace in 1918. Economic readjustments and the social upheavals resulting from the war caused widespread economic losses, and while conditions varied greatly from one country to another over the next decade, perhaps more so than in any earlier period, a fundamental change in attitude toward the jobless was apparent nearly everywhere. State responsibility for helping the unemployed was no longer controversial—the methods and the amounts of assistance remained debatable but not the principle itself.

In Europe, revolution, actual and potential, with its threat to extinguish private-enterprise capitalism, supplied much of the pressure, but probably concern for the welfare of unemployed ex-soldiers was the chief reason for the shift in public opinion and public policy. After so much pointless slaughter, the survivors must not be allowed to rot in idleness. In newly reconstituted Poland, one writer explained, "the authorities felt unable to refuse help to ex-service men or to war prisoners and civilian deportees who were returning in huge numbers

[1] *English Poor Law History* (New York, 1963), II: 668. Hobson had made essentially the same point in the 1890s. See above, pp. 123–24.

from Russia and Germany." In the Republic of Austria, with Communist revolutions exploding to the north and east, the government went so far as to try to compel large employers to increase their work force by 20 percent. This was impractical (and far from common) but more aid to the unemployed with no, or very few, questions asked was almost universal. Between 1919 and 1925 Italy, Austria, and Poland created compulsory unemployment-insurance systems, financed by workers, employers, and the state. By 1925 there were altogether fifteen national systems, eight of them voluntary, along the lines of the Ghent plan, the rest patterned after the British compulsory model.[2]

Of the major industrial powers, Great Britain's postwar experience was the most complex. During the conflict full employment had resulted in the accumulation of large reserves in the new unemployment-insurance fund. In 1916 coverage was extended to workers in the munitions industry and allied fields, bringing over a million more people into the system. The adjustment to peacetime production after the war was much smoother than the experts had expected, but beginning in the summer of 1920 unemployment rapidly increased (and remained a chronic problem for the next two decades). Tens of thousands of servicemen were seeking jobs. These men had risked their lives for the nation; either to ignore their needs or to treat them as charity cases was unthinkable. With militant trade unions also calling for "work or maintenance," the government swiftly enacted a temporary "out-of-work donation" covering virtually all workers, the first national direct-relief program in British history.

Once the policy of aiding the jobless without qualification had been adopted, there was no politically safe way to terminate it except by making unemployment insurance universal. In 1920 all but agricultural workers and domestics were brought into the system; roughly three out of four wage earners were covered. The insurance reserve fund soon evaporated, yet with unemployment high and rising and with the fear of revolution reaching panic proportions, the government dared not reduce the benefits or increase worker contributions. The system soon lost all but the pretense of actuarial soundness.[3] When prices rose, payments were increased; when large numbers failed to find jobs before their benefit periods expired, the period was first extended and then made indefinite; supplementary payments

---

[2] Max Lederer, "Social Legislation in the Republic of Austria," *International Labour Review*, 2 (1921), 6–7; H. Baumgart, "Polish Labour Legislation," *ibid.*, 7 (1923), 852; "The International Labour Organization and Social Insurance," *ibid.*, 11 (1925), 778–79; M. R. Carroll, *Unemployment Insurance in Austria* (Washington, 1932), pp. 8–9, 19–28.

[3] The original rate structure had been reached through guesswork—it assumed an unemployment rate among the groups covered of 8.5 percent, but without any real evidence.

were made to those with children without regard for what they had contributed; the waiting period before payments began was shortened. Need rather than benefits earned became the criterion for receiving "insurance," the cost being met out of general revenues. As William Beveridge, who watched the transformation of the system he had helped to create with growing alarm, put it, "everything that could be called system disappeared."[4]

Thus, without formal acknowledgment, without repealing the ancient poor laws, the British abandoned the principle of less eligibility and the mean restrictions of past centuries on the granting of public assistance to the unemployed. Almost without a contest, the radical demand of 1918–19 for "work or maintenance" (by-product of the Russian Revolution, echo of the French) won acceptance, the state settling upon the more easily achieved alternative.

Defeated Germany followed a somewhat different but related pattern. The constitution of the Weimar republic contained a "right to work" guarantee that could perhaps best be characterized as an expression of good intentions. During the strife-torn demobilization period, the government set up an office for economic demobilization to make payments to all the jobless similar to the contemporary British "donations," and undertook a "productive work relief" program, employing the jobless on road repair, soil conservation, canal and dam building, and similar projects. The thriving network of employment exchanges was taken over by the state in 1919. By the summer of that year, the job situation was beginning to improve, and during the terrible inflation of 1922–23 relatively few were without work.

But after monetary stability was restored, unemployment rose sharply. The government then instituted a system of unemployment aid financed by worker and employer contributions. This was not a true insurance system, however, because applicants had to demonstrate need, not merely that they had lost their jobs. Early in 1926 the German economy once again began to improve; a boom developed and unemployment fell. Under these favorable circumstances the Reichstag in 1927 passed an unemployment-insurance act even more comprehensive than the British—agricultural workers and domestic servants were included in the coverage. The Germans tried harder than the British to maintain the distinction between insurance payments (*Arbeitslosenhilfe*) and outright public assistance (*öffentliche Fürsorge*), classifying aid given to those who had exhausted their benefits without finding work as loans, but by the end of the decade rising unemployment had put the system far in the red.[5]

In France and the United States, the unemployment-insurance idea made no significant headway, in part because unemployment was a less serious problem in those countries. Only a relative handful of French skilled workers participated in state-subsidized union unemployment-insurance plans. During the brief economic crisis that followed the outbreak of war in 1914, the French had established a central fund to back up departmental and municipal unemployment-relief programs. After the war ended the fund was retained, administered by local committees of employers and workers. The network of employment exchanges was also strengthened and extended during the war; in the early twenties well over a million jobs a year were filled through these exchanges. Actually, because of its low birth rate and the enormous casualties of the war, France was suffering from a shortage of labor; Spanish, Italian, Belgian, Polish, and other foreign workers (over three million individuals by 1929) flocked into the country.[6]

The American experience was initially much like the German and British. Conversion from a war to a peacetime economy caused unemployment to soar after the armistice. With between three and six million workers idle (no one knew exactly how many) the federal government for the first time was compelled to face the issue. In 1921, at the urging of Secretary of Commerce Herbert Hoover, President Harding summoned a conference on unemployment, its purpose, according to Hoover, being to launch a "war" against the problem. (Actually Hoover intended it to serve only educative and inspirational functions.) The conference recommended an investigation of the relation between business cycles and unemployment and the creation of a permanent committee on unemployment, which was put not in the Department of Labor but in Hoover's domain. But the conference was dominated by representatives of business and industry and no doubt also influenced by the President's introductory admonition against proposing anything that would require "either palliation or tonic from the public treasury," a point reinforced by Secretary Hoover. It had little to suggest beyond the usual ideas about spreading out seasonal work, improving the new U.S. Employment Service, which had been organized in 1918, and stepping up public-works expenditures in bad

[5] Frieda Wunderlich, "Die Bekämpfung der Arbeitslosigkeit in Deutschland seit Beendigung des Krieges," *Schriften der Gesellschaft für Soziale Reform*, 75 (1925), 38–46; M. R. Carroll, *Unemployment Insurance in Germany* (Washington, 1930), pp. 23–25, 32–39, 48–59; W. A. Lewis, *Economic Survey: 1919–1939* (New York, 1969), pp. 24–27, 40–41; O. Weigert, "The Development of Unemployment Relief in Germany," *International Labour Review*, 28 (1933), 169.

[6] Roger Picard, "Labour Legislation in France during and after the War," *ibid.*, 13 (1926), 889–91; Tom Kemp, *The French Economy: 1913–1939* (London, 1972), p. 95.

times. Harding's strictures aside, the standing committee confined itself largely to encouraging municipal relief agencies; it gave no serious consideration to the idea of compulsory unemployment insurance. The troubles plaguing the British system at the time gave the experts pause, as did the fact that the American Federation of Labor was dead set against any federal labor legislation. ("Place in the hands of the government the right to determine who is or who is not entitled to governmental insurance," the AFL convention declared in 1919, and "the government will determine then what will constitute justifiable reasons for unemployment." In 1922, Samuel Gompers, the venerable president of the Federation, denounced unemployment insurance contemptuously as a "dole."[7]

After the postwar depression American unemployment soon fell back to more acceptable levels, further reducing interest in insurance. A few important businessmen experimented with company-financed unemployment-insurance schemes, most notably the label manufacturer Henry S. Dennison; Herbert S. Johnson, the wax manufacturer; and William G. Procter, president of Procter & Gamble, the soap company. In 1923, as part of a complex plan for stabilizing production, Procter guaranteed five thousand of his employees forty-eight weeks' work a year. These private programs were supposed to prevent unemployment; if they functioned perfectly, the companies would never have to pay a cent in benefits. They were primarily intended to enhance employer credibility; to persuade workers and stockholders that other measures designed to keep factories running steadily and harmoniously—market analysis, careful scheduling, scientific management, profit sharing, worker training, various paternalistic employee-benefit devices—were in their common interests. This "New Emphasis" was thus a more ambitious variant of the Beveridge approach—unemployment could be reduced by organization and planning.

The New Emphasis was also related to the corporatist point of view that Eugène Buret had expressed in the 1830s, a view that was attracting the attention of "enlightened" conservatives in all the industrial countries at the time. During the war, labor and management had been compelled by governments to cooperate in regulating production and distribution, and in setting wage rates without strikes, all in the inter-

---

[7] *Report of the President's Conference on Unemployment* (Washington, 1921), pp. 22–23, 27, 29; Carolyn Grin, "The Unemployment Conference of 1921," *Mid-America*, 55 (1973), 83–107; Daniel Nelson, *Unemployment Insurance: The American Experience* (Madison, 1969), pp. 36–39, 76; Joseph Dorfman, *The Economic Mind in American Civilization* (New York, 1959), IV: 35–36; M. R. Carroll, *Labor and Politics: The Attitude of the American Federation of Labor toward Legislation and Politics* (Boston, 1923), p. 73; Milton Derber and Edwin Young, *Labor and the New Deal* (Madison, 1957), p. 245.

ests of efficiency and orderly expansion. In the postwar period, corporatists envisaged a planned but privately owned economy organized around trades and professions, workers and employers sharing in decision making, the system supervised by the state, their hope being that through cooperation businessmen could avoid the waste associated with competition, the loss of private control associated with socialism, and the class conflict associated with capitalism. The American version tended to play down the role of government and to say little about sharing decision making with the work force, but the desire of men like Dennison to improve the welfare of workers was nevertheless genuine. And so long as the economy was expanding their schemes worked quite well. They did not, however, attract a mass following among workers or employers.[8]

The fate of unemployment insurance in the United States during the twenties illustrates how local conditions affect the transit of ideas. In Great Britain, where insurance received its first full-scale test, it had to be seen as no more than a palliative, for unemployment remained high and even increased despite (by 1926) no fewer than fifteen acts of Parliament dealing with the subject. In America, where no substantial unemployment-insurance systems existed, relatively low levels of unemployment made the problem less urgent. Proponents were thus both tempted and pushed to make exaggerated claims in its behalf; they argued that insurance would prevent unemployment. Just as workmen's compensation laws had encouraged employers to install safety devices in their plants, thus reducing industrial accidents, so unemployment insurance would encourage employers to regularize output and spread work evenly in order to avoid having to contribute to the support of laid-off workers.[9]

This optimistic argument was made most persuasively by Professor John R. Commons of the University of Wisconsin and his student John B. Andrews, the latter author of *A Practical Program for the Prevention of Unemployment in America* (1914). It was shared by most American economists during the 1920s. The economists dealt with unemployment primarily as it related to business cycles (a subject of particular interest in the United States) and to technological change. The great authority on cycles, Wesley Clair Mitchell, was by the end of the decade growing somewhat alarmed by the trend of events. "We are leaving [the depression of] 1921 well behind us," he noted in 1929, "and there are signs that the caution inspired by that disastrous year is wearing thin." But most students of cycles were at least hopeful that the wondrous new

[8] Nelson, *Unemployment Insurance*, pp. 28–30, 40–58; C. A. Chambers, *Seedtime of Reform: American Social Service and Social Action, 1918–1933* (Ann Arbor, 1967), pp. 175–76.

[9] Nelson, *Unemployment Insurance*, pp. 105, 113; Beveridge, *Unemployment*, p. 276.

Federal Reserve system would, by its manipulations, check the ups and downs of cycles and thus reduce unemployment. Professor Alvin Hansen of the University of Minnesota, author of *Cycles of Prosperity and Depression in the United States, Great Britain, and Germany* (1921) and *Business-Cycle Theory* (1927), predicted that fluctuations in economic activity of all kinds would become less severe as part of an "increasing social adjustment to the capitalistic method of production." Professor Sumner Slichter of Cornell, possibly influenced by the New Emphasis argument, suggested in 1927 that unemployment would soon cease to be a problem because businessmen, becoming conscious of the cost of cyclical unemployment to themselves, would find ways to reduce it.

As for technological unemployment, American economists tended to minimize its importance. One who studied the effects of the linotype machine on printers concluded that, except for some older workers who could not adjust to the new device, few lost their jobs. Another, Paul H. Douglas of the University of Chicago, took the orthodox position that mechanization did not permanently reduce the number of jobs, although he admitted that individual workers could be temporarily idled by technological advances and that society had a responsibility to aid them. The most elaborate investigation of the period, labor economist Isador Lubin's *The Absorption of the Unemployed by American Industry* (1929), painted a darker picture—almost half of the workers Lubin studied were still out of a job and many of those who had found work had been compelled to accept reductions in income. Lubin's suggestions for dealing with technological unemployment, however, were not startlingly original—better employment exchanges, insurance, countercyclical public works.[10]

Although the Soviet Union was not yet an important industrial power, its experience with and policies toward unemployment were in some ways the most significant of the postwar years. At the time of the 1917 revolution, the Russian economy was as predominantly agricultural as the American had been at the time of the American Revolution —only about one worker in ten was engaged in industrial production. Moreover, the economic dislocations associated with the Russian Revolution hit the small industrial sector particularly hard; in 1921 there were fewer workers engaged in manufacturing in the country than in 1897. Thereafter, economic growth resumed, but the expansion was accompanied by an increase in unemployment as large numbers of rural people flocked into the cities in search of factory jobs. By early 1929 about 1.7 million in a labor force of some 12 million wage and salaried workers were idle.

[10] Dorfman, *Economic Mind,* IV: 373–74; V: 546–49, 542–43, 517–18, 534, 537–38.

But in 1928 Stalin inaugurated the first Five Year Plan, an all-out effort to do away with private enterprise in Russia and substitute a state-owned "command economy." Hectic, and despite the emphasis on planning essentially improvised industrial expansion was given the highest priority. The state poured money into the construction of factories and the development of natural resources. By the end of 1929 unemployment was shrinking rapidly and soon an actual shortage of factory workers began to develop. In October 1930 the government boldly announced that unemployment no longer existed. To demonstrate that this was indeed the case, the Soviet unemployment-insurance system was dismantled.

There is no reason to doubt that unemployment other than the inevitable idleness caused by the shifting of labor from one activity to another did disappear in Russia at this time, fulfilling the promise of the Soviet constitution that "the right to work is insured by the socialist organization of the national economy." The forced-draft expansion of capital-goods production resulted in a steady growth of capacity and kept the whole work force busy. The stress on output without regard for cost led, however, to what became known as "hidden unemployment," the squirreling away of labor by plant managers without regard for efficiency in order to increase production. Moreover, the guarantee of a job was accompanied by an insistence that everyone work. Something approaching forced labor was decreed; only a doctor's certificate would henceforth be acceptable as a reason for refusing a job assigned by a state labor exchange. Although it proved very difficult to enforce, this aspect of the Soviet system was seized upon by critics—if workers were, in effect, tied to their jobs like slaves, of course they could never be unemployed. Nevertheless, the dramatic Soviet boast that unemployment had been abolished had a large impact on the capitalist world, especially during the depression-ridden decade of the 1930s.[11]

Whatever local conditions were and no matter how economists might differ in their precepts and prescriptions, awareness of the unemployment problem had by the 1920s become general, study of the subject institutionalized. Unemployment was one of the major concerns of the International Labor Organisation of the League of Nations; immediately after its establishment in 1919, the ILO began collecting statistics on unemployment, and soon it was publishing this

[11] S. M. Schwarz, *Labor in the Soviet Union* (New York, 1952); pp. 5–6, 8–9, 50–51, 81; W. W. Eason, "Labor Force Materials for the Study of Unemployment in the Soviet Union," National Bureau of Economic Research, *The Measurement and Behavior of Unemployment* (Princeton, 1957), pp. 390–91; Moshe Lewin, *Political Undercurrents in Soviet Economic Debates* (Princeton, 1974), pp. 97–101.

material, summaries of reports and investigations in different countries, and many special articles on the subject, separately and in its
journal, the *International Labour Review*. As early as 1923 an ILO book-
let, *Remedies for Unemployment*, surveyed "the state of the question in
different countries." This study dealt with practical matters—exchanges, insurance, and the like—but the next year the *Review* published an unsigned article, probably written by Henri Fuss, chief of the
ILO Employment Service, dealing with economic theory. "Bank Credit
and Unemployment" claimed to have discerned the emergence of a
new school of economists. It lumped together thinkers with some very
different ideas, among them Wesley Clair Mitchell, Irving Fisher of
Yale, the Swedish economists Knut Wicksell and Gustav Cassel, Ralph
G. Hawtrey of the British Treasury, A. C. Pigou, and the brilliant
Cambridge professor John Maynard Keynes. What these economists
had in common was that all were insisting that industrial stability could
be achieved by manipulating interest rates.[12]

This concept, tactically similar to the idea of a countercyclical public-works policy, was based on the assumption that when economic
activity began to flag, easy credit would revive it by encouraging entrepreneurs to invest borrowed capital in productive enterprises. Conversely, raising interest rates would act as a brake on booms, thus
preventing "overexpansion" and ultimate collapse. The resulting lev-
eling of the swings of the business cycle would surely reduce unemployment. Viewed more narrowly, in bad times cheap credit would
stimulate investment and thus make new jobs. This appeared to be the
more pressing need in the immediate postwar period.

The argument that easy lending policies stimulated economic activity by encouraging investment and increasing the volume of money in
circulation, thus causing prices to rise, was first fully enunciated by
Ralph G. Hawtrey in *Good and Bad Trade*, one of the many works on the
dynamics of business cycles published just before the Great War. But
although central banks certainly continued to regulate interest rates,
by 1924 the idea of stimulating the economy by increasing the supply
of money was in bad odor. If the immediate result of the restoration
of peace in 1918 had been to overwhelm ancient prejudices against
indiscriminate public assistance to the jobless, in the following years
rampant inflation had created a new prejudice, equally powerful,
against "unsound" government finance. The German paper-money
avalanche of 1922–23 was only the worst of the postwar inflations.
Prices in Austria had soared to 14,000 times their prewar level, in
Hungary to 23,000 times, in Poland to 2.5 million times, in the Soviet

[12] "Notes on Unemployment Problems," *International Labour Review*, 7 (1923), 302;
"Bank Credit and Unemployment," *ibid.*, 9 (1924), 78–94.

Union still higher. Of the lesser inflations, Belgium's currency had fallen to about a quarter of its 1914 value, France's to about a fifth. In most of the smaller European countries the decline was to between one-tenth and one-fiftieth. In addition to the United States, only Great Britain, Switzerland, Holland, and the Scandinavian nations got their currencies close to prewar levels relative to gold, and even in these, prices in the mid-1920s were some 50 percent higher than in 1913.

Once the price explosion had apparently subsided, political leaders of nearly every persuasion along with a large majority of the world's economists were agreed that preventing a renewed outburst must have the highest priority. But statisticians examining the relationship between unemployment and the price level in different nations were beginning to notice some interesting trends. After an ILO survey of world conditions early in 1925, the author of the *International Labour Review*'s summary concluded: "Of the many and varied factors affecting the unemployment situation, the general movement of prices . . . appears to be the most important." The next year, in a signed article, Henri Fuss called attention again to the relationship; he put the causal connection in the form of a question, but his own opinion was unmistakable. And by 1927 Fuss was stating the principle flatly: when prices rose, unemployment declined.[13]

The tension between this observation and the fear of inflation (along with the equally profound if less acute commitment to classical laissez-faire ideas) governed thinking about the unemployment problem in the 1920s. Sweden, for example, went back on the gold standard in 1924; thereafter the economy expanded, prices held firm, but unemployment rose to about 10 percent of the work force. Swedish economists—and they were among the most brilliant of their generation—blamed the unemployment chiefly on high wages and thought that more rather than less deflation was in order. If the cost of living could be brought down to 1914 levels, perhaps working people would be willing to accept a reduction in wages. The Swedish government was anything but insensitive to the unemployment problem. It set up a Commission on Unemployment in 1927 to study the subject, staffed by Gunnar Myrdal, Dag Hammarskjöld, and other top-flight social scientists. But concern about high wages, about too much state interference, and about the importance of balancing the budget persisted in Sweden well into the next decade. In 1933 Myrdal proposed a

[13] "Unemployment in 1924 and the Beginning of 1925," *ibid.*, 12 (1925), 223; Henri Fuss, "Unemployment in 1925," *ibid.*, 14 (1926), 203–31; Fuss, "Money and Unemployment," *ibid.*, 16 (1927), 601–17. The American economist Irving Fisher was equally positive: "When prices fall unemployment increases. When prices rise unemployment decreases—for a time." "Banking Policy and Unemployment," *American Labor Legislation Review*, 16 (1926), 24.

public-works program designed to stimulate the economy, but even at that late date he cautioned against "unsound" government financing.[14]

The most interesting clashes of opinion about unemployment policy again took place in Great Britain. Although British unemployment rose to unprecedented levels in the 1920s, the desire to put the pound sterling back on the gold standard, which had been abandoned of necessity after the war, was widespread. The wish to do so at the pound's prewar value of a little less than five American dollars was only less broadly based. Such a valuation would, however, act as a brake on economic growth. It would also make British goods more expensive in foreign markets, further depressing the very "export" industries in which unemployment was already heavy. This problem probably explains why so much of the most advanced economic thinking of the period was British.

In the summer of 1923, in an effort to strengthen the pound, the Bank of England raised the rediscount rate from 3 to 4 percent. John Maynard Keynes promptly denounced the move as "one of the most misguided . . . that has ever occurred," and a few months later published *A Tract on Monetary Reform.* Both inflation and deflation, Keynes wrote, were undesirable; stability of values was the monetary ideal. When the value of money rose or fell, some interests benefited, others suffered, but the gains and losses were unearned and better avoided. Postwar inflation had injured holders of fixed securities and benefited debtors, but by eroding the value of savings it had reduced investment and thus precipitated a depression that injured all classes. Inflation brought windfall profits to businessmen, but by discouraging investment it hurt their businesses far more. Many workers lost during inflationary periods because their wages did not keep up with price increases, and all labor suffered when inflationary booms were followed by depressions. But given conditions as they existed in Great Britain at the time, Keynes believed that deflation such as was bound to result from an increase in the bank rate was the greater evil. "It is worse, in an impoverished world, to provoke unemployment than to disappoint the *rentier.*"[15]

Moreover, stability of internal prices was far more crucial to prosperity than stability of a nation's currency on international exchanges. Keynes opposed Great Britain's returning to a gold standard and especially doing so at the prewar rate. The old self-adjusting gold

[14] Erik Lundberg, *Business Cycles and Economic Policy* (Cambridge, Mass., 1957), pp. 19–20, 94–96, 117–19.

[15] R. F. Harrod, *The Life of John Maynard Keynes* (New York, 1971), p. 395, 405; J. M. Keynes, *Essays in Persuasion* (New York, 1963), p. 91–98, 103.

standard no longer existed, he claimed. Since, as a result of the war, the United States controlled most of the world's gold, "a dollar standard" had replaced it. Neither the dollar nor any other currency conformed to the price of gold; instead, the value of gold "almost entirely depends on the policy of the Federal Reserve Board." Maintenance of the price depended, Keynes wrote, on "the collaboration of an [American] public understanding nothing with a Federal Reserve Board understanding everything," a situation he did not expect to long endure.

Keynes was soon also recommending a massive (£100-million-a-year) public-works program focused on housing, road improvement, and the development of electric power. At the same time he urged discouraging overseas investments; the capital would create more British jobs when invested at home. "I abandon *laissez faire* not enthusiastically, not from contempt of that good old doctrine, but because, whether we like it or not, the conditions for its success have disappeared," he wrote in *Does Unemployment Need a Drastic Remedy?* (1924).[16]

Keynes was one of a relatively small group of economists thinking along these lines. In Germany, L. Albert Hahn of the University of Frankfurt had insisted in a book published in 1920 that lowering interest rates would reduce unemployment. Even before the war, Irving Fisher had called for stabilizing prices by varying the gold content of the dollar, and in 1924 he attacked the gold standard with weapons almost identical with those employed by Keynes in his *Tract on Monetary Reform.*[17] Keynes was better known than most economists, however, famous or notorious (depending on one's viewpoint) ever since the appearance of his analysis of the Versailles Treaty, *The Economic Consequences of the Peace,* with its eviscerating pen portraits of Wilson, Clemenceau, and Lloyd George and its persuasive assault on the heavy reparations payments exacted from the Germans by the treaty. Besides being a first-rate theoretical economist and a man of great practical experience in the financial world, he was a talented writer who could explain difficult economic concepts in language that ordinary persons could understand. He had also a gift for controversy, a penchant for hyperbole, and a sharp wit; his talents made him a formidable debater, but he sometimes employed them so devastatingly as to hurt his own cause.

Keynes never, for example, recommended inflation as an end in itself, and he admitted that runaway inflation such as had occurred in Germany was an unmitigated disaster. But when he attacked the gold

16 Keynes, *Essays in Persuasion*, pp. 196, 203–204; Harrod, *Keynes*, pp. 403–405.
17 L. A. Hahn, *Volkswirtschaftliche Theorie des Bankkredits* (Tubingen, 1920); Hahn, "Compensating Reactions to Compensatory Spending," *American Economic Review*, 35 (1945), pp. 28–29; Dorfman, *Economic Mind*, IV: 289–91.

standard and its mossback defenders, his quotable sarcasms were almost sure to alarm moderates. In the *Tract*, his evaluation of the relative importance of bondholders and unemployed workers, however sensible from the point of view of the public interest, was so matter-of-fact in tone as to suggest that he was prepared to undermine the inviolability of private property and the sanctity of contract to put the idle back to work. He made defenders of the gold standard appear to be hopelessly out-of-date, writing in one passage of their "primitive passion for solid metal" and in another of their belief in hard money "consecrated by the wisdom and experience of Dungi, Darius, Constantine, Lord Liverpool, and Senator Aldrich." And with the runaway German inflation in everyone's mind, he remarked:

> The tendency of money to depreciate has been in past times a weighty counterpoise against the cumulative results of compound interest and the inheritance of fortunes. It has been a loosening influence against the rigid distribution of old-won wealth and the separation of ownership from activity. By this means each generation can disinherit in part its predecessors' heirs.[18]

Keynes's manner and style aside, the desire to return to the gold standard was almost universal in Great Britain. Doing so, the argument ran, would eliminate the danger of inflation and insure Britain's continued role as a power in international finance. It would presumably stimulate world trade, usher in an era of prosperity, stability, and international cooperation, and serve symbolically to ring down the curtain on the hectic readjustment period that had followed the Great War. Most of the economists who believed that price stability would moderate cyclical fluctuations reasoned that the gold standard would make the achievement of stability easier, because international movements of gold would automatically set in motion balancing pressures on domestic prices.

Returning to the gold standard at the prewar ratio of $4.86 to the pound attracted equally broad support, partly for sentimental and psychological reasons, partly because, since Great Britain was still a creditor nation owed large sums in pounds, lowering the value of British money would "needlessly" depreciate these assets. Keynes thought that the $4.86 rate overvalued the pound by 10 percent and he seems to have been approximately correct; other experts at the time, however, thought the overvaluation much smaller and many believed there was no overvaluation at all. R. G. Hawtrey, one of the most prescient of the more conservative English economists, recog-

[18] Keynes, *Essays in Persuasion*, pp. 87, 197; Harrod, *Keynes*, p. 400.

nized that the old ratio would cause a dangerous contraction of the currency, but nonetheless favored it on the ground that any lower rate would be interpreted abroad as a sign of British financial weakness.[19]

As for work relief, the argument during the 1920s revolved around the question of its efficacy as a means of steadying and perhaps stimulating the economy, rather than as a way of exacting a price in labor from persons who had become public charges. In the immediate postwar period the Labour party proposed a large public-works program to be financed by borrowing. "It is one of the foremost obligations of the Government," a party pronouncement ran, "to find, for every willing worker . . . productive work at standard rates. . . . The Government can, if it chooses, arrange the public works . . . in such a way as to maintain the aggregate demand for labour in the whole kingdom (including that of capitalist employers) approximately at a uniform level from year to year." This policy—probably the brainchild of Sidney Webb—was not adopted when the Labour party came to power in 1924 and again in 1929. No more than 1 percent of the British work force was employed on public projects at any time during the decade.

Therefore, relatively little was said about the practical difficulties of public-works projects that had loomed so large in most earlier discussions. Critics—most of the important British politicians were in this camp—were almost literally obsessed with the idea of reducing the national debt, which had grown so much during the war. Any additional expenditure would slow debt retirement and was therefore resisted. As the historian K. J. Hancock has noted, with a single unimportant exception all the chancellors of the exchequer of the period were "slaves to the debt" and thus opposed to increasing public construction.[20] Critics also took the position that if the state pumped more money into the economy to pay for additional projects, the effect would be inflationary, and if it raised the money by borrowing or through taxation it would merely divert capital from the private sector without increasing total activity. This was essentially the wages fund idea of classical economics—the germ of the concept went back at least as far as Adam Smith's *Wealth of Nations*, which describes public borrowing as a device for "the perversion of some portion of the annual produce which had before been destined for the maintenance of productive labour, towards that of unproductive labour." In its twentieth-century form, critics stressed the presumed lack of effect on employment over all. "When . . . a government gives work to the

[19] A. J. Youngson, *Britain's Economic Growth: 1920–1966* (London, 1968), pp. 30–31, 271–77; Sidney Pollard, ed., *The Gold Standard and Employment Policy Between the Wars* (London, 1970), pp. 125–26, 139.
[20] Pollard, *Gold Standard*, pp. 99–121.

unemployed," one official report ran, "it is diminishing employment with one hand while it increases it with the other. It takes work from people employed by private individuals, and gives it to people selected by the State." Philip Snowden, the leading financial expert among Labour party leaders, got off what he obviously thought was a very clever remark when he called the advocate of a scheme for spending money on public works at the expense of reducing the debt a "charwoman economist" who believed that Englishmen could live by taking in one another's washing.[21]

Keynes was by no means the only English economist to challenge this line of reasoning. As early as 1908 in his inaugural lecture as professor at Cambridge, A. C. Pigou, who seldom concerned himself with practical questions related to his field, and who mistrusted politicians of all persuasions, nonetheless attacked what later became known (somewhat unfairly to that institution) as the "Treasury view." In *Industrial Fluctuations* (1927), Pigou pointed out that the amount of capital available to hire workers, which he called "the labour purchase fund," was not a fixed sum. "In times of depression" (certainly whenever there was considerable unemployment) capital that was in "storage" could be put to work "without it being necessary for any transference to be made in the aggregate." In addition, funds so invested, by creating jobs, would check another drain on capital, the "sums annually devoted, through unemployment insurance, charity and the Poor Law, to the relief of persons who have been brought low through the effects of intermittent employment."[22]

The more sophisticated opponents of public works did not challenge Pigou's reasoning in detail but insisted on the one hand that the amount of capital available from such sources would not support an effective program, and on the other that a program large enough to have a significant impact on unemployment would require an enormous bureaucracy and would be plagued by waste and inefficiency. These arguments were difficult to meet. By the end of the decade Keynes and a few other economists were working out a more complicated justification—the sums invested in public works would trigger further economic expansion as the wages earned were spent and as the suppliers of materials and services expanded their operations to meet the government-inspired demand. "Greater trade activity would make for further trade activity, for the forces of prosperity . . . work with cumulative effect," Keynes wrote in 1929. This was the idea of the "multiplier," soon to be more formally explicated and mathematically

[21] Adam Smith, *The Wealth of Nations* (New York, 1937), p. 878; A. C. Pigou, *Industrial Fluctuations* (London, 1927), p. 291.
[22] Pigou, *Industrial Fluctuations*, pp. 291–92.

demonstrated by one of Keynes's students, R. F. Kahn.[23]

But no British government of the decade attacked the unemployment problem by expanding public spending. In March 1929, Lloyd George's Liberal party proposed a "deliberate policy of national development" designed to "conquer unemployment" in two years by building roads and low-rental housing and improving the telephone and electrical networks. Lloyd George claimed that his program would create jobs for 600,000 people; its cost—£250 million—could be met by bond issues, and would be recouped from income from the projects and the reduced costs of maintaining the unemployed. The plan caused a great stir. In a pamphlet, Keynes and another economist, Hubert D. Henderson, answered the question *Can Lloyd George Do It?* with a ringing affirmative, while the reigning Conservative government marshaled a series of studies to show that the wartime Prime Minister could not. Winston Churchill, Chancellor of the Exchequer in the Conservative government, stood firmly (albeit with a politician's inevitable qualifications) for "the orthodox Treasury dogma"—"very little additional employment . . . can, in fact, and as a general rule, be created by State borrowing and State expenditure." The Labour party's response, which the historian Robert Skidelsky has called "a slovenly document," criticized Lloyd George for failing to offer a "sound and permanent" solution to the problem, and also for the "madcap finance" on which his scheme was predicated; thus the party managed to appear radical and conservative at the same time without making any substantial proposal of its own.

All three parties were talking past one another. Lloyd George and his cohorts stressed the economic stimulation that his program would produce, his critics its cost and the practical difficulties in the way of organizing and running it on short notice. In the election that followed this debate, no party won a majority, a fairly clear indication that the nation (indeed, no nation) had decided how best to deal with unemployment. Labour, the party with the least coherent program, formed the new British government. That autumn prices on the New York Stock Exchange collapsed. By the following spring the world was becoming aware that a major cyclical depression was under way.[24]

Later in 1930 William H. Beveridge published a new edition of his classic *Unemployment: A Problem of Industry.* Beveridge had left government service with a knighthood in 1919 to become director of the newly founded London School of Economics. (The revision of *Unemployment* served as Sir William's doctoral thesis, for although he was

[23] Robert Skidelsky, *Politicians and the Slump: The Labour Government of 1929–1931* (Middlesex, 1970), p. 70; Harrod, *Keynes*, pp. 237–38.
[24] Skidelsky, *Politicians and the Slump*, pp. 67–77; Beveridge, *Unemployment*, pp. 313–14.

director of the school and had served a term as vice chancellor of the parent University of London, he needed the degree to become an official member of the university!) The new edition—actually an entirely new work was appended to the original, which was reprinted without alteration—was Beveridge's effort "to show how a theory of unemployment deduced from facts known in 1909, has stood the test of experience, and what has happened to policies based on that theory."[25]

Once again Beveridge's analysis was even-handed, informed, but without much originality, a summary of what was known and thought about the subject. The record of two decades of experience, he admitted, was depressing. British unemployment since 1919 had run nearly three times the prewar average. Labor exchanges had reduced frictional unemployment very little; unemployed casual labor remained a serious problem. Unemployment insurance had failed to provide adequate protection for the jobless; aid for the unemployed had "grown portentously," but "always in the direction of becoming relief and nothing else." Although somewhat more sanguine about reducing unemployment through public works than he had been in 1909, he still considered this approach of limited usefulness. After neatly summarizing the controversy among the theoreticians and coming down (with certain qualifications) on the side of Keynes and Pigou, he emphasized the practical difficulties in the way of "finding work to be done which is at once valuable for public purposes, suited to the kind of men unemployed, and either within reach of their homes or so placed that housing can be provided, without excessive cost," a large order.[26]

Great Britain's current unemployment, he explained, rose from different causes than the prewar variety, the most direct one being that wages were too high. "So long as employers . . . can increase the value of their production by more than the cost of production, they will tend to demand more labour; as soon as they find that the addition of another man and his production will bring the price which they can command for their product below the cost of producing it, they will stop expanding their staffs." The latter situation had predominated during the decade of the 1920s. Money wages had risen during the war and the ensuing inflation; they had not declined during the following period of deflation. The increased strength of labor unions and the existence of unemployment insurance and the dole were the positive and negative forces preventing competition from pushing wage rates down. Put differently, "the higher standard of life of those who are in

[25] Beveridge, *Unemployment*, p. viii–ix; Beveridge, *Power and Influence* (London 1953), p.212.

[26] Beveridge, *Unemployment*, pp. 418, 345, 321–23, 352, 288–94, 414–15.

regular work is to some extent won at the cost of unemployment of those who are not."[27]

These "abnormal" conditions might be corrected by reducing the labor supply, by increasing worker productivity, by lowering wages, or by raising prices. Of these approaches the first would be the most effective—but it was impracticable. The last would be the most easily accomplished—but it would mean inflation. In common with the great majority of experts Beveridge dismissed this "solution" out of hand— "the inevitable after-effects of such a policy rule it out."[28] To lower wages would be extremely difficult, and might well weaken incentives, thus undermining efficiency. Raising productivity was therefore the most desirable answer to the problem, but recent experience indicated that the rate of improvement was slowing rather than speeding up. Unless organized labor would encourage rather than resist technological change, and forgo wage increases until business profitability had been increased (conditions unlikely to be met) Beveridge did not expect much from this approach.

His final word was a mixture of hope and skepticism. "If we wish to get back to the level of unemployment that ruled before the war, we must either lower our standards of life or bring production up to justify them. . . . If we think the cost of curing unemployment too high, we may continue instead to pay for unemployment; the post-war situation puts frankly the question, how much unemployment we are prepared to carry in order to avoid surrender of standards of life once gained."[29]

Beveridge, of course, was writing on the edge of the abyss. Vaguely he sensed its presence, but like nearly all his contemporaries he discounted the danger. His earlier treatment of business cycles had been, he confessed, "inadequate." Clearly they were a major cause of unemployment, but fortunately the primary cause of cyclical fluctuations had at last been discovered. It was "the inherent instability of credit," and the analyses of economists like R. G. Hawtrey provided "the first and longest step to full explanation of the trade cycle." It now appeared at least possible that cycles had been a passing and (in historical perspective) a brief phenomenon. True cycles had not existed before the middle of the nineteenth century; they came into being only with the emergence of heavily capitalized industries and "a central bank

[27] *Ibid.*, pp. 368–69, 361, 417.

[28] *Ibid.*, p. 416. He also dismissed with a single footnote—far more peremptorily than in the 1909 edition—the Hobsonian reasoning that high wages reduced unemployment by shifting wealth from the saving rich to the consuming poor. "High wages are among the many good things for which there are many better arguments than the bad argument that they cure unemployment," he pontificated. P. 371n.

[29] *Ibid.*, p. 417, 419.

adopting a simple and automatic credit control." With the development of the credit management techniques of the American Federal Reserve system and with the tendency of nations to break with a fixed gold standard, perhaps cycles would cease to exist. "It may be that the catastrophe of 1920–1 (perhaps one should now say the collapse of 1930) will prove the last kick of the dying [cycle] system." But prophecy was idle, he added, and he contented himself with the conclusion: "The future of cyclical fluctuation in the changed and changing monetary conditions of the world is obscure."[30]

[30] *Ibid.*, pp. 330, 332, 342, 344, 413.

9

The Great Depression

In failing to understand the seriousness of the world economic situation in 1930 Sir William Beveridge was being no more obtuse than the overwhelming majority of experts in the fields of economics, business, and politics. And with good reason; predicting what was to come would have been most difficult, for the extent, duration, and profundity of the decline that we now call the Great Depression was without precedent. Although some nations were hit sooner than others and suffered more extensive losses, every country and virtually every sector of the economy of every country felt the depression's numbing impact: Australian wheat farmers, Brazilian coffee growers, German manufacturers of cameras and chemicals, American automobile makers, British shipbuilders—the list is endless. The decline continued until early 1933, varying only in the rate at which prices and production fell, and when activity at last began to pick up it did so with agonizing sluggishness. Not until 1936 and 1937 did production begin to reach the levels of 1929. Then the world economy again sounded the depths, plunging into what was euphemistically called the "recession" of 1938. Only the outbreak of World War II brought the Great Depression to an end.

Unemployment on a scale never before experienced was a major characteristic of this depression, its most persistent aspect. Unemployment was proportionately highest in the United States and Germany but only less serious in other heavily industrialized countries. Every country had more idle workers in the early 1930s than in any previous period. And even when recovery occurred, the ranks of the jobless remained much larger than in the 1920s in most nations. As late as 1940, some ten million Americans were still unemployed. It is fair to say that, while unemployment is probably better understood as a symptom than as a disease, most of those who concerned themselves with the economic problems of the thirties saw it as the central problem of their age.

Yet despite decades of past effort by some of the best minds of the century, unemployment resisted even accurate description. In the 1890s the heretic John Hobson had called it "perhaps the most illusive term which confronts . . . modern industrial society." In *Unemployment* (1913), Pigou, the pillar of the established order, wrote: "Unemployment is one of those many terms in common use, the general significance of which is understood by all, but which it is, nevertheless, somewhat difficult to define with accuracy," and in *The Theory of Unemployment,* published twenty years later, Pigou was still forced to admit that it was not a "clear-cut conception." In 1906 Pigou's predecessor at Cambridge, Alfred Marshall, noted that different nations defined the term differently, " 'Arbeitslosigkeit' . . . means something very widely removed from 'Unemployment.' " During the 1930s, officials of the International Labor Office were making the same complaint. A French economist, writing in 1931, called unemployment *"un mot élastique."*[1]

Economists could not even agree as to what constituted the minimum amount of unemployment that might be hoped for in an industrial society—how small could Marx's "industrial reserve army" be? In the prosperous 1920s, Americans tended to think that *any* unemployment was a social disaster. In the winter of 1928–29, at the peak of the American boom, the National Federation of Settlements made a study of 150 unemployed families. In a foreword to the Federation's published findings, *Case Studies of Unemployment,* the social worker Paul U. Kellogg complained that "in our most prosperous years we had a body of one million unemployed." Kellogg considered a million far too many; he implied that zero unemployment was possible. But in the late 1920s, a million amounted to about 2 percent of the civilian labor force of the United States, in modern thinking surely full employment. Even Sidney and Beatrice Webb, who were certainly well informed about the subject, could write in 1928 that British unemployment had never fallen below 2 percent in "the best of times during the past half-century," as though 2 percent represented substantial unemployment.[2]

The professional economists of the thirties accepted some unemployment as a fact of industrial life, but they did not know how much

[1] J. A. Hobson, *The Problem of the Unemployed* (London, 1896), p. 1; A. C. Pigou, *Unemployment* (London, 1913), pp. 12–13; Pigou, *The Theory of Unemployment* (London, 1933), p. 3; Pigou, *Memorials of Alfred Marshall* (London, 1925), p. 429;

[2] Marion Elderton, ed., *Case Studies of Unemployment* (Philadelphia, 1931), p. xi; Sidney and Beatrice Webb, *English Poor Law History* (London, 1963), II: 634. See also W. T. Foster and Waddill Catchings, *The Road to Plenty* (Boston, 1928), p. 7, where it is suggested that one million jobless Americans represent high unemployment.

was "normal," or what "normal" meant. The author is of a comprehensive British survey of world unemployment, published in 1935, concluded that "a certain degree of unemployment appears to be inevitable even in times of prosperity," though as readers of Beveridge they claimed that "this 'normal' unemployment . . . can undoubtedly be lessened by better organization of the labour market." They suggested that normal unemployment in Great Britain amounted to about half a million persons in a work force of a little more than 12.6 million, about 4 percent, whereas actual British unemployment during the interwar years never fell below a million persons. Royal Meeker, a former United States Commissioner of Labor, estimated in 1930 that normal unemployment in the United States ranged between 5 and 9 percent. He admitted that he was merely guessing, and, in fact, there were probably fewer persons without jobs in the 1920s than he thought, but the point is that he was using "normal" in the sense of "actual."[3]

As the depression of the 1930s deepened, the tendency was to accept larger and larger percentages of unemployment as normal in the sense, minimal. "Unemployment," wrote the French novelist Jules Romains in 1936, "has unfortunately taken on an almost normal character. . . . It has little chance of disappearing in a world undergoing industrial transformations and a constant readaptation of techniques." The Bishop of York complained two years later that the British people had "become accustomed to a high degree of unemployment" and were complacently accepting government aid to the jobless as a substitute for finding them work.[4]

One monumental difficulty in resolving the question of how much unemployment was too much was the inconsistency, the unreliability, and even the absence of statistical information. It is not surprising that the jobless had seldom been counted systematically before the idea "unemployment" was conceived, but thereafter, beginning with the pioneer Hobson, who bewailed the "miserably defective character" of British estimates, everyone who studied the subject was struck by the need for better data.

For many countries in the 1930s the most important sources (other than information gathered in periodic censuses) were nongovernmental, chiefly records collected by labor unions. These differed in value depending upon the percentage of workers in unions and their repre-

[3] Royal Institute of International Affairs, *Unemployment* (London, 1935), p. 441; Royal Meeker, "The Dependability and Meaning of Unemployment and Employment Statistics in the United States," *Harvard Business Review*, 8 (1930), 392.

[4] Jules Romains, *Visite aux Americans* (Paris, 1936), p. 139n.; Pilgrim Trust, *Men Without Work* (Cambridge, 1938), p. xi.

sentativeness of the laboring population; upon the skill, industriousness, and objectivity of union officials; and upon the purpose of the recording process, which affected the willingness of union members to provide information. All these factors varied from one country to another, and within countries over time.

Nations that made relief payments to unemployed workers ran labor exchanges where those receiving aid must register. The records of these bodies made up another source of data, but again, they applied different standards; in some the grants were hedged about with many difficult qualifications and in others payments were so small and job opportunities so few that numbers of the unemployed did not bother to apply and were thus not counted. In many instances those in need were helped by family or friends, or were too proud to accept what they considered charity. Where unemployment-insurance systems were in effect, still another source of information existed, but aside from the fact that few countries had such insurance, the systems did not cover all types of workers and made payments only for limited periods; thus these statistics were also incomplete and somewhat unrepresentative.

In nearly all cases the result of weaknesses in the statistical techniques was to understate the number of unemployed. It became increasingly apparent that millions of persons who were without work were not being counted. In 1932 statisticians at the German Institut für Konjunkturforschung concluded that there were 2 million "invisible" unemployed in that country, individuals who could not qualify for benefits or who had somehow dropped out of sight. Polish unemployment figures in 1933 showed an increase of about 150,000 over 1929 but a decline of employment of twice that number. In addition, according to one student of Polish conditions, there were a million idle peasants "ready at any time to accept employment in industry." The Japanese Bureau of Social Affairs estimated in 1930 that 378,000 workers were unemployed, but a Tokyo newspaper put the figure at 1.2 million, the gap resulting from the tendency of day laborers to slip through the government's statistical net. The French government estimated unemployment at 100,000 in October 1931, whereas the leader of the Socialists, Léon Blum, set the total at 650,000. Official French unemployment figures reached 503,500 in 1935, but at the same time the Ministry of Labor admitted that employment had fallen by 1.88 million since 1929.[5]

[5] "Some Recent Censuses of Unemployment," *International Labour Review*, 28 (1933), 51–52; Jan Rosner, "Measures to Combat the Depression and Unemployment in Poland," *ibid.*, 30 (1934), 160–63; Seishi Idei, "The Unemployment Problem in Japan," *ibid.*, 22 (1930), 507–509; Maurice Duperrey, ed., *Le chômage* (Paris, 1933), p. 132; Ministère du Travail, *Bulletin*, 42 (1935), 7–8.

When census takers asked questions about unemployment, more accurate totals could be reached. These were far larger—anywhere from two to five or six times greater—than those obtained by other methods. But even census figures had grave weaknesses. They reflected conditions at a particular point in time, which might correspond to a peak or trough in unemployment. They were frequently distorted by social attitudes: respondents who believed that the loss of a job reflected some personal inadequacy often hesitated to admit that they were unemployed. Furthermore, as with other sources, the census authorities did not all adopt the same definition of unemployment. The 1930 American census was widely criticized as having underestimated the jobless, chiefly because of a decision not to include persons reporting themselves to have been temporarily laid off. This decision led the census bureau expert on unemployment, Charles E. Persons, to resign in protest; economists concluded that the census was about 30 percent too low in its estimates. In 1937 a "voluntary" census of unemployment was taken in the United States, the count being accomplished by the dubious device of mailing questionnaires to heads of families. More than 7.8 million persons reported themselves as unemployed, but spot checks indicated that the actual number was closer to 10.8 million. The director of this census, John D. Biggers, underlining the discrepancy, had to admit: "We do not claim provable accuracy for any one figure."[6]

Of pre-depression American unemployment statistics, the best were those of the American Federation of Labor, and these were none too good. They were often carelessly compiled, and since only a small minority of the country's wage earners belonged to the AFL, they were a poor indication of the national situation. When President Harding's 1921 conference on unemployment tried to determine the number of jobless persons it found itself "without data even for an accurate estimate." It arrived at its figure (as one of its members later recalled) "by guess and by God."[7]

Worldwide, the inadequacy of the data did not result from a lack of effort by economists and statisticians. In 1910, at the peak of the first wave of interest in unemployment, an international conference, meeting in Paris, had studied the statistical problem, and in 1925 another conference of labor statisticians had laid down criteria for a uniform

[6] "Recent Censuses," pp. 46–47; P. H. Douglas and Aaron Director, *The Problem of Unemployment* (New York, 1931), pp. 12, 17; R. R. Nathan, "Estimates of Unemployment in the United States, 1929–1935," *International Labour Review*, 33 (1936), 55, 59–63; Broadus Mitchell, *Depression Decade* (New York, 1969), pp. 93–94.

[7] Meeker, "Meaning of Unemployment," p. 392; President's Conference on Unemployment, *Report* (Washington, 1921), p. 39; National Bureau of Economic Research, *The Measurement and Behavior of Unemployment* (Princeton, 1957), p. 585.

definition of unemployment and urged the industrial nations to adhere to them. In 1929 the International Labor Office began publishing a world index of unemployment, compiled quarterly by John Lindberg. Throughout the depression Lindberg struggled to improve the accuracy of this index, but he felt compelled to warn readers repeatedly of its inherent limitations. At best it revealed trends, he confessed. As an indication of the absolute numbers of jobless persons in any particular country it was suspect; to use it to compare unemployment in different countries was "impossible." "It is only by a stretch of the imagination that the name of unemployment statistics can be applied to all these different data," Lindberg admitted in 1934.

Under the pressure of prolonged mass unemployment the collection of statistics was expanded in many countries, but little was done to make the figures comparable internationally, or to measure part-time unemployment. In 1936 the ILO was still complaining of "the diversity which exists in the scope and method" of measuring unemployment, and it warned that the numbers in its world index "in most cases fall far short of reality." As late as 1939 the index, although by then somewhat improved, was prefaced with an admonition that its figures were merely approximations. "In very few countries do the statistics of unemployment approach completeness."[8]

Counting the jobless, however, represented only a small part of the effort that was made to examine and understand them during the Great Depression. Government agencies stepped up the collection and publication of data relating to the effects of unemployment on living conditions, school attendance, health, and other topics. Other investigators analyzed the records of relief agencies, public and private, in an effort to discover what types of persons were unemployed and how the loss of work affected their lives. Much use was also made of questionnaires. In 1931, for example, the New York City Welfare Council distributed a questionnaire to the city's social workers calling for information about the physical and psychological effects of unemployment on their clients. The replies represented the views of about 900 of these professionals serving some 100,000 families. In 1931 and again in 1933 the American Women's Association circularized its members in order to find out how many were unemployed and how their lives had been affected by the depression. More unusual was the tactic of the Polish Institute of Social Economy of Warsaw, which sponsored a prize competition for autobiographical essays by jobless persons. In an effort to make the autobiographies comparable, the institute drafted instructions describing what topics should be covered: occupation,

[8] *International Labour Review,* 26 (1932), 491–512; 28 (1933), 46–61; 29 (1934), 475; 33 (1936), 90; 39 (1939), 125.

length of unemployment, cause of the loss of work, relief secured, effects of unemployment on family health, the overall impact of joblessness on life.[9]

The questionnaire approach, while useful, had obvious limitations. By querying social workers and other professionals, fairly comprehensive responses could be obtained, but these were secondhand and perhaps biased. But depending on the unemployed to volunteer information raised a different question: were those who troubled to answer representative of the population being surveyed? The Polish essays made fascinating reading, but they reflected the views of articulate, intelligent, and motivated individuals, not necessarily typical of Poland's unemployed. The 1931 questionnaire of the American Women's Association was sent to all the association's 3,000 members. Nearly 2,000 returned it—a gratifyingly large percentage—but what of the others? Were those who did not answer more likely to be employed women who tossed the questionnaire aside as not applying to them, or jobless ones ashamed to admit their condition?

It is therefore not surprising that students of unemployment, like Villermé, Booth, and other nineteenth-century social investigators before them, went directly into the field in search of data. In 1931 two investigations were begun that have become classics, one in England, the other in Austria. The first was the work of E. Wight Bakke, an American graduate student sponsored by the Yale Institute of Human Relations. Bakke spent six months in the London suburb of Greenwich, which had an unemployed population of about three thousand. During this period he took lodgings with a working-class family. He frequented local pubs and employment offices, getting to know many of the jobless well, accompanying them as they searched for work. He interviewed numbers of these men repeatedly, recording their changing attitudes toward themselves, English society, the political situation; he even persuaded some of them to keep diaries of their routine activities for his own use. He published his findings in *The Unemployed Man* (1933).

The Austrian study was the work of a group of social scientists from the University of Vienna, led by Paul F. Lazarsfeld, Marie Jahoda, and Hans Zeisel. In the winter of 1931–32, the group settled down in Marienthal, a village not far from Vienna. This community of 1,486 persons was suffering from almost total unemployment. Early in 1930 the town's single industry, a textile mill, had closed its doors. The

[9] Lilian Brandt, *An Impressionistic View of the Winter of 1930–31 in New York City* (New York, 1932); Lorine Pruette, *Women Workers Through the Depression* (New York, 1934), pp. 16–23; Jan Rosner, "An Inquiry into the Life of Unemployed Workers in Poland," *International Labour Review*, 27 (1933), 378–92.

company went out of business and the mill was torn down. Aside from a few shopkeepers and local officials and a handful of men who had jobs in Vienna, everyone was without work and dependent upon the minuscule relief payments doled out by the Austrian government.

Convinced by earlier work that social research should combine "natural" data drawn from direct observation with "experimental" material created in response to the activity of the investigators, such as questionnaires, the Lazarsfeld team lived in close contact with the villagers for several months, studying their activities minutely. (In one project, a researcher sat in a room with a window opening on the main street and recorded how often each passer-by stopped while walking a certain distance.) The team compiled a file on each of Marienthal's 478 families and prepared detailed life histories of a sample of the population. They studied town records, election results, the volume of business in the taverns, and the books of the cooperative store. The experimental work included persuading eighty residents to write hour-by-hour diaries of their activities and getting forty families to keep careful track of what they ate at each meal for a week. They obtained essays written by school children on topics designed to reveal their expectations and values. They also collected and distributed clothing for the most needy, and they organized special classes, a free medical clinic, and an informal counseling service. The purpose of this complicated investigation, published under the title *Die Arbeitslosen von Marienthal,* was better to understand *unemployment,* not merely to discover what had happened to the people of Marienthal or to suggest ways of helping the jobless.

As the depression dragged on, field investigations proliferated. There were important studies of the unemployed by the Solvay Institute of Sociology in Belgium, by the Czechoslovakian Social Institute, the Polish Institute of Social Relations, the French Scientific Institute of Economic and Social Research, this last so elaborate that its findings were published in three volumes, the last not appearing until 1949. The London School of Economics sponsored a *New Survey of London Life and Labour,* a re-examination of the city in the manner of Charles Booth. This enormous project, which was directed by Hubert Llewellyn Smith, who had worked with Booth on the original study and with William Beveridge on the organization of the British employment exchanges and the unemployment-insurance system, was published in nine volumes between 1930 and 1935. In 1938 an important analysis of long-term unemployment in Britain sponsored by the Bishop of York came out under the title *Men Without Work.*

In the United States during the middle thirties, persistent high unemployment combined with the mood of hopeful experimentation inspired by the New Deal and the flourishing state of the social sciences in the universities to produce a small avalanche of investigations. That the two most innovative students of unemployment, Bakke and Lazarsfeld, were working in America after 1933 was doubtless a further stimulation. Bakke returned from England with his dissertation to teach at Yale and direct the Institute of Human Relations' unemployment studies. He was a co-author of the institute's *After the Shutdown* (1934), and his long field investigation of unemployment in New Haven led to *The Unemployed Worker* (1940) and *Citizens Without Work* (1940). Lazarsfeld came to the United States in 1933 and was soon involved in research on the unemployed under the auspices of the New Deal Works Progress Administration, serving as director of student relief in Essex County, New Jersey, for the National Youth Administration. He organized a large research program in which ten thousand young people in the city of Newark were interviewed in order to find out how many were without work, what kind of jobs the others held, how both groups used their leisure time. The WPA also prepared a translation of the Marienthal study, but since no publisher could be found it was distributed only in mimeographed form.[10] Lazarsfeld did, however, publish a summary of the book in English, an article describing the Polish autobiographies, and (in 1938) an analytical survey of recent research on the effects of unemployment. He also wrote, with Samuel A. Stouffer, *Research Memorandum on the Family in the Depression* (1937), one of thirteen volumes on aspects of the depression sponsored by the Social Science Research Council.

Stimulated at least in part by such examples, American researchers subjected the jobless and their families to batteries of tests, questionnaires, and interviews, seeking to isolate characterological traits that might explain their fate or reveal the psychological effects of idleness. Some compared the unemployed with persons in similar trades who were working; others studied vagrants; other persons on relief; still others those engaged on government work projects. Most of these studies were relatively small scale, and individually few were particularly significant. But their volume and variety attested to the great interest in investigating the subject.

Whatever the country, these studies varied greatly in scope and objectivity, and of course they revealed that individuals differed in the way they were affected by unemployment depending upon their intelligence, experience, and personalities, as well as upon the circumstances of their situation. As one researcher confessed, generalizing

[10] Later, when Lazarsfeld had the opportunity to publish it he refused because he had become dissatisfied with the sampling procedures he had used. It finally appeared in English in 1971 under the title *Marienthal: The Sociography of an Unemployed Community.*

about the effects of unemployment was "like trying to summarize a Persian rug." Yet it seems fair to say that contemporaries had a clearer picture of the effects of unemployment in the Great Depression than they did of its extent—statistical information about unemployment being so sketchy and inaccurate.

One of the surprising things revealed by research was that the depression did not appear to have had any dramatic effect on public health. It did not cause an increase in death rates or even slow the long-range trend toward increased longevity characteristic of the industrial nations. In 1932 the Surgeon General of the United States announced that with regard to health, "the country has never been as prosperous in its history as during the year 1931, so far as we are able to ascertain by statistics," and he released figures showing that the mortality rate had fallen from 12 per thousand in 1929 to 10.6 per thousand in 1932. He attributed this happy state of affairs in part to the "devoted self-sacrifice of the medical profession" in treating poor patients "regardless of possible remuneration," but he provided no statistical evidence on this point.

This is not to say that the health of many unemployed persons was not affected; common sense and much hard evidence indicate that it was. A British medical journal viewed the situation more realistically. "We know," it reported in 1933, "that at the present time a very large proportion of the population is imperfectly fed, but we cannot find the signs of it." In countries such as the United States that did not have national systems of relief in the early years, there were many cases of severe malnutrition and some of starvation, and even in Great Britain and Germany, where care of the needy was well organized and reasonably comprehensive, investigators found countless families suffering from hunger and various dietary deficiencies. National health statistics, however, did not reflect this suffering to any marked degree. The effects of malnutrition appear only slowly, and it was probably also true that statistically the improved diet available to full-time workers because of lower food prices counterbalanced the deficiencies endured by the minority that was unemployed.[11] In countries where unemployment was relatively low the national diet actually improved during the early thirties. In France the improvement was startling; between 1931 and 1935 the per-capita consumption of food increased by 5 percent (more than the rise between 1913 and 1930) and meat, milk, and fruit consumption rose even more. Similar trends were discernible in many other nations, including Great Britain, despite its chronically high

[11] Noreen Branson and Margot Heinemann, *Britain in the 1930's* (London, 1971), pp. 202–20; Pilgrim Trust, *Men Without Work*, pp. 133–35; R. P. Lopes, "The Economic Depression and Public Health," *International Labour Review*, 29 (1934), 793.

unemployment. When B. Seebohm Rowntree replicated his classic 1899 survey of *Poverty* in York in the mid-thirties he found enough improvement in living standards to title his new book *Poverty and Progress,* although the numbers living in poverty were still shockingly high.[12]

Both field studies of what unemployed families ate and estimates based on relief payments and the cost of food indicated that most of the jobless consumed enough calories to maintain weight. A French inquiry made in the middle of the depression put the daily caloric intake of the unemployed at slightly over 2,700 calories (for workers it was 3,150), a total generally conceded to be adequate. A British investigation made at about the same time calculated the intake of the unemployed at 2,850 calories per day, about 10 percent less than that of the typical worker. A German analysis of food prices and relief payments made during the grim winter of 1932–33 concluded that a jobless person could afford to purchase a little over 2,600 calories compared to about 2,850 for workers.[13]

However, the unemployed seldom ate enough of the right kinds of food. Conditions varied from one country to another according to the amount of aid provided and the general standard of living, and among individuals. But their consumption of fruit, vegetables, and especially high-protein foods fell off everywhere. As early as December 1930, milk consumption in New York City was running a million quarts a week below normal. Even in France, where the unemployed usually got enough proteins and vitamins, their intake of meat, dairy products, and vegetables was nevertheless much lower than that of workers. In poorer countries the dietary deficiencies of the unemployed were more serious. Lazarsfeld discovered that seven of ten families in Marienthal ate meat no more than once a week and that some of this meat was the flesh of cats and dogs. Pork consumption in Marienthal fell by about half, beef to only a small fraction of what it had been before the depression. Flour consumption, on the other hand, increased. In Vienna the records of the Office of Markets revealed a considerable drop between 1931 and 1932 in the number of cattle and pigs slaughtered and in the sale of eggs and fruits. In Hungary, where the condition of agricultural workers was particularly bad and where many of them therefore flocked into the cities, by 1932, 18 percent of the population of Budapest was on relief and getting, according to trade-

[12] Alfred Sauvy, *Histoire économique de la France entre les deux guerres* (Paris, 1967), II: 121; B. S. Rowntree, *Poverty and Progress* (London, 1941).

[13] Gabrielle Letellier *et al., Enquête sur le chômage* (Paris, 1949), III: 310; Pilgrim Trust, *Men Without Work,* p. 135; Lopes, "Depression and Public Health," p. 795.

union estimates, only about half the money needed to maintain a minimum standard of living.[14]

The nutritional problems of the jobless were complicated by bad management and by their widely noticed tendency to "waste" money on nonessentials. George Orwell noted in *The Road to Wigan Pier,* his report on conditions in the so-called "distressed areas" of Britain, that the unemployed consumed large amounts of sweets, chips, and "the Englishman's opium," tea, and that they were inveterate gamblers. In Marienthal nearly half of the evening meals consumed consisted only of bread and black coffee. Although the coffee had no nutritional value, it was "considered a food and also a luxury, and for that reason holds a central place in the diet of the poorest classes in particular." An unemployed Polish worker told a pathetic story about a child who asked his mother for milk in his coffee. The mother replied that the milk was already in the coffee, but that the cows were now giving black milk. When the child asked why this was so, she answered that the cows were not getting enough to eat, and had become angry.[15]

Investigations of unemployed French workers revealed a similar attitude toward "luxury" foods; they continued to devote substantial portions of their budgets to wine and coffee, despite the fact that a "purely rational analysis of their financial situation" should have led them to cut down on these items. A nurse in Alsace who visited unemployed workers in their homes described a poor family that used the *prime à natalité* received at the birth of a baby to purchase a "uselessly luxurious baby carriage." Many Belgian unemployed workers spent money raising pigeons, not to eat but in hopes of winning a worthless prize, and Lazarsfeld reported the case of an almost destitute fifty-year-old woman who bought a curling iron on the installment plan. The German journalist and sociologist Siegfried Kracauer, watching ragged young people laying out 50 pfennige at a Berlin movie theater, decided that they attended "less for pleasure than to drive away the ghost of bad times." The film was a kind of medicine, he concluded.[16]

[14] *New York Times,* December 6, 1930; Letellier, *Enquête sur le chômage,* III: 202–3, 209; Marie Jahoda, P. F. Lazarsfeld, and Hans Zeisel, *Marienthal: The Sociography of an Unemployed Community* (Chicago, 1971), pp. 26, 30; Lopes, "Depression and Public Health," pp. 789–90; M. Incze, "Condition of the Masses in Hungary," *Acta Historica,* 3 (1954), 12, 19–20, 25–32, 51–67; Mark Mitnitzky, "The Economic and Social Effects of Industrial Development in Hungary," *International Labour Review,* 39 (1939), 459–73.

[15] George Orwell, *The Road to Wigan Pier* (New York, 1961), pp. 84–89; Lazarsfeld, *Marienthal,* pp. 27n., 55; Rosner, "Unemployed Workers in Poland," p. 388.

[16] Letellier, *Enquête sur le chômage,* III: 41; Claude Thouvenot and Arnette Minot, "Incidence de la crise de 1929 sur les consommations en Meurthe-et-Moselle," *Annales de l'Est* (1970, no. 3), 239; Philip Eisenberg and P. F. Lazarsfeld, "The Psychological Effects of Unemployment," *Psychological Bulletin,* 35 (1938), 360; Siegfried Kracauer, *Strassen in Berlin und anderswo* (Frankfurt-am-Main, 1964), p. 93.

Descriptions of ragged clothes and bad housing conditions also fill the unemployment studies of the 1930s. Investigators reported finding children unable to go to school because they had no shoes, families living in crowded squalor or evicted for nonpayment of rent. It was sometimes noted that landlords allowed tenants to stay on even when far in arrears, out of pity or because they preferred not to leave buildings vacant and at the mercy of vandals, but the sight of the poor living in tiny huts designed as toolsheds on garden allotment plots, and the mushrooming of shantytowns on wasteland on the edges of great cities from Australia to the Argentine—sardonically called Hoovervilles in the United States, *bidonvilles* (tin-can cities) in France, humpies in Australia—suggests that eviction was far from uncommon. In the spring of 1935 two Indiana University sociologists found about twenty thousand unemployed men living in state-operated shelters in the city of Chicago. Most of these unfortunates were ill educated and of low intelligence, men who before the depression had been casual laborers at best. Many exhibited signs of emotional instability. But a number of them—a small percentage but several hundred nonetheless—were high school and college graduates who had held down good jobs before the depression struck. In Budapest in the early thirties hundreds of homeless unemployed professional workers were living in an army barracks, and eating leftovers in the university cafeteria until the dean ejected them on the ground that they were having "a prejudicial effect, morally, on the students." Inadequate housing was, of course, a problem for many working families, in good times as well as bad, but the jobless, compelled to spend larger and larger proportions of their declining funds on food, often had to liquidate their meager possessions merely to stay alive.[17]

In a sense, demonstrating that many who were without work were inadequately fed, clothed, and sheltered was only documenting the obvious; the reports of researchers on the psychological effects of unemployment were somewhat more surprising. While individuals reacted in widely different ways, nearly every survey, whatever its scope, whatever the method of investigation, revealed essentially the same patterns. These were spelled out early in the depression by the Lazarsfeld team's analysis of Marienthal, by Bakke's study of Greenwich, and in the autobiographies of unemployed workers gathered by the Polish Institute of Social Economy. When workers lost their jobs

[17] Thouvenot and Minot, "Consommations en Meurthe-et-Moselle," p. 242; F. A. Bland, "Unemployment and Relief in Australia," *International Labour Review*, 30 (1934), 53; Enrique Siewers, "Unemployment in Argentina," *ibid.*, 31 (1935), 798–99; E. H. Sutherland and H. J. Locke, *Twenty Thousand Homeless Men: A Study of Unemployed Men in Chicago Shelters* (Chicago, 1936), pp. 34–35, 52–69; Incze, "Masses in Hungary," pp. 87–88.

their response, perhaps after a brief period of waiting for something to turn up, was to search feverishly for a new one. Then they became discouraged, sometimes emotionally disorganized. Finally, after months of continuous idleness, most either sank into apathy or adjusted to their condition, leading extremely circumscribed lives in apparent calm.

This evolution, or at least its final stage, apathy, had been noticed by many careful observers in earlier times. Often it was attributed to poverty per se, as when Eugène Buret spoke of the *"facile résignation"* with which the French factory workers he was studying viewed their condition. One of Charles Booth's assistants reported a laborer saying: "Whenever I am out of work I feel like a bloody dog." In the 1890s Paul Göhre, an idealistic young German who spent three months as a factory hand, described "the inexpressibly depressing effect of being obliged to trudge from factory to factory, from shop to shop, always offering one's abilities and capabilities, and always in vain," and an American professor who made a similar experiment recorded the discouragement that came with rejection—the awareness that "you are a superfluous human being." In 1910, B. Seebohm Rowntree reported in more detail the feelings of an unemployed English plumber, who, after weeks of "hoping against hope," was told at the local labor exchange to check in only once a month. "I turned away, and the only remaining strength in my body seemed to completely forsake me. I staggered into the street, a completely world-forsaken man."[18]

But the investigators of the 1930s called attention to the pattern and to its universality. In *The Unemployed Man,* Bakke recorded the process as it evolved in the case of "A," a young Greenwich truck driver. Bakke met A at a political rally three days after he had been laid off. "There's plenty of jobs for a man with my experience," A said. "I've never been out more than a week or so before. I'll soon be back." Three weeks later, after having moved in with his parents and answered want ads without success, he was discouraged but still hopeful. After another five weeks, however, he told Bakke, "I'm beginning to wonder what's wrong with me," after another three, "either I'm no good, or there is something wrong with business around here. . . . Even my family is beginning to think I'm not trying." Finally, four months after losing his job, A became utterly despondent, complaining to Bakke of "the hopelessness of every step you take."[19]

[18] Eugène Buret, *De la misère des classes laborieuses* (Paris, 1940), I: 127; H. L. Smith, *New Survey of London Life and Labour* (London, 1932), III: 172; Paul Göhre, *Three Months in a Workshop: A Practical Study* (London, 1895), p. 72; W. A. Wycoff, *The Workers, An Experiment in Reality: The West* (New York, 1899), pp. 46–47; B. S. Rowntree, and Bruno Lasker, *Unemployment: A Social Study* (London, 1911), p. 240.

[19] E. W. Bakke, *The Unemployed Man: A Social Study* (London, 1933), pp. 64–67.

Lazarsfeld, who observed the people of Marienthal when they had already endured a long period without work, was more interested in their final adjustment to their situation. Studying closely the hundred most needy families in the village, he found four types. About half he classified as resigned to their fate; they had learned to accept a circumscribed existence, had no plans or expectations. Another quarter he called despairing—these were bitter, gloomy, frequently drunk, given to outbursts of misdirected rage. Another, smaller group were completely apathetic, heedless not only of the future but even of the present. Only about 16 percent of these people could be classified as "unbroken," and they, significantly, had slightly higher incomes than the rest. They continued to hope for work and had an optimistic outlook despite their suffering. Conditions in Marienthal as a whole were not quite so bad as this analysis of its poorest citizens indicated. Lazarsfeld estimated that nearly a quarter of the families in the town were unbroken and about 70 percent merely resigned. The despairing and the apathetic made up the rest.[20]

Since Marienthal was an extreme case, the relative numbers who were crushed or maimed by unemployment there may have been larger than elsewhere, although it seems equally possible that the universality of unemployment may have sustained many individuals. What was clear, however, in that village and in every locale where investigators examined the state of mind of the jobless, was that few persons could survive long periods of enforced idleness without paying a psychological price, even if their basic economic needs were met. Lazarsfeld called Marienthal *"die müde Gemeinschaft,"* the weary community. A Canadian researcher spoke of the "lowered morale and broken spirits" of the unemployed, their "hopeless despair," their "dependent attitudes." When Henri Fuss of the International Labor Office visited a British employment exchange, he found "an air of lassitude." The jobless, he said, "walk heavily and slowly." In Argentina, another writer noted, many of the unemployed "have gradually drifted away from all their connections and have come to look upon their past as another existence with which they have severed every tie."[21]

In 1931 New York City social workers, describing the reactions of their clients, stressed their general loss of pride and their tendency to avoid social contacts. In 1940, Mirra Komarovsky, who had studied a

[20] Lazarsfeld, *Marienthal*, pp. 45–65.

[21] H. M. Cassidy, *Unemployment and Relief in Ontario, 1929–1932* (Toronto, 1932), p. 253; Henri Fuss and D. C. Tact, "Unemployment Benefits and Measures for Occupying the Unemployed in Great Britain," *International Labour Review,* 27 (1933), 597–98; Siewers, "Depression in Argentina," p. 798.

group of unemployed New York families in the late stages of the depression, reported her general impression that "the [jobless] man suffers from deep humiliation." Unemployment, the psychologist Abram Kardiner noted in an article in *The Family*, produced feelings of shame and anxiety in its victims, leading eventually to apathy. When another psychologist administered a questionnaire designed to elicit social attitudes and personal values to eight hundred jobless men and women with records of previous steady employment, he also characterized their responses as apathetic; they appeared to react to the words of the items but not to their meaning. Still another psychologist gave a questionnaire prepared for the study of the mental state of psychotics to a group of English and Scottish unemployed workers. Many of the respondents displayed a "catastrophic" outlook toward life and were as "downcast" as mental patients.[22]

Novelists, reporters, and others who observed large numbers of the unemployed during the depression described the psychological effects of idleness in the same terms. Orwell visited a family in a mining town, all of them out of work, "grown-up sons and daughters sprawling aimlessly about . . . and one tall son sitting by the fireplace, too listless even to notice the entry of a stranger, and slowly peeling a sticky sock from a bare foot." Elsewhere in *The Road to Wigan Pier* Orwell wrote of men "gazing at their destiny with the same sort of dumb amazement as an animal in a trap," and "haunted by a feeling of personal degradation." Siegfried Kracauer compared a Berlin shelter to the waiting room of a railroad station where "the train never comes." At a labor exchange he found the mood dark and subdued. Everyone spoke in whispers and with resignation. "I have observed that many scarcely listen to the announcements of jobs," Kracauer wrote. "They are already too numbed to believe in their chance of being chosen."[23]

The American historian Ray Allen Billington, who was a director of the New Deal Writers' Project in Massachusetts in the late thirties, interviewed scores of applicants. A quarter of a century later he still recalled "their bleak, downcast eyes, their broken spirit." Maxine Davis, a journalist, spent four months in 1935 driving across the United States talking to young people; she was struck by the "sheep-

---

[22] Lillian Brandt, *An Impressionistic View of the Winter of 1930–31 in New York City* (New York, 1932), p. 17; Mirra Komarovsky, *The Unemployed Man and His Family—The Effects of Unemployment upon the Status of the Man in Fifty-Nine Families* (New York, 1940), p. 74; Abram Kardiner, "The Role of Economic Security in the Adaptation of the Individual," *The Family*, 17 (1936), 187–97; A. C. Tucker, "Some Correlates of Certain Attitudes of the Unemployed," *Archives of Psychology* (1940), no. 245; Nathan Israeli, "Distress in the Outlook of Lancashire and Scottish Unemployed," *Journal of Applied Psychology*, 19 (1935), 67–69.

[23] Orwell, *Wigan Pier*, pp. 60, 81; Kracauer, *Strassen in Berlin*, pp. 81, 72, 74.

like apathy" with which they accepted their state. The writer Sherwood Anderson, who also toured America in this period, came to a similar conclusion. "There is in the average American a profound humbleness," he wrote. "People seem to blame themselves."[24]

Although many Marxist novelists, especially in the United States, described the unemployed as militant, most novelists who wrote about the depression without this particular political bias pictured them as crushed by unemployment. The Englishman Walter Greenwood, whose *Love on the Dole* (1933) was one of the most widely read novels of the 1930s, put it this way:

> It got you slowly, with the slippered stealth of an unsuspected, malignant disease. You fell into the habit of slouching, of putting your hands into your pockets and keeping them there; of glancing at people, furtively, ashamed of your secret, until you fancied that everybody eyed you with suspicion.

Karl Lakner, the protagonist of the Austrian Rudolf Brunngraber's novel, *Karl and the Twentieth Century* (1933), emerges from World War I a cheerful, hard-working man fully capable of bearing misfortune. But repeated periods of unemployment and declining resources leave him with the "depressed look of the permanently unemployed." He becomes "utterly aimless," then "profoundly demoralized," and finally, after a futile attempt at robbery, he commits suicide. Johannes Pinneberg, the hero of the German Hans Fallada's *Little Man, What Now?* (1932), goes through similar experiences, reacts like Karl, and comes to almost as sad an end.[25]

Many Americans believed that the dependency resulting from unemployment was a more profound shock in their country than elsewhere because of the prevailing worship of self-reliance. In a nation that had almost no social insurance and provided relief for the destitute largely in the form of private charity until long after the economy had plumbed the depths, where labor unions preferred to obtain their goals by bargaining or striking rather than through legislation, unemployment was especially ego-eroding, or so the argument ran. Thus two sociologists wrote in 1936: "A man who has the traditional individualistic American idea that a man who is industrious and persevering can get and hold a job, receives a severe mental jolt when he finds himself unable to supply even the bare necessities of life." But

[24] R. A. Billington, "Government and the Arts: The W. P. A. Experience," *American Quarterly,* 13 (1961), 471; Maxine Davis, *The Lost Generation: A Portrait of American Youth Today* (New York, 1936), p. 27; Sherwood Anderson, *Puzzled America* (New York, 1935), p. 46.

[25] Walter Greenwood, *Love on the Dole* (London, 1969), p. 169; Rudolf Brunngraber, *Karl and the Twentieth Century* (New York, 1933), pp. 68, 203, 259, 265; Hans Fallada, *Little Man, What Now?* (New York, 1933).

is much evidence that unemployment affected people in less individualistic societies in just the same way. "When for the first time I held out my hand for my 9 zloty of benefit," a Polish unemployed worker recalled, "I was filled with disgust for the whole of my previous existence." Orwell, eager to rouse the British jobless to act against the conditions that had produced their misery, was "horrified and amazed" to discover "that many of them were *ashamed* of being unemployed."[26]

The effects of prolonged joblessness, and particularly its psychological effects, go far toward explaining why unemployment did not generate more political protest, let alone revolutionary activity, among its victims. Many practical considerations combined to keep the unemployed from revolting, some of these being the international character of the depression, which made it difficult to believe that any one government was responsible for it; the lack of intellectually convincing suggestions as to how unemployment could be significantly reduced; the fact that the unemployed were everywhere a minority; fear of repression (which the majority seldom hesitated to apply when the jobless did make trouble); even gratitude for the aid which every society provided for those without work. But the numbing effect of prolonged idleness, part no doubt a result of diets low in proteins but also partly psychological, was also involved.

Protest, of course, there was: mass meetings, hunger marches, rent strikes, countless cases of petty theft by the destitute, outright violence. Such disturbances attracted wide attention and roused profound fears. "Unemployment is making the world tremble," a French businessman wrote in 1932. "There [in America] is the 'bonus army,' hundreds of thousands of the unemployed who besiege the capital. Facing us are the 'hunger marchers,' who tie up the heart of the British Empire. Elsewhere races become emaciated, nations break up and lose their sense of proper order." The very logic of the situation increased the feeling of many observers that the world was teetering on the verge of chaos. "The present crisis is so widespread in its effects and so dire in its consequences to those who suffer from them," a German commission on unemployment reported in 1931, "that social consequences of the most serious nature . . . are to be feared."[27]

But the protests of the jobless were sporadic, unfocused, and to a considerable extent merely rhetorical. A Washington reporter de-

---

[26] Sutherland and Locke, *Homeless Men*, p. 150; Rosner, "Unemployed Workers in Poland," p. 385; Orwell, *Wigan Pier*, p. 80.

[27] J. A. Garraty, "Radicalism in the Great Depression," L. H. Blair, ed., *Essays on Radicalism in American Life* (Austin, 1972), pp. 102–13; Duperrey, *Chômage*, p. 94; Ministry of Labour, *The Unemployment Problem in Germany* (London, 1931), p. 8.

scribed the American bonus marchers of 1932 as "the army of bewilderment," their behavior marked by "a curious melancholy." When, gathered eight thousand strong before the Capitol, they learned that the Senate had rejected the bonus bill, they meekly accepted the suggestion of their leader that they sing "America," and straggled back to their pitiful shacks on Anacostia Flats. Unemployed British hunger marchers occasionally used force to call attention to their plight, but most of the dozens of clashes between marchers and the police were provoked by the latter. In general the marchers conducted themselves with restraint and their leaders made great efforts to prevent breaches of the peace. They carried red banners, it is true, but most of their signs bore messages no more provocative than "down with the means test" and "against hunger and war." The culmination of the most successful of the great marches in early 1934 was the presentation of a petition to the House of Commons, phrased in the traditional language of petitioners ("[We] humbly desire to represent that great suffering has been caused to the unemployed . . . by the means test") and asking no more than "decent maintenance" or "employment at trade union rates." These most "militant" of victims of the depression were appealing for sympathy and succor, expressing, above all else, their dependency.[28]

Many students of unemployment in the thirties commented on the political passivity of the jobless, some with puzzlement, some with understanding. They collected innumerable individual statements expressing anger, resentment, and disillusionment with the authorities. "Unemployment is due to an agreement between the capitalists and the Government to crush the worker and make a slave of him," wrote a Pole. "I don't think things will improve until we have a revolution." "Just nationalise everything," said an Englishman. A researcher in an American municipal lodging house recorded the residents "giving the capitalist system hell in a big way." But such expressions were nearly always mere talk.

Those who studied the political attitudes of the unemployed also noted their lack of involvement. In Marienthal, always representative of the extreme case, the Lazarsfeld team reported a sharp falling off of *all* political activity. Elsewhere, however, most of the jobless displayed toward political issues the same apathy that characterized their whole lives. "When one is out of a job," a long-time-unemployed Dutch worker told an investigator in 1935, "one loses one's pleasure

[28] Roger Daniels, *The Bonus March: An Episode of the Great Depression* (Westport, Conn., 1971), *passim;* Wal Hannington, *Unemployed Struggles: 1919–1936* (London, 1936), pp. 219, 265, 282–83, 288; Allen Hutt, *Postwar History of the British Working Class* (New York, 1938), pp. 213–16.

in politics." Bakke found few radicals among the unemployed of Greenwich and no difference in political attitude between them and those with jobs. *He* seemed more indignant about how society had treated these people than they were themselves.

After a more detailed analysis of unemployment in New Haven Bakke came to the same conclusion. He attended a May Day meeting on the town common in 1934. A Communist orator delivered a powerful speech, but no one appeared to be following his argument, and when he ended with a call for a protest march to city hall, only a handful followed him. Bakke concluded that despite the depression nearly all the New Haven unemployed still accepted the capitalist system. On another occasion, after listening to several groups of men griping about conditions, he asked one of them where the local Communist headquarters was. The men bristled. "Take my advice and stay away from there," one of the men told him. To draw them out, Bakke began defending the Communist cause. Their response was twofold: Anyone who thought the Russian system was good was crazy. Communists were all foreigners; to support them was to be a traitor. "In the face of Communism," Bakke noted, "the most insecure American workman becomes a hero by defending American conditions."[29]

The writer Matthew Josephson, radicalized by the suffering he observed and read about in the early thirties, began visiting the dingy municipal lodging houses of New York. He found not rebelliousness but defeatism and lassitude. Once he treated three down-and-outers whose confidence he had won to a meal. "Things just can't go on like this," he said to them. They smiled faintly, but said nothing. Why didn't they complain about the dreadful conditions in the shelters? "We don't dare complain about anything. We're afraid of being kicked out." Why didn't they join the demonstrations that radicals in New York were organizing? They answered that they were " 'good Americans' and didn't go for the 'communist stuff.' " Later in the depression another American journalist who pictured himself as "frankly radical" and who described the efforts of various Communist groups in glowing terms spent seven months driving across the country and back taking the public pulse. As for the unemployed, he wrote, "the more I saw of them . . . the more I was depressed and outraged both by their physical and spiritual wretchedness and by their passive acceptance of their condition."

The Polish autobiographies revealed still another aspect of the polit-

[29] Rosner, "Unemployed Workers in Poland," p. 390; H. L. Beales and R. S. Lambert, eds., *Memoirs of the Unemployed* (London, 1934), p. 198; Sutherland and Locke, *Homeless Men*, p. 13; Lazarsfeld, *Marienthal*, pp. 40–41; Jan Beishuizen and Evert Werkman, *De magere jaren: Nederland in de crisistijd, 1929–1939* (Leiden, 1968), p. 126; Bakke, *Unemployed Man*, pp. 60–61, 149, 151, 236; E. W. Bakke, *Citizens Without Work* (New Haven, 1940), pp. 46–70.

ical passivity of the jobless. Lazarsfeld and a Polish sociologist studied them carefully; they remarked on the "inert" aggressiveness displayed in these accounts. The authors frequently manifested their rage and a desire for revenge, but often directed these feelings at their fellow sufferers, that is, at themselves. Of the fifty-seven published accounts, only two blamed the capitalist system for unemployment, only four could reasonably be described as expressing revolutionary attitudes. "The unemployed," the sociologists concluded, were "scattered, loose, perplexed and hopeless . . . *a mass only numerically, not socially.*"[30]

Among other similar observations, Edwin H. Sutherland and Harvey J. Locke, describing the residents of Chicago shelters, wrote: "While the men applaud anyone who makes a radical statement, they are generally indifferent to such radical programs as communism and fascism." Most of them insisted that all politicians were crooked and cynically sold their own votes on election day to the higher bidder, Democratic or Republican. When young Lauren Gilfillan, full of sympathy for the downtrodden, went to live among the poverty-stricken striking coal miners of western Pennsylvania in the early thirties, she discovered many Communists among them. But she portrayed the majority of the miners as anything but radical. "Oh, to hell with communism!" one of her new friends, himself an official of the Young Communist League, told her. "They're a lot of stupid lummoxes. Real miners ain't communists." In his autobiography, *There Was a Time*, Walter Greenwood described a conversation at a Labour party headquarters during the period before he wrote his best-seller, *Love on the Dole*, a time when he was himself unemployed. He was talking to a militant friend, one James Moleyns, when two other unemployed men came in. One of the newcomers announced angrily that he was "Fed up. Fed up to the blooming teeth." His unemployment benefits had expired and a former friend, now a successful businessman, had refused him even a temporary job as a laborer, which would have enabled him after an interval to collect insurance again. The cynical Moleyns urged him to try to get a doctor to declare him eligible for sick benefits, then added: "What the Government ought to do is freeze us solid, shove us in cold storage and bring us out when they need us." But the man merely continued to grumble about his faithless friend. "It was," Greenwood recalled, "as though he had not been listening."[31]

[30] Matthew Josephson, *Infidel in the Temple: A Memoir of the Nineteen-Thirties* (New York, 1967), pp. 75–81; James Rorty, *Where Life is Better: An Unsentimental Journey* (New York, 1936), pp. 9–10, 27–28; Bowhan Zawadski and P. F. Lazarsfeld, "The Psychological Consequences of Unemployment," *Journal of Social Psychology*, 6 (1935), 245–49.

[31] Sutherland and Locke, *Homeless Men*, pp. 160–61; Lauren Gilfillan, *I Went to Pit College* (New York, 1934), p. 259; Walter Greenwood, *There was a Time*, (Middlesex, 1969), pp. 150–52.

In 1934 two American political scientists, Gabriel Almond and Harold D. Lasswell, published the results of an ingenious experiment that throws much light on the political responses of the unemployed. They observed large numbers of people on relief who came to the complaints desk of a relief office and evaluated the relative aggressiveness or submissiveness of their behavior in these confrontations with the authorities. They then chose one hundred aggressive and another hundred submissive types and studied their case histories closely. They found, as might have been expected, that those in the aggressive group had displayed more assertiveness and had had more experience in manipulating people in their careers. They also had enjoyed higher standards of living than the submissive subjects. But the whole sample had shown little interest in radical politics; very few of those who behaved aggressively were affiliated with organized protest movements of any kind.[32]

These findings of contemporary investigators are confirmed by the most casual study of broad political trends. Nowhere did the unemployed mount a substantial political movement of their own, nor did any significant number of them join Communist or Fascist parties. In Britain there were roughly 3 million unemployed in 1932–33 but only about 15,000 Communist party members. In the United States the best estimate of unemployment in late 1932 is about 13 million; in the presidential election of that year only 103,000 persons voted the Communist ticket and only 882,000 the Socialist. (In 1912, when the electorate was only about one-third as large, over 900,000 Americans voted Socialist.) Many of the Communist and Socialist voters of 1932, probably a large majority of them, were not unemployed.

After the successful strikes of 1936 in France the Communist party made large gains, but most of the recruits were *working* men. The French unemployed, according to one recent student, behaved somewhat like the typical French *fonctionnaire*, tending to rely on the established authorities to take care of them.[33] Even in Germany, where the economic and social disintegration of the early 1930s favored extremist political movements, few of the unemployed were political activists. The Nazis strove mightily to recruit them, almost totally without success. By the fall of 1932 the jobless made up about 80 percent of the German Communist party, but the party had only 330,000 members, a small fraction of Germany's 6 million unemployed. Many more unemployed Germans voted Communist, whereas the British jobless remained loyal to the Labour party and the American unemployed

[32] Gabriel Almond and H. D. Lasswell, "Aggressive Behavior of Clients toward Public Relief Administrators," *American Political Science Review*, 40 (1934), 643–55.
[33] Annie Kriegel, *The French Communists: Profile of a People* (Chicago, 1972), pp. 75–77.

supported Franklin Roosevelt's New Deal. Political apathy did not apparently extend to total withdrawal from the political process, nor did it prevent the unemployed from voting their interests as they saw them. But they nowhere became an effective pressure group or an independent political force. Political activism was incompatible with joblessness. Insecurity caused the unemployed to be fearful and dependent. Fear and dependence eroded their confidence and destroyed hope. Lack of confidence and hopelessness undermined their expectations. Typically, when workers lost their jobs they had not suffered enough to become rebels. By the time they had suffered they had lost the capacity for militant protest.

10

The Great Depression: Responses

The depression which swept across the world in the 1930s may be compared to a blight or plague: it struck swiftly and without warning and caused much misery and suffering. Eventually it spread its poisons into every aspect of human existence—into politics, into social organization and culture, even into man's conception of himself. The most obvious symptoms of this plague were three: a massive decline of monetary values, the shrinking of demand and therefore of production, and unemployment on a scale never before experienced. Of these the most intellectually challenging was the first, because most clearly within the capacity of governments to eradicate if only they could find the proper medicine. The most baffling and frustrating was the decline of demand, for it created the paradox of poverty admidst plenty, of breadlines coexistent with overflowing granaries and children in tatters while shelves bulged with goods. But the most tragic was unemployment, product of the others both in the sense "result" and in the sense that it reflected a multiplication of the stifling evils of the times.

Unemployment was in moral terms also the most unjust aspect of the depression because it concentrated economic losses that if even roughly shared would have been far more easily borne. Although the output of goods declined sharply over a period of many years, there were never any real shortages and the economic machinery never ground to a halt. There were idle factories and abandoned farms, but even in the nations most profoundly affected the large majority of the people remained at work and able to support themselves. Put differently, in 1936 (when the depression was wrongly believed to be over), Wladimir S. Woytinsky, an economist working for the International Labor Office, estimated the total economic losses of the period 1930–1934 as roughly equal to the cost of the Great War of 1914–18, between 100 billion and 120 billion 1913 American dollars, a heavy price but not beyond the resources of a world population of perhaps 2 billion persons.[1]

But of course the losses were not equally shared. The metaphor of a plague is again apt. The depression seemed to choose its victims blindly, crushing this person and sparing his neighbor without apparent reason. Few could feel safe while it raged and therefore it struck fear in nearly every heart, but those seriously touched remained a minority.

Workers in some industries were harder hit than others. In general those producing durable goods, such as machinery, clothing, and housing, suffered more severely than those in food processing, utilities, and public service. Regional variations were also enormous, a celebrated example being the invisible but very real separation that split Great Britain into a relatively prosperous south and east and an economically devastated west and north. Younger workers were more afflicted than older ones, although those beyond early middle age, if they lost their jobs, found it most difficult to find new ones. Groups with low social status, such as blacks in the United States and foreign workers almost everywhere, were far more likely to be unemployed than others. On the other hand, those whose wages were traditionally depressed—women being the most notorious example—were somewhat less likely to be unemployed, other conditions being equal.

It is also true that many workers benefited from the depression because prices were falling faster than their wages, especially between 1930 and 1933. How many workers were in this fortunate position is impossible to say because statistics on part-time unemployment in the 1930s are almost nonexistent. Certainly short-time work was very common and in such cases the reduction in time worked often overbalanced the increase in real hourly wages. Even so, it seems likely that more than half the world's wage earners actually improved their standard of living, at least during the early thirties when the economic downturn was at its worst. Therefore, the depression separated the interests of workers and the unemployed and to some extent put them in conflict. Those with jobs were like diners eating a hearty meal in the window of a restaurant while outside a hungry crowd stared at them silently; they were painfully conscious that many unemployed persons were eager to take their places.

How deeply this awareness influenced particular workers would be difficult to determine, but it is possible to generalize at least about the attitude of organized workers toward the unemployed, during the

[1] J. A. Garraty, "Unemployment during the Great Depression," *Labor History*, 17 (1976), 133–34.

Great Depression and in earlier times as well. Although medieval guilds were as much organizations of capitalists as laborers, in their artisanal aspects they were prototypes of modern unions. Their history throws light on how workers look at other workers, especially potential ones. A statute of a French cobblers' guild stated the common attitude in the plainest words possible: "If our good king whom God protects would like his son admitted to this trade, it could not be done unless he first served three years' apprenticeship or married the daughter of a master." Another type of example is offered by the experience of Mayor Edward Livingston of New York in 1803, a period of bad times. Livingston proposed that the local Mechanics Society join with the city in setting up public workshops where the unemployed could make hats, shoes, and other goods. He asked craftsmen to hire and train extra helpers, whose wages would be paid by the city, and to manage the proposed workshops. The society turned down his plan on the grounds that it would "discourage" their current apprentices and drive down wages. When Livingston tried to go ahead without it, the society staged protests—the scheme would "destroy the freedom and independence of honest, frugal, and industrious workmen." The resistance of British artisans to the repeal of the Elizabethan Statute of Artificers in 1814 is still another illustration of this exclusionism; some sixty thousand London workers protested to Parliament at that time, arguing that they had a right to "the . . . exclusive use and enjoyment of their . . . arts and trades."[2]

In the nineteenth century, when organized workers faced a falling demand for their labor during depressions, they usually preferred to see some of their number discharged rather than to share the loss by having all work for lower wages. This was the pattern despite the reasoning of the classical economists that the opposite situation should prevail. There were exceptions, but apparently not very many. While he was making his study of French textile workers in the late 1830s, Louis René Villermé came across stories in the Paris newspapers of a group of machinists who, when their employer had announced that he must lay off all but a few veteran workers, had persuaded him to keep them all on at reduced wages instead. Villermé checked into the matter and discovered that the newspaper accounts were correct. But both the attention paid the incident by the press and Villermé's originally skeptical reaction suggest that such cases were rare. When the old French craft organizations, the *compagnonnages*, were revived after the Napoleonic period, they displayed the same

[2] Emile Coornaert, *Les corporations en France avant 1789* (Paris, 1968), p. 193; R. A. Mohl, *Poverty in New York: 1783–1825* (New York, 1971), pp. 116–36; E. P. Thompson, *The Making of the English Working Class* (New York, 1963), pp. 252–53.

anti-foreign attitudes as had their medieval predecessors.[3]

In the 1930s the union movement was more broadly based than in the nineteenth century and many unions were politically and socially quite radical. Union officials everywhere claimed to be deeply concerned about the fate of the jobless and there is no reason to doubt their sincerity. However, the fact remains that their first concern was nearly always for their own constituents. Since unemployed members tended to drop out of unions—and because of the conflict of interests between workers and the unemployed—this meant that unions reflected the attitudes of those with jobs. With only a handful of exceptions unions rejected work sharing as a means of coping with unemployment. Unions in the capitalist countries would have employed less blunt language, but they would not have disagreed with the position of the Soviet labor newspaper *Trud,* which declared in 1925:

> Unions fight for . . . the employment of those who are already organized. . . . Unemployed who are not union members will not agree with us on this issue because they want to get jobs. . . . Yet it must be stressed again that the unions will not and cannot undertake to protect all those who are not working.[4]

The major European unions, although rhetorically supportive of radical change, offered few constructive suggestions about creating more jobs. Most paid lip service to the idea of expanding public-works programs, but until late in the depression tacitly accepted the prevailing conservative dogma that public works must be financed without unbalancing national budgets, which drastically limited their extent. Beyond this, union proposals for dealing with unemployment were primarily self-protective. They advocated raising the school-leaving age, forcing married women out of the labor market, and instituting early retirement schemes—all measures that would reduce "unemployment" only by redefining the term—and they sought to "export" the problem, directly by calling for the repatriation of foreign workers, indirectly by advocating high protective tariffs and mounting campaigns urging consumers not to buy foreign-made goods. The faction-ridden French unions, for example, favored all these devices—some leaders even argued that unemployment could be reduced by birth control—and they stubbornly opposed efforts to rationalize antiquated French industry, insisting that mechanization would lead to wage cuts and reduce the number of jobs. But the relatively enlight-

[3] L. R. Villermé, *Tableau de l'état physique et moral des ouvriers* (Paris, 1840), II: 71n.; D. Roche, ed., *Ordres et classes* (Paris, 1973), p. 235.

[4] Garraty, "Unemployment," p. 135; S. M. Schwarz, *Labor in the Soviet Union* (New York, 1952), pp. 41–42.

ened Norwegian unions, which in the early years of the depression had sought to ration work among as many people as possible and which later supported a "pro-production" policy aimed at increasing the number of jobs, also launched a "Buy Norwegian Goods" campaign and tried to force married women out of the labor market.[5]

Organizations of those on the upper rungs of the vocational ladder, the professionals, were no different from the assembly-line workers and craftsmen in the unions. They used every means at their command to protect themselves, without regard for unemployed colleagues, present or future, domestic or foreign. In most countries doctors, lawyers, teachers, and other professionals sought to restrict entry into the universities, to stiffen examinations, to discriminate against women, especially married women, and to obtain stronger legal protections for professional titles of all sorts. Whereas before the depression most nations had merely required proof of competence before allowing foreigners to practice a profession in their territory, after its outbreak most strove to keep foreigners out. In France, previously most liberal in its attitude toward foreign professionals, laws were passed making it almost impossible for a foreigner to study medicine in the country and requiring that foreign doctors, even after becoming naturalized citizens, could not practice until they had performed military service or endured a five-year waiting period. A law of 1934 prohibited foreign lawyers from practicing in France until ten years after naturalization. The resistance of American professional groups to the admission of German-Jewish refugees after 1933 is another example of this attitude.[6]

Nearly all trade unions advocated government relief for the unemployed. They also favored unemployment insurance and in most instances were prepared to back systems involving worker contributions to insurance funds. But union support for both insurance and outright relief was not unqualified. The British Trade Union Congress fought hard, even when the Labour party was in power, against efforts to stiffen the requirements for obtaining public assistance and to reduce the amounts paid, but it is important to note that the dole (which was financed by general taxation) benefited unions by freeing them (and their employers) from responsibility for supporting their discharged

[5] R. Dufraisse, "Le mouvement ouvrier 'rouge' devant la grande dépression économique de 1929 à 1933," Denise Fauvel-Rouif, ed., *Mouvements ouvriers et dépression économique de 1929 à 1939* (Assen, 1966), pp. 168, 173, 176–82, 185–87; Alfred Sauvy, *Histoire économique de la France entre les deux guerres* (Paris, 1972), III: 186–87; E. Bull, "The Norwegian Labour Movement," *Mouvements ouvriers*, pp. 246–49.

[6] W. H. Kotschnig, *Unemployment in the Learned Professions* (London, 1937), pp. 179–90, 223–31, 243–45; "Remedies for Unemployment among Professional Workers," *International Labour Review*, 33 (1936), 310–20.

fellows out of the unemployment-insurance fund. It also reduced job competition that might have further depressed wages. The unions, in other words, implicitly accepted high unemployment as the price to be paid for maintaining the wage levels of persons with jobs. With the cost of living falling faster than wages, they became, in the words of historian Robert Skidelsky, "more interested in increasing the rate of unemployment benefit than in increasing employment." British craft unions tightened already strict controls on the admission of apprentices and even objected when the sponsors of clubs for the unemployed tried to help idle workers to keep themselves occupied and earn a few shillings by tailoring, carpentry, and other handicraft work. The steelworkers' union refused to cooperate with labor-sharing proposals intended to spread available work among more men even though, since steelworkers were paid on a tonnage basis and output per worker in the industry was rising, their earnings were increasing.[7]

Of all the major labor organizations, the German Labor Federation (Allgemeiner Deutscher Gewerkschaftsbund) had by far the most enlightened attitude toward the unemployment problem. Its leaders included a number of excellent economists, most notably Wladimir S. Woytinsky, who was director of research for the federation from 1929 to 1933; Fritz Baade, an agricultural marketing expert; and Fritz Tarnow of the carpenters' union, who was also a member of the Reichstag. Even in the 1920s the federation was urging policies aimed at increasing consumer demand, Tarnow arguing in *Why Be Poor?* (*Warum arm sein?*, 1929) that greater purchasing power would mean more jobs. Although socialists by conviction, these men were prepared to work within the capitalist system; they saw unemployment insurance as an entering wedge, "a step forward on the road to socialism." The tragic result of their insights, however, was that when mounting unemployment put the insurance fund deep in the red in 1930 they rejected a compromise that involved only a possible future reduction of unemployment benefits, even though rejection meant the certain fall of the pro-labor Socialist government. The fall of the government led to new elections which made the Nazis a power in the Reichstag and also to the very reduction of insurance benefits that the unions had hoped to avoid.

German labor was not, of course, responsible for Hitler's rise. Moreover, Woytinsky, Tarnow, and Baade went on to develop the so-called W-T-B Plan for stimulating consumption by inflating the currency,

---

[7] Robert Skidelsky, *Politicians and the Slump: The Labour Government of 1929–1931* (London, 1970), pp. 23, 61–63, 142–52, 293–301, 351–52, 433; W. C. Balfour, "British Labour from the Great Depression to the Second World War," *Mouvements ouvriers*, pp. 237, 247.

which the unions finally endorsed in 1932. But union intransigence in 1930 was surely a mistake, and also not unrelated to the conviction of union economists that maintaining the level of insurance benefits would help maintain the level of wages. The tragedy was compounded by the fact that after 1930 the unemployed tended to desert the Socialist party for the Communists. Indeed, according to Woytinsky, the president of the Socialist party, Otto Wells, opposed the W-T-B Plan on the ground that the party's first obligation was to the *employed*. Since so many unemployed voters were supporting the Communists and the Nazis, Wells said, let those parties look after their interests.[8]

In the mid-thirties the French labor federation (Confédération Générale du Travail) flirted with a number of rather imprecise "plans" for stimulating production, based on the Belgian Henri de Man's concept of a "mixed economy," one in which the state would control credit and nationalize certain key industries. In 1934 the CGT set up a bureau of economic studies to develop proposals. But the *planistes,* who included Georges Lefranc, secretary of the Institut Supérieur Ouvrier, Lucien Laurat, a prominent follower of de Man, and the economists Etienne Antonelli of the University of Lyons and François Simiand of the Conservatoire des Arts et Métiers in Paris, never attracted mass support for their ideas. They were also resisted by doctrinaire socialists ("before any plan, first . . . the total conquest of power by socialism") and other groups in the labor movement. In 1936, after the reunification of the Communist and non-Communist labor organizations, the CGT finally approved a plan on the de Man model that also called for large-scale public-works expenditures, but in the excitement following the political triumph of the Popular Front and the resulting wave of strikes the scheme was forgotten.[9]

As for the Communist-controlled unions, they expressed particular sympathy for the unemployed as the ultimate victims of capitalism, but preferred to wait for what they saw as the approaching collapse of the system before trying to do anything about the job shortage. Commu-

---

[8] Ursula Hüllsbüsch, "Die deutschen Gewerkschaften in der Weltwirtschaftskrise," Werne Conze and Hans Raupach, eds., *Die Staats- und Wirschaftskrise des deutschen Reichs 1929/33* (Stuttgart, 1967), pp. 136–40; Helga Timm, *Die deutsche Sozialpolitik und der Bruch der Grossen Koalition im März 1930* (Dusseldorf, 1952), pp. 128–29; Fritz Baade, "Fighting Depression in Germany," E. S. Woytinsky, ed., *So Much Alive: The Life and Work of Wladimir S. Woytinsky* (New York, 1962), pp. 162–68; W. S. Woytinsky, *Stormy Passage: A Personal History* (New York, 1961), p. 469.

[9] V. R. Lorwin, *The French Labor Movement* (Cambridge, Mass., 1954), pp. 71–72; Georges Lefranc, "Le courant planiste dans le mouvement ouvrier français de 1933 à 1936," *Le mouvement social,* 44 (1966), 69–89; Leon Jouhaux, *La C. G. T.: ce qu'lle est, ce qu'elle veut* (Paris, 1937), pp. 169–87; Michel Collinet, "Masses et militants: la bureaucratie et la crise actuelle de syndicalisme ouvrier français," *Revue d'histoire économique et sociale,* 29 (1951), 70.

nists (at least until 1934 after the Nazi seizure of power in Germany had caused a change in tactics) saw unions as mere agents of the party, designed to make workers class conscious and prepare them for the revolution; to concentrate on improving wages or working conditions would only delay the revolution by mitigating the evils of capitalism. The attitude of the French Confédération Générale du Travail Unitaire was typical: it opposed unemployment insurance based on worker and employer contributions on the ground that wages were too low to support the payments. "Social insurance is a *right* of the worker. The *bourgeoisie*, as the privileged class, should pay the cost."[10]

Communist labor leaders did try to play upon the dissatisfactions of the unemployed. In France they organized regional Committees of Unemployed and published irregularly a paper, *Le Cri des Chômeurs*. Especially in Great Britain and the United States, they attempted to organize the jobless to demand relief. In America the Communist Trade Union Unity League created a network of Unemployed Councils and announced an International Day for Struggle Against Worldwide Unemployment (March 6, 1930). Well-attended protest meetings, some leading to violence, were held in most large cities in the United States, and for a time the councils attracted many recruits. But the leadership soon diverted the movement to "abstract issues the jobless did not understand" and membership rapidly declined. Both the TUUL and the Unemployed Councils continued to exist and to support demonstrations by the unemployed, such as the Ford Hunger March of 1932, bloodily repressed by the Dearborn police and Ford company guards. But both organizations were essentially political groups, not labor unions, and had little effect on the attitudes of the unemployed. Similarly, the Unemployed Citizens' Leagues organized by A. J. Muste in 1932 attracted substantial support among the jobless of Ohio and Pennsylvania by working to improve relief programs and by organizing self-help projects. But the leagues were gradually politicized and consequently had little appeal to unemployed workers. Muste began to complain that the unemployed were "devoted to mere self-preservation," and by late 1934 he and other leaders had moved into the Workers Party, a Trotskyite group interested in the jobless only as "shock troops" for the revolution.[11]

[10] Antoine Prost, *La C. G. T. à l'époque du Front Populaire: 1934–1939* (Paris, 1964), pp. 123–30; Georges Lefranc, *Le mouvement syndical sous la troisième république* (Paris, 1967), p. 275.

[11] Police Reports to Minister of Labour, Jan. 13, 15, 1934, Archives Nationales, F⁷ (13562); D.J. Leab, " 'United We Eat': The Creation and Organization of the Unemployment Councils in 1930," *Labor History*, 8 (1967), 300–15; Roy Rosenzweig, "Radicals and the Jobless: the Musteites and the Unemployed Leagues, 1932–1936," *ibid.*, 16 (1975), 52–77.

The British National Unemployed Workers' Movement was a far more formidable phenomenon. It had a much larger influence among the unemployed, and its hunger marches and demonstrations against cuts in the dole attracted wide middle-class sympathy. It undoubtedly helped the jobless call attention to their suffering. But its Communist affiliations made it anathema to the trade unions that represented the bulk of British labor. Moreover, the NUWM had little to say about getting rid of unemployment. It concentrated on obtaining more government relief for those out of work; about all it could suggest for "reducing" unemployment were the conventional proposals for redefining it out of existence by keeping young people in school and retiring older workers early.[12]

The extent and persistence of unemployment during the Great Depression put pressure on economists to find ways of reducing it; consequently the volume of theorizing on the subject far exceeded that of any earlier period. The richness and variety of this literature makes generalization difficult.

Those who might perhaps still be called the classical economists focused on trying to explain why the automatic, balancing adjustments of the free market had not brought the depression to an end—and what might be done about it. The English theorist Pigou made the most elaborate effort; his *Theory of Unemployment* (1933) was one of the few works in the classical tradition that focused on the subject. In a system of completely free competition, Pigou wrote, wage rates would be so related to the demand for labor that everyone would be employed. In the real world, where the actions and policies of employers, labor unions, and governments restricted competition, this did not happen.

Pigou's conclusions were therefore quite different from those of his intellectual forebears. Reducing real wages would indeed lead to an increase in employment. But not merely by spreading a supposed wages fund among more people; the cuts would cause the total purchasing power of society to increase, because the cost of goods would go down along with wages and (Pigou's chief point) the incomes of the rest of society—doctors, lawyers, entrepreneurs, and so on—would not be directly affected by the wage cuts. Pigou thus directed the force of his argument at justifying deflation—for example, he claimed that if labor unions succeeded in maintaining wage rates during a period of declining prices the result would be to *reduce* unemployment: with

[12] Wal Hannington, *Unemployed Struggles: 1919–1936* (London, 1936), pp. 202–3, 232–33, 288; Noreen Branson and Margot Heinemann, *Britain in the 1930's* (London, 1971), pp. 28–32, 87, 90.

real wages rising, workers would consume more and would thus stimulate production and create more jobs. Why, after the protracted period of deflation that preceded the publication of *The Theory of Unemployment*, so many persons were still out of work did not, however, occupy much space in Pigou's book. At one point he suggested almost casually that the depression had been caused "by a general breakdown of confidence, whose origins are largely political," scarcely an enlightening statement.[13]

Pigou was never much of a stylist and his *Theory of Unemployment* is not the easiest of his works to follow. The reasoning of Lionel Robbins, a young economist at the London School of Economics who had assisted Beveridge in the 1930 revision of *Unemployment: A Problem of Industry*, was more accessible and also more typical of the classical approach.

In *The Great Depression* (1934) Robbins bestowed responsibility for the depression with magnificent impartiality upon employers, unions, and politicians. By entering into agreements to maintain prices, corporations were stifling demand. By fighting necessary wage reductions, unions were preventing manufacturers from making profits, thus from expanding output. By aiding shaky private enterprises, political leaders were preventing bankruptcies that would clear glutted markets, and by enacting tariffs and quotas and by manipulating the exchange value of their currencies, they were hampering essential international trade. Collectively they had destroyed the flexibility of the free-market economy, and their efforts to restore prosperity were only making the situation worse. To end the depression "property must be left to stand on its own legs."

Robbins was not insensitive to the sufferings that the depression had caused among the unemployed, and he confessed to a "natural reluctance" to suggest that anyone should have to get along with less than he already had. Nevertheless, he insisted that "the violence of the present depression and the magnitude of the unemployment" could have been avoided if wage rates had been allowed to fall when the depression first struck. "A policy which holds wage rates rigid when the equilibrium rate has altered, is a policy which creates unemployment." Labor unions were useful and socially desirable institutions, but they should "be guided by considerations of employment," not by the idea of maintaining wage rates; like corporations, they should get no state support.

As for governments, they ought to stop trying to "bite off more than they can chew." The practice of "intervening to prop up unsound

[13] A. C. Pigou, *The Theory of Unemployment* (London, 1933), pp. 252, 101–102, 236–37.

positions . . . must cease." Since the depression was an international phenomenon, the proper policy of every state should be to cooperate with other nations in seeking solutions to economic problems; maintaining free trade and the international gold standard were essential if self-adjusting free-market forces were to reassert themselves.[14]

Robbins's views were echoed by traditionalists in other countries. In France, the political philosopher Bertrand de Jouvenel wrote: "[The state] can neither know, nor want, nor do." French critics of government intervention spoke sneeringly of "Colbertisme," a return to discredited mercantilistic ideas. In 1931 Jacques Rueff, professor of economics at the Sorbonne and an unwavering foe of all forms of meddling with "natural" economic forces, published an article entitled "Unemployment Insurance: Cause of Unemployment" in the *Revue d'économique politique.* Insurance caused unemployment, Rueff insisted, by preventing wages from falling to a level at which everyone could find work. "At each moment," he wrote, his reasoning more typical of the thinking of 1831 than 1931, "the whole population is assured of finding work, but at a wage determined by the market. There can be no permanent unemployment unless one fixes a minimum wage higher than the level that would be established spontaneously."[15] In 1932 the Swiss economist Felix Somary described the tendency of governments to prop up failing enterprises as a "hopeless effort to bring cadavers back to life," and the German banker Hans Luther denounced as inflationary a proposal for putting 600,000 jobless people to work. The German economy was in a terrible state, Luther admitted, but if the recommendations of the advocates of make-work schemes had been adopted, conditions would be far worse.

As these examples suggest, most French and German academic economists remained as wedded to classical theory as Lionel Robbins: state intervention would stifle initiative, and in any case the task was too complicated for any organization to manage efficiently. Essentially they believed that the way to restore prosperity and thus to reduce unemployment was to enable producers to make profits, and that the way to make production profitable was to reduce the cost of labor. "Persistent mass unemployment," wrote the Austrian economist Ludwig von Mises, "is an unavoidable result of the effort to keep wages above the level they would find in the free market." Their proposals

[14] Lionel Robbins, *The Great Depression* (London, 1934), pp. 60–75, 186–90, 193, 160–72.

[15] Gaëtan Pirou, *La crise du capitalisme* (Paris, 1936), pp. 77–79; Henri Hatzfeld, *Du paupérisme à la sécurité sociale: 1850–1940* (Paris, 1971), pp. 48–50; Jacques Rueff, "L'assurance-chômage, cause du chômage permanent," *Revue d'économie politique,* 45(1931), 222 ff.

thus required further deflation, although by early 1933 prices had been falling for over three years.[16]

The counterargument of their critics was inflationary, although not always so stated. The more sophisticated of these critics called for dealing with unemployment by trying to stimulate consumption rather than production. If consumption could be increased, demand would come into balance with supply. Business profitability could then be restored by raising the prices of goods rather than by lowering the costs of making them. This was the argument that John A. Hobson had made in the 1890s, and which he continued to make thereafter. (In *The Economics of Unemployment,* published in 1922, Hobson claimed that the Great War had proved "the power of high consumption to maintain production" and that the way to prevent unemployment was to strengthen "the consuming powers of the community" by enacting progressive income taxes and increasing public spending. In his autobiography, published in 1938, he was still insisting that "the failure of consumer markets . . . to keep pace with the increase of producing power" was the cause of "depression and unemployment.") But Hobson did little to develop his position beyond where it had been in the 1890s and he remained, in his own words, "an economic heretic."[17]

Others, however, carried the consumptionist argument further. During the 1920s, two Americans, William Trufant Foster and Waddill Catchings, attracted considerable attention with what were essentially Hobsonian ideas. Neither Foster nor Catchings was trained in economics—Foster had an M.A. in English and a doctorate in education, Catchings was a wealthy lawyer and businessman—but although they were sometimes accused of oversimplifying complex ideas, their work received sympathetic attention from many economists. They agreed with Hobson that adequate consumption was the key to full employment, but stressed the importance of keeping production and consumption in balance. "If business paid back to consumers all the money it received from consumers, and consumers spent all the money," there would be no business cycles. Often industry did not do this because of what Foster and Catchings called "the Dilemma of Thrift." "Both corporations and individuals must save; yet if they do save, they cause a shortage of consumer buying." The main problem, however, was not the failure of consumption to keep up with output directly, but the lack of coordination between saving and investment. Savers and investors were not always the same people. Sums deposited

---

[16] Wilhelm Grottkopp, *Die grosse Krise: Lehren aus der Überwindung der Wirtschaftskrise 1929–32* (Dusseldorf, 1954), pp. 28, 49; Alfred Sauvy, *Histoire économique,* II: 347–48.

[17] J. A. Hobson, *The Economics of Unemployment* (London, 1922), pp. 6, 50, 81; Hobson, *Confessions of an Economic Heretic* (New York, 1938), p. 193.

in banks might earn interest without being productively employed—
"the fact that somebody *may* borrow the money . . . is immaterial as
long as nobody does borrow it."[18]

The way to achieve the necessary balance between saving and investment was through careful management of government spending—that
is, through fiscal policy. In *The Road to Plenty* (1928), Foster and Catchings' most widely read book,[19] they described how a new federal board
might collect data on the state of the economy and regulate government spending, particularly on public works, in accord with current
business conditions:

> Our Plan calls for a separate Federal Board, which shall itself gather and
> measure the data best adopted to show the adequacy of the flow of consumer
> income. . . . Having thus collected the needed information, the Board
> . . . shall determine when certain expenditures are to be made, which already
> have been provided for by Congress, under a policy of long-range planning
> of public works.

By thus regulating the timing of spending on roads, parks, rivers and
harbors, and other public construction projects, consumption could be
stimulated in an orderly manner in bad times. "Public works built in
this way might actually cost the country nothing; for if they were not
built, the country might lose more than they cost, through the idleness
of men and capital savings." Foster and Catchings were offering a
variation on the concept of countercyclical public works, certainly not
an original idea, but the coming of the Great Depression so soon after
the publication of *The Road to Plenty* added to their influence.[20]

John Maynard Keynes pushed the analysis forward in 1930 with *A
Treatise on Money*. Like Hobson, Keynes insisted in this work that thrift
was not always a virtue, but his crucial distinction was not between
saving and consuming but between saving and investment, between
thrift and enterprise. His central point, one made independently by the
Swedish economist Knut Wicksell, as well as by Foster and Catchings,
was that savers and investors were often not the same people and that
they seldom coordinated their activities. "Thrift may be the handmaid
and nurse of Enterprise. But equally she may not. And, perhaps, even
usually she is not."

[18] W. T. Foster and Waddill Catchings, *The Road to Plenty* (Boston, 1928), pp. 77,
158n., 159; A. H. Gleason, "Foster and Catchings: A Reappraisal," *Journal of Political
Economy*, 67 (1959), 156–72.

[19] The book described a fictional train trip during which a group of preternaturally
articulate, intelligent, and open-minded people of widely varying backgrounds discuss
economic problems.

[20] Foster and Catchings, *Road to Plenty*, p. 192; Joseph Dorfman, *The Economic Mind
in American Civilization* (New York, 1959), IV: 347–51.

Saving could exceed investment but investment could also exceed saving; in the former instance prices and output would decline and unemployment would increase, in the latter inflation and economic expansion would occur. The task of sound economic policy was to maintain price stability by keeping saving and investment as nearly in balance as possible, or perhaps to push investment slightly in advance of saving—a little inflation, Keynes suggested, would generate optimism and thus encourage expansion and innovation. Keynes was as clear about the choice between inflation and deflation as in his earlier work; he feared oversaving more than overinvestment. "If Enterprise is afoot," he wrote, "wealth accumulates whatever may be happening to Thrift; and if Enterprise is asleep, wealth decays whatever Thrift may be doing."[21]

Large government investments in public works would thus help balance saving and investment during depressions as well as stimulate consumption by putting money in the hands of previously idle workers employed on such projects. Keynes was only one of many economists urging this approach, for with unemployment so high in the industrial nations, it seemed, in the phrase of the American economist Paul H. Douglas, "good national housekeeping" to stimulate the economy by putting the jobless to work. In 1931, Richard Kahn's article on the multiplier effect of public works, which described how "money paid out by the Government to the builders of roads continues to be passed on from hand to hand," the expenditures producing "secondary" as well as "primary" employment, added to the force of this argument.[22]

According to Kahn, if the British government were to borrow £50 million and spend it on building and repairing roads, 250,000 jobs would be created directly. But when these workers and the suppliers of materials used in the construction spent the £50 million, they would cause other producers to expand output and, of necessity, to hire more workers; Kahn's equations indicated that another 150,000 or more people would find employment before the secondary effects had run their course.[23] The cost to the state would be much less than £50 million because the new workers would no longer need the support of the dole and because the additional economic activity would increase the government's income from taxes. The multiplier, Kahn added, worked most efficiently in a "closed system"—if Britain alone adopted

[21] R. F. Harrod, *The Life of John Maynard Keynes* (New York, 1971), p. 470.

[22] P. H. Douglas, *Controlling Depressions* (New York, 1935), p. 123; R. F. Kahn, "The Relation of Home Investment to Unemployment," *Economic Journal*, 41 (1931), p. 189.

[23] Theoretically, if the new workers had been previously without resources and if they and their employers spent all the £50 million on consumer goods, "the ratio of secondary to primary employment would be infinite" and "one man put to work on the roads would then place all the remainder of the unemployed into secondary employment."

the technique part of the benefit would go to foreign countries because some of the new expenditures would be devoted to imports. "The more a country approximates to a closed . . . system the greater the ratio of secondary to primary employment." The United States, with a more self-contained economy, could profit from public works more readily than Britain. But by controlling foreign investments and placing tariffs on imports any nation could increase the secondary benefits. The particular beauty of the multiplier, according to Kahn, was that it functioned best when it was most needed.

> At normal times, when productive resources are fully employed . . . the building of roads carries with it little secondary employment and causes a large rise in prices. But at times of intense depression . . . the amount of secondary employment is then large and the rise in prices is small. . . . The greater the depth of the depression, the greater is the expansion of employment. . . . If there is ever any justification for expenditure on "public works" as a means of reducing unemployment, the justification is greatest when depression is most severe.[24]

The concept of the multiplier was easy enough to understand, but for many persons in responsible positions difficult to believe. Kahn's mathematics might appear to refute, say, Sir William Petty's seventeenth-century statement, "a hundred pound passing a hundred hands for Wages, causes 10000 l. worth of Commodities to be produced," but Petty's seemed a sounder principle on which to base public policy. Then there was the stumbling block of trying to create work by borrowing. By insisting that public-works programs would not cause inflation, Kahn was trying to counter the arguments of those who believed that governments should reduce their expenditures and balance their budgets in hard times. The fear of inflation remained both widespread and in many quarters profound. That Germans remembered the disaster of 1922–23 with alarm was understandable. Writing of that time in his autobiography, the banker Hjalmar Schacht used words like "political outlawry," "loss of capital," "ruin," "corruption," "child mortality," and "crime." But many Frenchmen apparently found the "memory" of the inflation caused by the printing of assignats at the time of the French Revolution equally vivid—one modern historian speaks of "an almost sentimental attachment to the stability of money," although the franc, far from being stable, was in fact rising in value as the depression deepened. And even in the United States, where the postwar inflation had been comparatively modest, many economists tended to dismiss out of hand policies that might erode the value of

[24] Kahn, "Home Investment," pp. 189–91, 184, 196–97, 182.

the dollar. The labor economist Leo Wolman, speaking on the unemployment problem at a meeting of the American Academy for the Advancement of Science in 1932, rejected "the proposal to borrow heavily for public improvements" with the to him definitive statement: "Increases in public spending are essentially of an inflationary character."[25]

Nevertheless, even in Germany, some economists were moving in the direction Kahn and his mentor Keynes were pointing. By the early 1930s a group gathered around Institut für Konjunkturforschung (Institute for Business Cycle Research) were advocating make-work programs and measures to increase consumer purchasing power. The Institut studied economic trends from the perspective of the American business-cycle economist Wesley Clair Mitchell. Although founded only in 1925, by the early 1930s it was world famous as a center for the collection and analysis of statistics. But its generally pessimistic forecasts prejudiced the German government and most German business interests against it, and academic economists tended to disdain its practical, nontheoretical approach. The Institut was indeed concerned with economic policy (what the Germans call *Wirtschaftspolitik*) rather than theory, and its leaders adopted a manipulative attitude toward the economy. (Since detailed and precise statistical information was essential if the economy was to be managed intelligently, why not manage the economy once the data had been collected?)[26]

Ernst Wagemann, director of the Institut, and others of this group reasoned that if the government had adequate knowledge of economic trends it could apply the proper stimulants at the correct point in the business cycle; thus recovery could be speeded without the risk of inflation. This "active business cycle policy" *(aktive Konjunkturpolitik)* could best be effected through public works; indeed, the approach was essentially a more sophisticated variant of the countercyclical public-works argument. Robert Friedländer-Prechtl, a mining executive, and Heinrich Dräger, a Lübeck manufacturer, were among its leading German advocates. As early as 1931 Friedländer-Prechtl, in his magazine *Die Wirtschafts-Wende* was arguing that "secondary, tertiary, and quaternary waves" of employment would be "set in motion" if the government undertook a massive road-building program. Two billion marks, so invested, would make half a million jobs directly, four million in-

[25] A. I. Monroe, ed., *Early Economic Thought* (Cambridge, Mass., 1951), p. 205; Sauvy, *Histoire économique*, II: 352; Hjalmar Schacht, *My First Seventy-six Years* (London, 1955), p. 163; Maurice Vaïsse, "Le myth de l'or en France," *Revue d'histoire moderne et contemporaine*, 16 (1969), 475; Leo Wolman, "Employment Stabilization through Public Works," C. F. Roos, ed., *The Stabilization of Unemployment* (Bloomington, 1933), p. 90.

[26] C. W. Bullock *et al.*, *Beiträge zur Konjunkturlehre* (Hamburg, 1936), pp. 9–12, 20; Grottkopp, *Grosse Krise*, 12n., 32.

directly. The next year Dräger's *Arbeitsbeschaffung durch produktive Kreditschöpfung* (creating work by creating credit) advocated the expenditure of five billion marks a year on housing, dams, roads, sports facilities, and other public works, the money to come from unsecured long-term low-interest loans by the Reichsbank to the producers of "useful" goods.[27]

Dräger, aware of his countrymen's particular fear of inflation, was prepared to see his proposal implemented by stages, but he insisted that the inflationary effects would be negligible because of the vast amount of unused capacity in the depressed German economy. This reasoning was in accord with Kahn's multiplier theory, although there is no indication in Dräger's book that he knew of Kahn's work. The multiplier concept was, as another of the German "Reformers," Wilhelm Grottkopp, later wrote, "in the air" everywhere by 1931. The German labor unions' W-T-B Plan was drafted in 1931, and in that year in the United States, John Maurice Clark of Columbia University wrote: "If someone employs 100,000 people and pays them wages, they spend the wages, and that money spent employs other men." Also in 1931 the American press lord William Randolph Hearst demanded that the government appropriate some $5 billion for public-works jobs for the unemployed. Hearst's reasoning reflected, albeit crudely, the multiplier concept: borrowing for public works would increase employment; the employment in turn would bring back good times and make possible repayment of the debt.[28]

Keynes effectively summarized the most advanced thinking of his school of thought in the summer of 1931 in a lecture at the University of Chicago, the opposite point of view being presented by Professor Karl Pribram of the University of Frankfurt. When investment is greater than saving, said Keynes, boom conditions prevail and unemployment declines. When savings are greater than investment, the reverse is the case. To reduce the current unemployment, investment should be encouraged by raising prices and lowering interest rates. It was true that there might be difficulties—chiefly psychological in nature. "The dilemma of a rich country," Keynes admitted, was that conditions "make it more and more difficult to find an outlet for our savings." Furthermore, there might be some conflict between restoring the confidence of investors and entrepreneurs and the policy of deliberately holding down long-term interest rates. But this was in essence "a technical banking problem." Low interest was the "vital necessity."

[27] Grottkopp, *Grosse Krise*, p. 124; Heinrich Dräger, *Arbeitsbeschaffung durch produktive Kreditschöpfung* (Dusseldorf, 1932), pp. 44–45, 23–24, 58, 89, 96.

[28] Dräger, *Arbeitsbeschaffung*, p. 49, Grottkopp, *Grosse Krise*, p. 125; Dorfman, *American Mind*, V: 763; W. A. Swanberg, *Citizen Hearst* (New York, 1961), pp. 429–30.

Pribram rejected Keynes's whole argument. Reducing interest rates would not stimulate investment when bad times made the likelihood of earning a profit "problematical." Propping up prices and wages during depressions meant "redistribution of the income of the population to the advantage of the employed workers" rather than of the unemployed. Moreover, the kind of precise prediction of economic trends necessary to manipulate interest rates and other prices intelligently was not possible. Expanding public-works programs in order to stimulate the economy required borrowing money that European nations at least could not conveniently raise. No shortcut to recovery existed. Wages must be allowed to fall. There were excellent moral and practical reasons for trying to help the jobless, but one must not expect large results—the unemployed must face the fact that their period of suffering was not yet over.[29]

The existence of directly conflicting arguments, persuasively advanced by intelligent economists, did not inspire general confidence in any particular approach to the unemployment problem, let alone persuade political leaders to undertake expensive new programs. Yet as time passed and the high unemployment persisted, pressure mounted for some sort of action. In good times and bad, every government employed, in addition to what may be called its regular bureaucrats, a certain amount of labor on construction projects, either directly or through private contractors. As unemployment increased all sought to put additional hands to work. Most administrations, however, were deeply concerned about deficits, and as their incomes shrank during the depression finding money for public works programs became more difficult. No nation accepted the Keynes-Kahn analysis during the thirties, although some found ways of expanding outlays on public-employment projects enormously. Of the industrial powers, the United States and Germany, where unemployment was most acute in the 1930s, developed public-works programs on a large scale; Great Britain and France, on the other hand, made little use of the technique. The pattern in other countries varied—for example, Sweden relied heavily on the device, Belgium very little. Nations as economically and geographically diverse as Uruguay and Poland attacked their unemployment problems with expanded public-employment schemes.[30]

[29] Quincy Wright, ed., *Unemployment as a World Problem* (Chicago, 1931), pp. 21–22, 28–29, 35–42, 125–48.

[30] Marquis Childs, *Sweden: The Middle Way* (New Haven, 1936), pp. 149–57; Bertil Ohlin, "Economic Recovery and Labour Market Problems in Sweden," *International Labour Review*, 31 (1935), 681, 684; Jan Rosner, "Measures to Combat the Depression and Unemployment in Poland," *ibid.*, 30 (1934), 175; C. Charlone, "The Economic and Social Situation of Uruguay," *ibid.*, 33 (1936), 614; Charles Roger, "New Deal for Belgium," *Foreign Affairs*, 13 (1933), 625, 634.

In America President Herbert Hoover expanded federal construction projects as soon as the seriousness of the depression became evident, but cutbacks in state and local projects occasioned by the shrinking of tax revenues greatly lessened the impact of his efforts on the economy. Hoover's policies, moreover, were considered quite reckless by his critics. Franklin Roosevelt's charge during the 1932 presidential campaign that Hoover's was "the greatest spending Administration in peace times in all our history" can be dismissed as political rhetoric, but the supposedly dispassionate and surely intelligent commentator Walter Lippmann denounced Hoover's budget message of December 1931, which, he wrote, "offers the spectacle of the government of the richest country in the world unwilling to economize enough and unwilling to tax enough to balance its accounts." The historian Allan Nevins, another intelligent and well-informed observer, singled out this statement as evidence of Lippmann's insight into the needs of the times. "It will be noted," Nevins wrote in the introduction to a collection of Lippmann's columns published in 1932, "that Mr. Lippmann was insistently calling for a program of budget-balancing as a first and fundamental step toward recovery before any of our political leaders did so."[31]

With between 13 and 16 million people jobless in early 1933, the first New Deal Congress appropriated $3.3 billion for public works, and during the winter of 1933–34 the Civil Works Administration put more than 4 million people to work. President Roosevelt, however, was of two minds about how much the government could safely borrow to finance such programs. (When Keynes during a visit to the White House in 1934 evidently tried to explain the multiplier concept to him, Roosevelt was only confused by what he called Keynes's "rigamarole of figures.") But while New Deal public-works expenditures did not turn the economy around, they did support millions of unemployed workers, and not merely unskilled laborers—imaginative special programs found jobs for many writers, artists, musicians, students, and other classes of workers not directly employed in most government projects. The German effort, begun in 1932 and expanded by the Nazis after their seizure of power, was on a relatively larger scale and succeeded in reducing unemployment more, and more rapidly, than the American. It was accomplished without causing inflation because it was combined with the kind of tough controls possible under a dictatorship, rather than because the Nazis adopted "Keynesian" policies.[32]

[31] Allan Nevins, ed., *Walter Lippmann: Interpretations, 1931–1932* (New York, 1932), pp. 75, viii.

[32] J. A. Garraty, "The New Deal, National Socialism, and the Great Depression," *American Historical Review*, 78 (1973), 909–10.

The British government, despite continuing high unemployment, did not attempt to create work on a large scale; no more than 59,000 persons were ever so employed during the thirties, and in 1937 only 303 men were working on government projects. The well-established unemployment-insurance system, buttressed by the dole (officially known by the euphemism "transitional payments") created a formidable political obstacle for those in favor of work relief in Britain: to compel the unemployed to accept public-service jobs by threatening to cut off the dole resembled the detested work-or-starve practice under the old poor law. The pressure of the "Treasury view" of public works was, of course, a further reason for British inactivity in this field.[33]

Unemployment was less acute in France because so many foreign workers—usually the first to be discharged everywhere—were more or less compelled to return to their homelands. The government did encourage local authorities to expand their public works by paying part of the interest on municipal loans for such projects, but national public works were on a very small scale.

Both French and British politicians hewed to extremely conservative financial policies, budget balancing being an obsession in both countries. "I love the working class," Premier Pierre Laval told the National Assembly in 1932. "I am mayor of a heavy populated Paris suburb and I have seen the ravages of unemployment. . . . The government will never refuse to go as far as the resources of the country will permit. But do not ask it to commit acts that would unbalance the budget." Just about every French and British premier of the decade made similar statements—in 1935 Pierre Etienne Flandin dismissed the idea of public works on budgetary grounds, although by his own admission he was receiving "hundreds of heart-rending letters each day" from unemployed workers. As these examples show, national policies toward work relief were not influenced by the most advanced economic theories of the time nor were these policies closely related to the sympathy of particular administrations toward the jobless.[34]

Except in Germany, where by late 1936 unemployment had been reduced to negligible proportions, and perhaps in Sweden, where a massive public-works program financed by borrowing was instituted in 1933, government job-creation efforts did not succeed in bringing unemployment down to pre-depression levels. Under such circumstances, the search for solutions became increasingly frantic. Almost

[33] B. B. Gilbert, *British Social Policy: 1919–1939* (Ithaca, 1970), 193; T. W. Hutchinson, *A Review of Economic Doctrines: 1870–1929* (Oxford, 1953), pp. 420–21.

[34] Edouard Bonnefous, *Histoire politique de la troisième république* (Paris, 1962), V: 103; Ministère du Travail, *Bulletin*, 42 (1935), 119.

any proposal could find a hearing; the times favored nostrums and panaceas.

Some sought salvation in settling the jobless on the land; no idea better reflected the disillusionment with industrial society that the prolonged depression had provoked. That industrial workers unfamiliar with rural life could be transformed into yeoman farmers was highly unlikely, but the idea had a powerful emotional appeal, well expressed in such films as the American *Our Daily Bread,* in which a group of unemployed families rehabilitate a rundown farm,[35] and the French *Harvest,* where a single determined individual (supported by the love of a good woman) revives an abandoned village by growing a bumper crop of wheat.

One form that this "back to the soil" movement took was the work camp. Unlike the turn-of-the-century labor camps, which had tried to "recondition" down-and-outers and prepare unemployed urban workers for emigration, most of the camps of the 1930s housed unemployed youths. Although much useful conservation work was accomplished, in nearly every case the chief purpose of the camps was not to employ the jobless productively, much less to stimulate the economy, but to improve the morale of youths for whom no jobs existed. As Henri Fuss of the International Labor Organization wrote in summarizing a study of youth camps on three continents, "their object is to protect young people from the demoralising effects of unemployment by keeping them occupied." The best-known of these institutions, the New Deal Civilian Conservation Corps and the Nazi youth camps, were clearly designed with this goal in mind. The camps would keep unemployed young men "off the city street corners," President Franklin Roosevelt said. Adolf Hitler put it this way—the purpose of the camps was to prevent young Germans from "rotting helplessly in the streets."[36]

Resettling unemployed workers in rural areas, which also attracted considerable support during the 1930s, had even less impact on unemployment. Those who pushed for rural resettlement had mixed motives. To the argument that the international industrial system had broken down, requiring each nation to seek economic self-sufficiency, was added both disillusionment with urban society and a romanticization of the preindustrial past and the virtues of country life. Adam Stegerwald, minister of labor in Germany under Chancellor Heinrich

[35] Consider also the climactic scene in *Mr. Deeds Goes to Town,* in which the hero distributes titles to farms to an eager crowd of unemployed men.

[36] Henri Fuss, "Unemployment among Young People," *International Labour Review,* 31 (1935), 660; S. I. Rosenman, ed. *The Public Papers of Franklin D. Roosevelt* (New York, 1938), II: 81–82; Max Domarus, ed., *Hitler: Reden und Proklamationen* (Munich, 1965), I: 212.

Brüning, was an ardent advocate of resettlement. Industrialization and urbanization had gone too far, had run their course in Germany. The day of "over-organized mammoth corporations and trusts of the American type" was ending. Finding work for the jobless was important, Stegerwald admitted, but not as important as getting people back on the land. Not many unemployed industrial workers were actually settled on farms or even in suburban areas in Weimar Germany, and still fewer under the Nazis, despite Adolf Hitler's professed belief that farmers were "the foundation and life source" of the state. In the United States, President Roosevelt supported resettlement with equal enthusiasm but only a trivial number of jobless families were moved to rural areas during the New Deal years.[37]

Similar efforts in Great Britain, where there was high unemployment and relatively little agricultural land in proportion to the population, and in France, where there was less unemployment and much more farmland, were also unsuccessful. A British commentator concluded in 1936 that "in placing industrial workers on the land we are definitely sentencing them to a lower . . . standard of life." French workers often returned temporarily to family farms when out of work, and after 1935 the government provided transportation subsidies, help in finding housing, and relief payments for six months for unemployed people who would remove to rural areas. Through the late 1930s, however, only a handful of unemployed industrial workers—a mere 39 from the Paris region where unemployment was heavier than elsewhere in France—had taken advantage of the offer.[38] French urban dwellers, one sociologist noted, displayed *"vives répugnances"* for rural life, while the farmers preferred a "more malleable" work force. As the economist Michel Augé-Laribé, General Secretary of the National Confederation of Agricultural Associations, said, "Agriculture cannot offer much hope of employment to unemployed industrial workers. Farmers do not care about engaging workers who have to be taught practically everything." Many farmers in France and elsewhere also disapproved of the back-to-the-soil movement because they believed that any increased agricultural activity would further depress prices.[39]

Although the back-to-the-soil movement concentrated on celebrat-

[37] Hennig Köhler, "Arbeitsbeschaffung, Siedlung und Reparationen in der Schlussphase der Regierung Brüning," *Vierteljahrsheft für Zeitgeschichte,* 17 (1969), 290–91; Garraty, "New Deal and National Socialism," pp. 919–21.

[38] A similar program in Argentina to help unemployed workers in Buenos Aires return to the provinces was only slightly more effective. Siewers, "Unemployment in Argentina," p. 792. P. L. Yates, "The Land and the Unemployed Industrial Worker in Great Britain," *International Labour Review,* 34 (1936), 352.

[39] Gabrielle Letellier et al., *Enquête sur le chômage* (Paris, 1938), pp. 317–19; Michel Augé-Laribé, "Labour Conditions in French Agriculture," *International Labour Review,* 25 (1932), 51.

ing the virtues of rural life, its negative aspect—the rejection of machine civilization—was probably more significant. This rejection took many other forms, such as renewed worry about the problems of technological unemployment. Traditionally, critics of mechanization had merely claimed that machines replaced workers faster than they could be absorbed in other industries. Now they added the argument that mechanization was causing overproduction, glutting markets, driving down prices, and thus making the depression worse. This view led in the United States to the New Deal experiments with crop limitation under the Agricultural Adjustment Act, and with restrictions on the output of manufactured goods under the National Recovery Administration codes. Almost everywhere that public-works programs were developed to fight unemployment, the emphasis was on projects that required large numbers of people, that is, ones that used labor rather than machinery.

In France, support for this *malthusianisme économique* was particularly powerful; it resulted in laws limiting the production of wheat and wine, and even in a measure prohibiting the construction of new shoe factories and the expansion of existing facilities for two years. In extreme forms the argument against mechanization took on an almost Luddite aspect; one French economist suggested that "destruction may become a means of public safety," another urged that the government buy up new inventions to keep them from being developed, a third claimed that the "rationalization" of industry had created "a permanent residue of unemployed workers."[40]

Other economists, however, sought salvation in mechanization. Alvin Hansen, now a professor at Harvard, concerned by what seemed to him increasing signs that "the great era of growth and expansion" was ending, called for "a more rapid advance of technology than in the past" in order to create "private investment opportunities adequate to maintain full employment." The brief American vogue of technocracy provides an unsophisticated example of this concept. Technocracy was the ultimate glorification of engineering and technical efficiency; merely by organizing production and distribution with scientific precision, the technocrats insisted, prosperity and full employment could be restored.[41]

A still-less-sophisticated illustration of the faith in the power of machine production to eliminate unemployment was that advanced by

[40] Sauvy, *Histoire économique*, II: 371–72, 361, 365. This attack on mechanization should not be confused with the argument that machines were dehumanizing labor and depersonalizing life in general, a well-known French example in this period being the novelist Georges Duhamel's critique of American civilization, *Scènes de la vie future* (1930).

[41] Alvin Hansen, "Economic Progress and Declining Population Growth," *American Economic Review*, 29 (1939), 1–13; Dorfman, *Economic Mind*, V: 647–49.

a French writer, Jacques Duboin, in *La grande relève des hommes par la machine* (1932), a widely read tract similar in style and format to Foster and Catchings' *Road to Plenty*. The book describes a series of conversations supposedly held at the Alpine retreat of one Dr. Hermondan, an omniscient hermit-sage. Machinery, the doctor declares after demolishing the suggestions of his various guests, is the savior of humanity. "At a rate daily more rapid, mechanization makes possible the multiplication of output without any increase in labor." Unemployment is therefore only "the irrefutable proof of great technical progress." Instead of trying to create more jobs, society should take advantage of the efficiency of machine production and reduce the amount of work done by individuals. This can be achieved by shortening the work day and by lowering the age of retirement. All the 300,000 unemployed workers in France could be immediately rehired if job holders over fifty-five were pensioned off. Instead of restricting output, allow the marvelous engines of production free rein. In an "economy of abundance" there will be plenty for everyone. "The time for retirement will arrive at 55, at 54, at 50, depending on technical progress," Duboin's hero insisted. "Life is not only a matter of creating wealth," he added. "There are other things: study, the arts, science, sport, in short, everything that makes life worth living." The choice was clear—"either slide more and more rapidly down the path of disorder that leads to ruin, or adapt rationally to the new situation made possible by science."[42]

Amid the cacophony of insistent, clashing voices, national governments struggled to deal with their unemployed. The crudest way to get rid of the jobless was to export them. Between 1922 and 1933 the British managed to place over 400,000 of their subjects in Commonwealth nations under the Empire Resettlement Act of 1922, but more commonly foreign workers rather than the native born were encouraged or compelled to leave. France, which had eagerly welcomed foreign labor after the Great War, turned its Service de la Main-Oeuvre Étrangère to the task of canceling work permits and making sure that no foreigner held a job that a native Frenchman could fill. Between 1931 and 1933, more than half a million Poles, Spaniards, Italians, and other foreigners were repatriated. However, many more remained; in 1936 there were an estimated 25,000 jobless aliens in Paris alone. In other countries, similar patterns developed. Thousands of workers in the southwestern United States were forced to return to Mexico. Across the Pacific, other thousands of Javanese straggled back from remote provinces of the Dutch East Indies and from elsewhere in

[42] Jacques Duboin, *La grande relève des hommes par la machine* (Paris, 1932), pp. 23, 291, 310, 337.

Southeast Asia, causing problems for their native villages, while at the same time, many Europeans in the Dutch possessions, thrown out of work, pulled up stakes and headed home.[43]

But, if foreigners usually were the first victims and if other unemployed people seldom received as much help as they needed, the trend was toward more comprehensive support of the jobless and toward a more sympathetic understanding of their problems. Of the major industrial nations, only France, citadel of bourgeois complacency, adopted a niggardly attitude toward relieving the suffering of those without work. The official position of the government, repeatedly enunciated by the Ministry of Labor, was: "The state cannot pretend to eliminate or reduce unemployment, since its intervention does not affect the cause of the trouble." The ministry established requirements for those seeking aid that seem more like obstacles than controls, and praised its *fonctionnaires* for "not allowing unemployed workers to get aid unless they met all the requirements." A circular of 1932 made not mere unemployment but "the impossibility" of obtaining work a criterion for receiving public assistance. The state also devoted enormous energy to checking up on those who did qualify for aid—aid that amounted to only a few francs a day—to make sure that no undeserving person was feeding at the public trough. In 1935 some 323,000 francs were extracted from people found to have obtained relief improperly.

Nevertheless, even in France, more, and more generous, relief was forthcoming as conditions worsened. In the watch-manufacturing town of Besançon, for example, nine out of ten watchmakers were out of work during the summer of 1932. They received cash grants from the Besançon *fond du chômage* (90 percent of which came from the central government). In addition, private charities, the church, and the local military garrison pitched in to help, setting up soup kitchens and a shelter for the homeless, and providing additional financial aid.[44]

In the United States, supposedly the last bastion of individualism, a dramatic change in government policy came with the election of Franklin Roosevelt as President. Traditionally public assistance to the unemployed had been a local responsibility, and despite mounting evidence that local resources were inadequate, Herbert Hoover had resisted

[43] Hertha Kraus, *Aiding the Unemployed* (New York, 1934), p. 81; Letellier, *Chômage*, pp. 294–97; Georges Mauco, "Alien Workers in France," *International Labour Review*, 33 (1936), 192; "Labour Conditions in the Dutch East Indies in 1931," *ibid*, 29 (1933), 237–38; G.C. Kiser and David Silverman, "Mexican Repatriation during the Great Depression," *Journal of Mexican-American History*, 3 (1973), 139–58.

[44] Ministère du Travail, *Bulletin*, 42 (1935), 286; *ibid.*, 43 (1936), 171; Letellier, *Chômage*, p. 249; M. Daclin, *La crise des années 30 à Besançon* (Paris, 1968), pp. 79, 89–92, 119.

expending federal funds for relief purposes. But Roosevelt had no scruples about federal assistance; at his urging Congress swiftly created a Federal Emergency Relief Administration and provided it with $500 million for distribution through state and local agencies. A few months later the government also undertook the aforementioned emergency public-works program under the Civil Works Administration. Thereafter, throughout the depression, it provided money and jobs for the aid of the unemployed on a large scale.

In retrospect, the controversy that the New Deal measures roused seems without much substance. Drawing public funds from national sources rather than local scarcely amounted to a revolution, and it is hard to see how President Hoover (and the millions who agreed with him) could have believed that relief originating in Washington would damage the "moral fiber" of recipients more than aid coming from a particular state or city government. But, substantial or not, the controversy was real and also historically significant, since it helps explain why Roosevelt (although not himself worried about the supposed moral impact of federal aid on the national character) was reluctant to press for as much aid as those of his advisers who had been persuaded by the arguments of economists like Keynes and Kahn were recommending.[45]

The most important result of the high unemployment of the depression in the United States was the passage in 1935 of a national unemployment-insurance law. The measure did not come earlier because of the same popular prejudice against expanding federal authority and also because of disagreements among the advocates of insurance. The idea that an unemployment-insurance system could *prevent* unemployment, which had been advanced before the Great War by John R. Commons and others, was put to the test in Commons's own state of Wisconsin in 1932. The Wisconsin law required each company employing ten or more workers to build up an unemployment reserve fund, financed by the employer but administered by the government, from which that employer's workers would draw benefits when unemployed. The law provided that once the fund had reached a sum equal to $75 for each worker, the employer would not have to add to it except to make up for what was paid out to workers that had been laid off—presumably, therefore, employers would use every means possible to spread out work to avoid having to discharge anyone.

Other supporters of insurance preferred some variant of the British system, with workers as well as employers contributing to a single national fund. The issue was complicated by the opposition until 1932

[45] A. M. Schlesinger, Jr., *The Coming of the New Deal* (Boston, 1959), pp. 263–68, 275.

of many important labor leaders to any compulsory insurance system and their resistance thereafter to employee contributions, and by fears that no system could remain actuarily sound in the face of political pressures. There were also genuine constitutional concerns—it seemed likely that the Supreme Court would throw out any law setting up a nationally administered system. To get around the constitutional problem, Senator Robert F. Wagner of New York introduced a bill calling for a national payroll tax against which employer payments into any state insurance fund could be offset—thus federal law would force all states to enact unemployment insurance laws, yet not interfere with the Wisconsin system or for that matter prevent other states from devising whatever forms of insurance they wished.[46]

President Roosevelt's position on unemployment insurance was not unlike Winston Churchill's in 1910, although he played a much smaller role in planning and pushing through the necessary legislation. Like Churchill, he did not allow the lack of detailed knowledge to keep him from espousing the principle whole-heartedly. He actually told Secretary of Labor Frances Perkins that he favored "cradle to the grave" insurance for all Americans against illness, unemployment, and old age, "operated through the post offices," but aside from insisting that workers should contribute to the insurance fund so as to have an irrefutable claim to benefits, he did not commit himself to any particular system. He accepted the idea of separate state insurance embodied in Wagner's bill, and when experts who wanted a centralized system objected, he pointed out the political and constitutional problems and put them off with the bromide "We cannot eat the whole cake at one meal." The Social Security Act of 1935 insured against both old age and unemployment. By leaving the particulars to the individual states it created a confused and inequitable unemployment-insurance system. But, under the impetus of the tax offset provision, all the states swiftly established systems. Despite its limitations, the act was, as the historian Arthur M. Schlesinger, Jr. wrote, "a tremendous break with the inhibitions of the past" and in the American context a "prodigious achievement." With its passage all the important industrial nations except France had compulsory unemployment-insurance systems, as did Poland, Austria, several Balkan countries, and a number of the British Commonwealth nations.[47]

Nevertheless, after half a decade of depression, the number of unemployed in the world, while declining, remained enormous. The

[46] Daniel Nelson, *Unemployment Insurance* (Madison, 1969), pp. 128, 157–61, 198–200.

[47] Frances Perkins, *The Roosevelt I Knew* (New York, 1946), pp. 282–83; Schlesinger, *Coming of the New Deal*, pp. 313–15; International Labor Organization, *Unemployment Insurance Schemes* (Geneva, 1955), pp. 18–41.

ILO index for August 1935, the month Roosevelt signed the Social Security Act, stood at 188 (1929 = 100), having descended with agonizing slowness from a peak of 291 reached in the autumn of 1932. In Great Britain and the United States between 15 and 20 percent of the work force was still idle, and even in Nazi Germany, where the figures were improving rapidly, the unemployment rate stood at over 9 percent. In France, unemployment was increasing. Elsewhere the situation varied—in Japan the rate was under 5 percent, in the Netherlands, over 34.[48]

Meanwhile, in Cambridge, England, John Maynard Keynes was putting the finishing touches on a new book bearing the unpromising title *The General Theory of Employment, Interest, and Money*. He had sent proofs to his old student Dennis H. Robertson, author of *A Study of Industrial Fluctuation* (1915) and *Banking Policy and the Price Level* (1926), and to Ralph G. Hawtrey of the Treasury. Robertson and Hawtrey objected to Keynes's theory in general and in detail; after an extended exchange of letters he came reluctantly to the conclusion that they did not grasp what he was trying to say. Another of Keynes's students, Roy F. Harrod of Oxford, later his biographer, did understand the theory; he read Keynes's proofs "with a sense of his mighty achievement." But even Harrod had doubts, particularly about Keynes's ridiculing of so much of classical economics. "Where I differed," Harrod recalled, "was in regard to his allegation that the traditional theory of interest did not make sense. It seemed to me that this . . . would make too much dust and would give rise to irrelevant controversies." Keynes made a few changes as a result of Harrod's comments, but he was determined to make his case as he saw fit.[49] The *General Theory* was published in February 1936. It resulted in an economic revolution.

[48] *International Labour Review*, 35 (1937), 565; *ibid.*, 33 (1936), 92–95.
[49] Harrod, *Keynes*, pp. 520–23.

11

The Keynesian Revolution

John Maynard Keynes's *General Theory of Employment, Interest, and Money* is so well known as to require only the most cursory summary, yet the work has been so influential, its argument so central to the development of unemployment policy in modern times, that it demands extended discussion. Readers during the 1930s found the book startling (to some it was shocking, even outrageous) on two levels. It offered a new way of observing and organizing economic science, and it did so in a style that was at times coldly precise and mathematical, at other times epigrammatic, satirical, hyperbolic.

It is a question whether on balance Keynes's clever language in the *General Theory* advanced or impeded the impact of his ideas. He explained his new formulations so vividly that the most unsophisticated reader could follow them, but he was writing also (indeed primarily) for economists, for many of whom his irreverent and overstated criticisms of earlier theorists made accepting his argument emotionally difficult. To compare the classical economists to "Euclidean geometers in a non-Euclidean world,"[1] might amuse and also instruct ordinary citizens. But remarks like this one were not calculated either to amuse or to persuade professionals who were aware of the enormous intellectual achievements of the classical authorities.

In his biography of Keynes, Roy Harrod called attention to his hero's tendency in informal conversations to *"épater le bourgeois"* and push his arguments "to a point of extravagance." Under such circum-

[1] The full passage runs: "The classical theorists resemble Euclidean geometers in a non-Euclidean world who, discovering that in experience straight lines apparently parallel often meet, rebuke the lines for not keeping straight—as the only remedy for the unfortunate collisions that are occurring." *The General Theory of Employment, Interest, and Money* (New York, 1964), p. 16.

stances, as Harrod says, the tendency did no harm to his influence; whether or not it was counterproductive when exercised in a formal treatise is another question. "The *General Theory*," one of Keynes's leading American admirers admitted, "is arrogant, bad-tempered, polemical, and not overly generous in its acknowledgments." Wilhelm Lautenbach, who was later sometimes referred to as "the German Keynes," while appreciative of the contribution of the *General Theory* criticized Keynes for failing to give proper credit to the Swedish economist Knut Wicksell, and also noted with some misgivings the sarcasm and tone of "passionate harshness" *(eifernde Strenge)* that permeated Keynes's discussion of orthodox classical theory.[2]

As we have seen, Keynes's explanation of the causes of unemployment had been largely worked out before 1935. But in the *General Theory* he extended and refined the argument. When employment increased, income increased. When income increased, consumption increased—"but not so much as income." Keynes spoke of a person's "propensity to consume," a variable that tended to decline as income rose. (Here he was following the line of reasoning that ran back to Hobson.) Therefore, if all the increase in employment was devoted to making goods for consumption, production would outstrip demand and employers would be compelled to lay off workers. Lowering money wages could not reverse this trend, Keynes insisted. Lower wages would mean lower prices, but fixed costs would remain unchanged; new investment would therefore be discouraged and unemployment would actually rise. Moreover, *rentiers* would end up with a larger share of total income, and since they were as a class well-to-do, this would cause a reduction in the general propensity to consume and thus also lead to more unemployment. And so, Keynes concluded, "to justify any given amount of employment there must be an amount of current investment sufficient to absorb the excess of total output over what the community chooses to consume."[3]

But the willingness to invest was independent of the propensity to consume; it reflected the relation between what Keynes called the marginal efficiency of capital (roughly, the expectation of profit) and interest rates. If the marginal efficiency of capital rose or if interest rates fell, investment would increase and unemployment decline. The actual amount of unemployment, its "equilibrium level," was thus fixed by the current propensity to consume and rate of investment. Full

[2] R. F. Harrod, *John Maynard Keynes* (New York, 1971), pp. 532, 539; P. A. Samuelson, "The General Theory," S. E. Harris, ed., *The New Economics: Keynes's Influence on Theory and Public Policy* (New York, 1965), pp. 148–49; Wilhelm Grottkopp, *Die grosse Krise* (Dusseldorf, 1954), pp. 38–39n.; Wilhelm Lautenbach, "Zur Zinstheorie von John Maynard Keynes," *Weltwirtschaftliches Archiv* 45 (1937), 493–522.

[3] Keynes, *General Theory*, pp. 27, 262, 267.

employment was "a special case," possible but unlikely if entrepreneurs were left to their own devices. During depressions, for example, income fell and the ratio of consumption to income increased—
investment therefore declined. But Keynes now rejected the "oversav-
ings" explanation of depressions and with it his own argument in the
Treatise on Money that saving and investment were not always equal.
Looked at one way, he noted, all income was either consumed or
invested. Seen from another perspective, saving was what was left after
consumption was subtracted from income. Therefore, saving and investment *had* to be equal, despite the fact that the two functions were
often performed by different people. The key to understanding this
almost paradoxical statement lay in what Keynes called "the *bilateral*
character" of transactions between producers and those who purchased their output. Income depended upon—was impossible without
—consumption or investment, because to obtain income a producer
had to sell his output, either to a consumer or to another producer,
that is, to an investor. Thus, "the excess of income over consumption,
which we call saving, cannot differ from the addition of capital equipment which we call investment. . . . Saving, in fact, is a mere residual."[4]

But the equilibrium of saving and investment might well occur at a
level substantially below full employment. Especially in well-to-do
countries, where consumption occupied a smaller proportion of output than in poor ones and where, since capital was relatively abundant,
new investment was less likely to be profitable, there was a tendency
for the economy to stabilize at a level below full employment. "We
oscillate," Keynes wrote, "round an intermediate position appreciably
below full employment and appreciably above the minimum employment a decline below which would endanger life."

This reasoning seemed plausible in the light of the experience of
Great Britain and other industrial countries during the Great Depression, but it directly contradicted classical theory, especially Say's law
that supply created its own demand and the dogma that when the
supply of labor exceeded demand wages would fall until all willing
workers were employed. "Workers," Keynes wrote in a typical sally,
"are instinctively more reasonable economists than the classical
school, inasmuch as they resist reductions of money-wages . . . even
though the existing real equivalent of these wages exceeds the marginal disutility of the existing employment."[5]

The problem as Keynes saw it was to stimulate investment, a task
that he thought could be managed in two ways. One was by reducing
interest rates. Classical theory held that an interest rate was the "price"

[4] *Ibid.*, pp. 14, 61–65.
[5] *Ibid.*, pp. 254, 30, 14.

that reflected the relation between investment (demand) and savings (supply). Rates responded passively to increases and decreases in these elements, the changes being part of a self-regulating process of adjustment that kept investment and savings always in balance. In Keynes's terminology the classical writers considered saving and investment "determinants," whereas he believed—and here he was breaking new ground—that they were "determinates," the determinants being the propensity to consume, the marginal efficiency of capital, and the rate of interest. He advanced another new concept, "liquidity preference," the desire of the owner of wealth to keep it readily available in the form of money. Interest, Keynes suggested, was "the reward for parting with liquidity," the rate a "highly psychological phenomenon" that measured "the unwillingness of those who possess money to part with their liquid control over it."[6]

But why would anyone with money to invest prefer to hold cash? Keynes had a startling answer to this question: the preference for liquidity could be "speculative," an indication of "*uncertainty* as to the future of the rate of interest." It therefore had little to do with any particular rate. Interest payments, in other words, were rewards for not hoarding rather than for not spending. From this subtle but vital distinction it followed that if a "monetary authority" committed itself to maintaining over a long period *any* reasonable rate of interest, liquidity preference would be low, willingness to lend correspondingly high. Keynes, of course, believed that the rate should generally be quite low in order to stimulate the investment that was essential for the maintenance of full employment.[7]

The other way to increase investment was for the government itself to do the investing. In making this point Keynes relied heavily, and with full attribution, upon R. F. Kahn's concept of the multiplier, which he related closely to his own concept of the propensity to consume— the greater the propensity the larger the multiplier. His discussion of the idea of government borrowing for public works, which he had pressed for so energetically but futilely in Britain, produced one of his most extravagant (and for this reason best known) attacks on conventional economic thinking, one which also illustrates the unusual shifts of style and purpose that characterize Keynes's book. Only a few pages after a passage full of technical mathematics designed to distinguish between his own version of the multiplier effect and Kahn's, a passage incomprehensible to nonspecialists, he wrote, obviously venting his exasperation with advocates of the Treasury view: " 'Wasteful' loan expenditure may nevertheless enrich the community on balance. Pyra-

[6] *Ibid.*, pp. 183–84, 167, 202.
[7] *Ibid.*, pp. 174, 205.

mid-building, earthquakes, even wars may serve to increase wealth, if the education of our statesmen on the principles of classical economics stands in the way of anything better." If the government were to bury banknotes in "disused coalmines" and "leave it to private enterprise on well-tried principles of *laissez-faire* to dig the notes up again," unemployment would disappear and the wealth of the nation would increase. Such an absurd practice would differ little from gold mining, which "adds nothing to the real wealth of the world." But "just as wars have been the only form of large-scale loan expenditure which statesmen have thought justifiable, so gold-mining is the only pretext for digging holes in the ground which has recommended itself to bankers as sound finance."

Seemingly carried away by the argument, Keynes then launched into an explanation of the special value of gold mining as an economic stimulant "if we are precluded from increasing employment by means which at the same time increase our stock of useful wealth." The enterprise, being highly speculative, was little affected by high interest rates. Increases in the supply of gold did not reduce the marginal utility of the metal, whereas the building of more houses had the effect of lowering rents and thus of discouraging further investment in construction. The "fabled wealth" of ancient Egypt, Keynes professed, was doubtless due to investments in mining precious metals and building pyramids, "the fruits of which, since they could not serve the needs of man by being consumed, did not stale with abundance." And he concluded with a passage at once bitter and poignant. Having followed the advice of "prudent" financiers not to "add to the 'financial' burdens of posterity by building them houses to live in . . . we have no such easy escape from the sufferings of unemployment." These sufferings must apparently be accepted "as an inevitable result of applying to the conduct of the State the maxims which are best calculated to 'enrich' an individual by enabling him to pile up claims to enjoyment which he does not intend to exercise at any definite time."[8]

Despite this and similar bleak prognostications, and despite the continuing resistance of governments to deficit spending as a way of reducing unemployment, Keynes considered government expenditure the key to solving the problem. He believed that holding down interest rates to encourage private investment was highly desirable, but since independent decisions to invest were influenced by many factors besides the cost of borrowing, ranging from the "political and social atmosphere" to "the nerves and hysteria and even the digestions and reactions to the weather" of individual businessmen, he was "some-

[8] *Ibid.*, pp. 128–31.

what sceptical" of relying only on monetary policy as an economic stimulant. During really severe depressions, "the collapse in the marginal efficiency of capital may be so complete that no practicable reduction in the rate of interest will be enough" to tempt producers to borrow. So recovery must ultimately depend upon government spending. "I expect to see the State, which is in a position to calculate . . . on long views and on the basis of the general social advantage, taking an ever greater responsibility for directly organizing investment," he wrote, adding in another place: "I conclude that the duty of ordering the current volume of investment cannot safely be left in private hands."[9]

Keynes's accomplishment, one of the major intellectual achievements of the century, was to devise a new way of understanding how the capitalist system functioned. The general theory was not entirely original; Keynes himself acknowledged his debt to earlier thinkers, including Hobson, Malthus, and many preclassical writers on economic subjects whose "practical wisdom," especially their disapproval of high interest rates, he warmly praised. (He quoted Locke, for example, to the effect that "High Interest decays Trade.") But Keynes's theory had both a scope and a precision that none of the work of these earlier writers possessed. What Keynes once wrote concerning his teacher Alfred Marshall's *Principles of Economics*—that it provided a "Copernican view" of the subject—applies with at least equal force to the *General Theory*.[10]

The importance of the theory, its qualities as an intellectual construct aside, was that it suggested a way of managing a free economy so as to maximize and then stabilize output, and thus to do away with sharp cyclical fluctuations and also with unemployment. After Keynes, full employment seemed a realizable goal of public policy; apparently the industrial reserve army of Malthus and Marx could be permanently demobilized.

But the initial reaction to Keynes's book was anything but enthusiastic. Most economists outside Keynes's circle found his claim to have devised a new way of organizing the concepts of their science to be greatly exaggerated, if not entirely without foundation. Although granting that the general theory deserved "the widest and most scrupulous consideration," the reviewer in the *Times Literary Supplement* suggested that "Keynes' main contentions are less revolutionary than he is inclined to indicate." Pigou admitted that Keynes had thrown light on "certain aspects of economic analysis whose vital importance

[9] *Ibid.*, pp. 162, 316, 164, 320.
[10] *Ibid.*, pp. 340, 344; J. M. Keynes, *Essays in Biography* (New York, 1963), p. 183; L. R. Klein, *The Keynesian Revolution* (New York, 1966), pp. 124–52.

for practice had not been seen before," but insisted that despite his title he had by no means produced a synthesis of economics comparable to what Einstein had done in physics. Pigou was annoyed by Keynes's "sarcastic comment[s] upon other people" (in addition to many barbs aimed at the classical writers, the *General Theory* contained a special appendix demolishing Pigou's *Theory of Unemployment*). Pigou's conviction that the way to reduce unemployment was to cut wages remained unshaken, and he rejected the idea of the multiplier. And he concluded his review with a turn of phrase worthy of his target: "We have watched an artist firing arrows at the moon. Whatever be thought of his marksmanship, we can all admire his virtuosity."

Pigou later moderated his criticism of Keynes's theory, but as late as 1950 he was still insisting that it was "limited in scope." Elsewhere among British commentators, an equal lack of enthusiasm prevailed; in 1937, the editors of the *Economist*, summing up the experience of the first four years of the American New Deal, described public works as "an unduly 'expensive' form of increasing employment," and remarked somewhat wistfully of Roosevelt's programs: "It is only a rich country that can afford to deal with its unemployment in this expensive, unremunerative way."[11]

American economists were, if anything, more skeptical of Keynes's theory than the British. A reviewer in the *Political Science Quarterly* dismissed it as no more than "an interesting exhibit in the museum of depression curiosities." Frank Knight of the University of Chicago described Keynes's treatment of the great classical writers as "caricatures," the general theory as a mixture of exaggeration, logic chopping, fuzzy thinking, and plain error.[12] Alvin Hansen—later a leading exponent of Keynesian economics—reviewed the *General Theory* twice, in each case disparaging it as no more than a symptom of the depression. It was "not a landmark," indeed, anything but the foundation of a new school. After summarizing Keynes's argument, he predicted that the theoretical structure would be picked to pieces by critics. The theory of interest would "certainly be challenged" and the theory of equilibrium below full employment was "not tenable" except "under conditions of relative stagnation of technical progress."[13] And Hansen

[11] *Times Literary Supplement*, March 14, 1936, p. 213; *Economica*, (1936), 115–32; Harrod, *Keynes*, p. 534; A. C. Pigou, *Keynes's "General Theory," A Retrospective View* (London, 1951), p. 61; editors of the *Economist*, *The New Deal: An Analysis and Appraisal* (New York, 1937), pp. 26, 14.

[12] *Political Science Quarterly*, 51 (1936), 60; *Canadian Journal of Economics and Political Science*, 3 (1937), 401–19.

[13] Hansen's "conversion" to Keynesian economics was much influenced by his growing fear of economic stagnation caused by the slackening of population growth and technological advances. In 1938 he wrote: "The frontier for the entire world is largely gone and population is approaching stabilization. . . . In view of the possibility of a

stated flatly: "There is . . . no inherent imperious law of the economic system that precludes full employment." Even Lauchlin Currie, a member of the Board of Governors of the Federal Reserve system who, as an important behind-the-scenes figure in the Roosevelt administration, had been advocating deficit financing of public works and other practical measures favored by Keynes, found the general theory unsatisfactory as a theoretical explanation of how the economy functioned. Anyone who expected to find in it "the answer to an economist's prayer" was "doomed to disappointment," Currie wrote. "All too often we find that familiar things are being described in unfamiliar language . . . and that precision and definiteness are being purchased at the expense of reality." Keynes's claim that a precise value could be assigned to the multiplier effect of investments proved to be unfounded when tested against actual data. His argument for low long-term interest rates as a stimulus to investment did "not follow in any way from his formal framework of analysis," and adopting the monetary policy he recommended would under certain circumstances be both "fruitless" and "dangerous."[14]

European economists offered mixed reactions to Keynes's book. Germans in general were favorably predisposed toward Keynes as an economist because in his *Economic Consequences of the Peace* he had criticized the heavy reparations payments exacted from Germany by the Versailles Treaty. More specifically, the German "Reformers" grouped around the Institut für Konjunkturforschung had long been advocating expanding public works as an economic stimulant and therefore found his reasoning on this subject appealing, just as they had approved of the distinction he had drawn between savings and investment in the *Treatise on Money*. The *General Theory* was published in German within months of its appearance in English, with a special foreword by Keynes in which he wrote: "I may perhaps expect less resistance to my theory from German readers than English." On the other hand, most German theoretical economists were very conservative, especially—and understandably after the great inflation of the early 1920s—on questions of monetary policy. Even the Reformers found Keynes's attitude toward inflation objectionable, although they said little at the time. The conservatives were horrified by his cavalier treatment of the subject. One reviewer of his *Treatise on Money*, which

---

slowing down in capital-consuming technological innovations, the problem of structural, or secular unemployment . . . is almost certain to present itself." *Full Recovery or Stagnation?* (New York, 1938), pp. 28–29.

[14] *Journal of Political Economy*, 44 (1936), 667–86; *Yale Review*, 25 (1936), 828–30; National Industrial Conference Board, *The Economic Doctrines of John Maynard Keynes* (New York, 1938), p. 15, 25–26.

was translated into German in 1932 as *Vom Gelde,* commented that the book should have been titled *Vom Missbrauch des Geldes, On the Mishandling of Money.* Carl Krämer, the economist who had translated the *Treatise on Money* into German, wrote a long and favorable review of the *General Theory* in which he ranked Keynes among the "towering thinkers" whose work had changed "the basic way of perceiving economics." However, Krämer added, while suitable for nations with ample currency reserves, no restrictions on the use of private capital *(Kapitalfreizügigkeit),* and mature *(ausgebauten)* industrial systems—nations that had not experienced the losses involved in runaway inflation—Keynes's ideas were not useful for present-day Germany, where the economy was closely regulated, where there was no lack of investment opportunities for the foreseeable future, and where there was no need to restrict savings or stimulate consumption.[15]

As for France, it is almost correct to say that the general theory had no influence there at all—the French had closed their minds to Keynes long before the depression and for the same reason that German readers were prejudiced in his favor—his attitude toward reparations. *The Economic Consequences of the Peace* caused consternation in France. Reviewers in serious journals (the popular press ignored the book) denounced it and its author—"an aberration," "pro-German propaganda," "the novel by M. Keynes," the man who "has stolen from France the fruits of her victory." Although some French economists certainly read Keynes's later writings, few of them found anything positive to say about them. The *Revue d'économie politique* published a rather routine essay on his *Treatise,* part of a series on the work of foreign economists, and a doctoral thesis on his monetary theories appeared in 1933. The *Revue* ran an intelligent and scholarly but carping critique of the *General Theory* in 1937, written by Etienne Mantoux (who later published a major attack on Keynes's book on the peace treaty). Keynes was overrated as a theoretician, Mantoux claimed. The thinking behind the general theory was muddled. Keynes's "serpentine" mind, his "disconcerting faculty of changing his opinions frequently," lay at the root of his reputation for profundity, while his popular prestige was the result of his penchant for sarcasm and his polemical skills, not "cold reason." Mantoux called special attention to Keynes's argument in favor of public works, quoting the passage about burying bank notes *in extenso* and characterizing both the argument and the principle as absurd. Keynes presented himself as seeking to preserve capitalism, but if put into practice his ideas would alter the established system profoundly. His easy-money theories

[15] Grottkopp, *Grosse Krise,* pp. 231, 235–37; *Schmollers Jahrbuch,* 61 (1937), 316, 325.

would also increase the risk of serious inflation, and not only, as Keynes insisted, if adopted during periods of full employment. There were currently over a million and a half unemployed workers in Britain, yet prices were rising at a disturbing rate. "English economists," Mantoux noted somewhat smugly, considered unemployment "an unbearable challenge" to their theories. Getting rid of it had become "the alpha and omega of British economics."[16]

Mantoux was at least aware of what Keynes had written. Many of his confrères were not. Indeed, no full-length analysis of the general theory appeared in France until the publication of Jean Domanchi's *La pensée de John-Maynard Keynes* in 1943, and the *General Theory* was not published in a French translation until after World War II. French economists during the thirties were, to put it charitably, uncreative. According to Roy Harrod, "they did not move easily among the latest ideas of Anglo-Saxon or Swedish theorists." In the universities, classical economics still reigned. Prominent professors such as Charles Rist, Gaëtan Pirou, and Jacques Rueff bewailed the inadequacy of French statistics and the lack of work "explicative of economic reality," but claimed to be powerless to correct the situation.[17]

The impact of Keynes's proposals on contemporary political leaders was equally limited in the years immediately following the publication of the *General Theory*. One reason, of course, was that his ideas were at variance with conventional wisdom; indeed, his analysis of the causes of unemployment appeared to fly in the face of common sense. With millions living in straitened circumstances, with governments struggling to reconcile shrinking revenues with escalating relief expenditures, with everyone fearful of the future, the natural reaction was to economize, conserve, hold out. When Keynes said, as he did as early as 1931 in a radio address, "Whenever you save five shillings you put a man out of work for a day," and when, in the *General Theory*, he wrote that "in contemporary conditions the growth of wealth, so far from being dependent on the abstinence of the rich . . . is more likely to be impeded by it," he was denying the practical virtue of thrift as well as outraging conventional morality.

Yet Keynes was himself partly responsible for the fact that his advice was so often rejected. (He wrote in the preface to a collection of some of his essays that his efforts to sway public opinion resembled "the croakings of a Cassandra.") The fondness for sarcasm and hyperbole

16 François Crouzet, "Réactions françaises devant 'Les conséquences économiques de la paix' de Keynes," *Revue d'histoire moderne et contemporaine*, 19 (1972), 6–26; *Revue d'économie politique*, 51 (1937), 1557–90.

17 Harrod, *Keynes*, p. 373; Charles Rist, ed., *"L'enseignement économique en France et à l'étranger* (Paris, 1937), pp. 183–86, 21, 58–59.

that cropped up from time to time in his technical work pervaded his articles and speeches aimed at a wider audience. In the 1920s he could annoy conservatives by referring to Prime Minister Stanley Baldwin as "Queen Baldwin," and almost coincidentally goad radicals by referring to *Das Kapital* as "an obsolete economic textbook which I know to be not only scientifically erroneous but without interest or application for the modern world." Immediately after his reference to the unfortunate effect of saving five shillings in his just-mentioned radio speech in 1931, he said:

> Therefore, oh patriotic housewives, sally out to-morrow early into the streets and go to the wonderful sales which are everywhere advertised. You will do yourselves good—for never were things so cheap, cheap beyond your dreams. Lay in a stock of household linen, of sheets and blankets to satisfy all your needs. And have the added joy that you are increasing employment.

When the British government introduced a 15 percent salary reduction for teachers, he wrote: "That the school-teachers should have been singled out for sacrifice as an offering to the Moloch of finance is a sufficient proof of the state of hysteria and irresponsibility into which Cabinet Ministers have worked themselves." The government's budget, he said, represented "a policy of Bedlam."[18]

To say the least, such language was not calculated to persuade the politicians. The urge to balance national budgets in hard times persisted everywhere, although the compelling need to help the jobless and shrinking yields from taxes combined to prevent the budgets from balancing. No chief of state in the major industrial nations during the 1930s knew very much about economic theory of any variety. After his first meeting with Keynes in 1934, Franklin Roosevelt told Secretary of Labor Frances Perkins that Keynes seemed to him "a mathematician rather than a political economist," the President's use of this old-fashioned term a clear indication of his lack of sophistication in the discipline.[19] Adolf Hitler put a large-scale public works program into effect in Germany, building in addition to the *Autobahn* network of modern, limited-access highways many enormous and unattractive public buildings, thus giving currency to the word *Pyramidenbau*, pyramid building. But Hitler too knew little formal economics. ("Less today . . . than I thought I knew a few years ago," he confessed in 1934). Moreover, Nazi policies were certainly not Keynesian, since they were aimed at restricting consumption and preventing inflation.

[18] J. M. Keynes, *Essays in Persuasion* (New York, 1963), pp. v, 264, 300, 152, 163–64.

[19] Keynes, for once containing his tongue, merely reported to Secretary Perkins that he had "supposed the President more literate, economically speaking." Frances Perkins, *The Roosevelt I Knew* (New York, 1946), p. 226.

French political leaders also lacked much understanding of modern economics, not surprisingly in the light of the state of the discipline in that nation during the 1930s. Even the Socialist Premier Léon Blum, although an intelligent and intellectually inclined person, was economically unsophisticated; the leading French authority on the period, Alfred Sauvy, once quipped that Blum's ignorance of economics was matched only by his sincerity.[20]

However, events (not the general theory or the opinions of reviewers) pushed political leaders toward the policies that Keynes had been advocating. By 1937 the world economy was on the mend. In the United States output finally surpassed the level of 1929 early in that year and unemployment was down to 7.7 million. Conditions in France improved rapidly in late 1936 and early 1937 following the reforms instituted by Blum's Popular Front government, while in Britain the recovery was relatively even greater than in France and the United States. In Germany, boom conditions prevailed. But just when the depression seemed at last to be ending came a decline more precipitous than that of 1930–31. The causes of this "recession" of 1937–38 varied from country to country, but in nearly all there was a clear relationship between the downturn and cutbacks in public spending. The relationship was most evident in America. Roosevelt had reduced public-works and relief expenditures sharply in June 1937 at the same time that contributions to the new social security system were cutting into workers' spendable incomes. The reaction was almost immediate; by August a decline was noticeable and by the end of the year output had plummeted and unemployment was soaring. The French boomlet came to a sudden end for more complex reasons; nevertheless, Premier Blum's decision to call for a "pause" in government spending in an effort to balance the budget coincided with its termination.

These circumstances played into the hands of those who favored easy-money policies and large public-works expenditures for whatever reason; and the existence of Keynes's *General Theory* gave all an added weapon in the struggle to influence policy. In the United States, Keynes himself tried to persuade President Roosevelt, sending him in February 1938 "some bird's eye impressions" of the recession. He was most uncharacteristically restrained, even ingratiating, describing himself to Roosevelt as "an enthusiastic well-wisher of you and your policies." Along with low interest rates and unemployment relief, he said, New Deal public-works expenditures had been a major force for

[20] J. D. Heyl, "Hitler's Economic Thought: A Reappraisal," *Central European History*, 6 (1972), 92; René Erbe, *Die nationalsozialistische Wirtschaftspolitik im Lichte der modernen Theorie* (Zurich, 1958); Alfred Sauvy, *Histoire économique de la France entre les deux guerres* (Paris 1967) II: 303.

recovery. The Securities and Exchange Commission was doing "splendid work," and the New Deal support of collective bargaining had been "essential." As for the opposition of businessmen to the necessary policies—this was Keynes's one reversion to his typical style in the letter—businessmen are "perplexed, bemused, indeed terrified, yet only too anxious to take a cheerful view."

> You could do anything you liked with them [he went on], if you would treat them (even the big ones), not as wolves and tigers, but as domestic animals by nature, even though they have been badly brought up and not trained as you would wish.

But the very success of New Deal measures had led to an "error of optimism." Public-works outlays had been "greatly curtailed in the past year." They ought to be resumed swiftly on a large scale and concentrated in the housing industry and perhaps railroads. But whatever the details, a policy of promoting investment was "an urgent necessity."[21]

Roosevelt paid no more heed to this letter than to Keynes's earlier efforts to educate him, but by April, with unemployment again above ten million, he had yielded to the pressures of the "spenders" in his administration. He then asked Congress to appropriate $3 billion for public projects, and he called also for the reduction of interest rates. The government, he said, was intervening to "take up the slack" in the faltering economy. By the end of the year the American economy had bounced back and unemployment had been reduced by nearly a million. By this time also, the German, British, and French governments were spending heavily on armaments; unemployment declined in Britain and France and disappeared in Germany.

The experience of the recession and the subsequent recovery made Keynesians of more and more economists. For example, a massive study of *Security, Work, and Relief Policies* in the United States, begun shortly after the recession by the National Resources Planning Board, not only attributed the downturn to the premature balancing of the federal budget, but also adopted a Keynesian explanation of the causes of unemployment and the ways by which it could be reduced.[22]

Then in 1939 came the war and soon unemployment ceased to be a problem.[23] Unbalanced budgets, heavy public investments, low interest rates—inadvertently, the industrial nations adopted Keynesian

[21] J. M. Keynes to F. D. Roosevelt, February 1, 1938, Roosevelt papers, Hyde Park, N.Y.

[22] E. W. Hawley, *The New Deal and the Problem of Monopoly* (Princeton, 1966), p. 410; National Resources Planning Board, *Security, Work, and Relief Policies* (Washington, 1942), pp. 322–28.

[23] In the United States, however, there were still over 8.1 million jobless in 1940, and as late as 1942 there were 2.66 million, nearly 7 percent of the industrial labor force.

policies, and in doing so eliminated unemployment. Similar policies had produced similar results during World War I, but at that time no theoretical explanation of what was happening existed; now, quite suddenly as such things go, the Keynesian logic appeared irrefutable. In 1940 British Prime Minister Winston Churchill, he who, as recently as 1929, had named and defined the "orthodox Treasury dogma" that Keynes had so long assaulted, made Keynes his close economic adviser. In 1942 Keynes became Lord Keynes of Tilton. As late as 1939 the standard American economics texts were still dismissing the subject of unemployment in a few pages, but no less a critic than Alvin Hansen had changed his mind about the general theory and young graduate students like Paul A. Samuelson, the future Nobel laureate, originally skeptical, were being caught up by a new excitement as they puzzled over Keynes's equations and realized their significance.[24]

The herald of the new view was once again the durable William Beveridge. (Soon, like Keynes, he would be made a peer in recognition of his long public service.) In 1937, writing in the journal, *Econometrica*, Beveridge was still bleakly predicting that unemployment would never return to pre-1914 levels, which he estimated to have averaged around 4.5 percent. In his last speech as director of the London School of Economics in that year, he attacked Keynes's *General Theory* on the ground that it was based too much on assumptions and not enough on observation. But, when he began a new survey of unemployment in 1943, his view had altered radically, how radically the title of his report, *Full Employment in a Free Society*, made clear. Full employment, which Beveridge defined as "having always more vacant jobs than unemployed men," was a realizable goal. "The labour market should always be a seller's market." Since "deficiency of total demand" was the prime cause of unemployment, the number of available jobs depended upon the volume of spending. Therefore, when private spending proved inadequate, government should take up the slack. "Full employment means ensuring that outlay in total is sufficient. Only the State can ensure that." The idea that the national budget ought to be balanced annually was in error; instead, the government "must be prepared at need to spend more than it takes . . . in order to use the labour and other productive resources which would otherwise be wasted in unemployment." Fear of a large national debt was thus without foundation. Furthermore, interest rates should be kept as low as possible—"a policy of cheap money should be regarded as an integral part of any plan for full employment." Beveridge, in other words, had become a Keynesian; indeed he paid specific tribute to Keynes, whose "epoch-making" book, he said, was, if not the "last word on the problem," a

[24] Samuelson, "The General Theory," pp. 145–46.

work of "fundamental importance" and the harbinger of a "new era of economic theorizing about employment."[25]

Full Employment in a Free Society was swiftly translated into all the major European languages and even into Chinese and Hebrew, but it was actually less original and less influential than Beveridge's first study of unemployment in 1909. Almost coincidentally with his completion of the manuscript of *Full Employment* in May 1944, the British government released a White Paper on Employment Policy, which was (Beveridge's words) "a ceremonial scattering of [the] ashes" of the Treasury dogma. It was also an almost total acceptance of Keynes's general theory. "The maintenance of a high and stable level of employment," the White Paper stated, was now one of the government's "primary aims and responsibilities." The paper endorsed low interest rates, large-scale public-works projects, and other techniques designed "to prevent total expenditures from falling away."

> The power of public expenditures, skillfully applied, to check the onset of a depression has been underestimated. The whole notion of pressing forward quickly with public expenditure when incomes were falling and the outlook dark has, naturally enough, encountered strong resistance. . . . Such resistance can, however, be overcome if public opinion is brought to the view that periods of trade recession provide an opportunity to improve the permanent equipment of society by the provision of better housing, public buildings, means of communication, power and water supplies, etc.

Even the sacrosanct idea of "a rigid policy of balancing the Budget each year regardless of the state of trade" was abandoned, although "the principle" that it must balance in the long run was firmly sustained.[26]

Despite such obeisances to old-fashioned concepts of sound finance, the White Paper was a document of major significance, the forerunner of many similar national pronouncements. Early in 1945 the Canadian government announced "unequivocally" that "a high and stable level of employment" was "a major aim of Government policy," and its description of the tactics it would pursue in achieving this end was thoroughly in line with the general theory. The budget, for example, was to be employed as "a balance wheel of the economy," and the government was prepared deliberately to increase the national debt in order to carry out "its employment and income policy." Australia also

[25] W. H. Beveridge, *Power and Responsibility* (London, 1953), pp. 253, 259; W. H. Beveridge, *Full Employment in a Free Society* (New York, 1945), pp. 18–19, 26, 187, 136, 148–49, 93–97.

[26] Beveridge, *Power and Responsibility*, p. 331; Beveridge, *Full Employment*, p. 260; *White Paper on Employment Policy* (New York, 1944), pp. 3, 16, 22, 25.

issued a policy statement on full employment in 1945 accepting "responsibility for stimulating spending . . . to sustain full employment," and Article 55 of the United Nations Charter declared full employment to be one of the major aims of that organization. The next year a UN conference called for international action to maintain employment, including the "timing" of public-works projects and the "synchronization of credit policies so as to ease terms of borrowing."[27]

Then in 1946 the American Congress passed an Employment Act which declared "creating and maintaining . . . useful employment opportunities" to be "the continuing policy and responsibility of the Federal Government." Although this act was hedged about with even more qualifications than the British White Paper, its passage was a landmark in the history of national economic policy, and also of American political history, for it set up a Council of Economic Advisers, the influence of which on public policy was to be enormous. In its first report the council described the Keynesian techniques that should be used to stabilize the economy, concluding:

> The agents of government must diligently study and vigorously use a democratic and statesmanlike control of the public purse to put a brake at certain strategic points where boom forces develop dangerous trends, and to stimulate employment and production and support purchasing power when and where it becomes unduly depressed.[28]

Even more remarkable than the "conversion" of the United States Congress to the new economics was that of the National Constituent Assembly of France, which included in the preamble of the constitution of the Fourth Republic the statement: "Everyone has the right to work and the right to obtain employment." The new constitution also created an Economic Council charged with advising the Council of Ministers about "a national economic plan for full employment," and before very long a French economist was writing of Keynes's "grandiose vision" and bemoaning the fact that "masters" of his caliber were being replaced by narrow specialists.

The immediate postwar period provided further demonstrations of the influence and efficacy of the Keynesian techniques. Many economists had feared that the disruptions associated with the conversion from a war to a peacetime economy would cause unemployment to soar. After the defeat of Germany, for example, Paul Samuelson predicted that five million Americans would lose their jobs or at least suffer greatly reduced work time as a result of government cutbacks in

[27] *Federal Reserve Bulletin*, 31 (1945), 536–49; United Nations, *Conference on Trade and Employment* (1946), pp. 4–5.
[28] Council of Economic Advisers, *First Annual Report* (Washington, 1946), p. 18.

spending made possible by the ending of the two-front war. With the fall of Japan, concern that another great depression would follow increased and, in the United States, influenced the passage of the Employment Act of 1946. The pent-up demand for consumer goods and the investment of billions in the reconstruction of Europe demonstrated that these fears were groundless, and thus strengthened the confidence of economists and political leaders that Keynes's explanation of the causes of unemployment was correct. In 1947 a diehard like Jacques Rueff could still write about the "Fallacies of Lord Keynes' General Theory," but he was by then distinctly in the minority within the economics profession. In that year Alvin Hansen, probably the most influential of the American converts, compared the significance of the *General Theory* with that of *The Wealth of Nations*. "Demand," he wrote in *Economic Policy and Full Employment*, "does not mean 'need' or 'desire'; it means 'outlay' or 'expenditure.' Adequate total *demand* means an adequate volume of expenditure whether by individuals, businesses, or government." Taxes must be raised and lowered "as a countercyclical device," and "modern economic analysis favors the maintenance of a low rate of interest." Public investment was also "high on the priority list," but by whatever means "a policy of conscious and controlled compensatory action is absolutely essential" to "hold the economy in balance."[29]

In 1951 the British government announced that it would henceforth never tolerate a jobless rate of more than 3 percent and "hoped" to hold the rate below 2 percent. (Currently it was 1.6 percent.) Elsewhere conditions varied, but mass idleness such as had plagued the world in the 1930s had become a thing of the past. Or so it seemed.

---

[29] Colette Cordebas, "Quelques réflections sur la pensée économique contemporaine," *Revue d'économie politique*, 73 (1963), 260; Jacques Rueff, "Fallacies of Lord Keynes' General Theory," *Quarterly Journal of Economics*, 61 (1947), 343–67; Alvin Hansen, *Economic Policy and Full Employment* (New York, 1947), pp. 18, 141, 148, 183, 249.

12

The End of the Golden Age

The extraordinary prestige of Keynesian economics after World War II resulted in part from the extraordinary economic expansion that occurred in those years. In the United States, the pent-up demand for homes, automobiles, and other consumer goods long in short supply because of wartime restrictions triggered the boom. Unemployment, essentially nonexistent during the war, held below 4 percent thereafter except during a brief recession in 1949–50. Britain and the Scandinavian countries also experienced only negligible unemployment in the postwar period, and while many persons were jobless in Germany and the occupied countries whose economies had been disrupted, massive American aid applied to the task of reconstructing shattered cities and replacing destroyed factories brought the unemployment rate down sharply, especially after 1950.

The confidence inspired by this happy state of affairs did not, however, cause economists to forget about unemployment, for proper management required a vigilant supervision of what became known as "economic indicators," of which unemployment was a major component. By closely observing changes and shifts of direction in a country's gross national product (a new term soon familiar to everyone as GNP), its trade balances, money supply, and price level, along with unemployment and other statistics, experts claimed to be able to manage the economy, preventing downturns from gathering momentum and checking booms before they caused the economy to "overheat" (another addition to the vocabulary of the subject). For this reason the decline of unemployment was accompanied by increased efforts to count and classify accurately the unemployed.

The United States, so laggard in this area before the Great Depression, made the most significant advance in keeping track of the jobless.

In 1937 WPA officials attempted to *estimate,* as distinct from actually count, the unemployed, publishing an analysis of a questionnaire survey. Out of this experience statisticians developed the idea of conducting periodic surveys of sample households, and beginning in 1940 WPA interviewers were sent each month to selected homes to gather information about the work status of all residents. The Census Bureau took over this work in 1942 and eventually the project became the joint responsibility of the Census and the Bureau of Labor Statistics. By the late 1950s a rotating sample of about 35,000 households was being queried each month.[1]

The chief advantage of the survey method was that it put the classification of the working and nonworking populations in the hands of supposedly objective professionals. To separate those of the idle who were able and willing to labor from the loafers and incompetents was as difficult in the 1950s as it had been in the 1550s, but the interview technique made for more valid distinctions. Instead of asking those without jobs if they wanted work and were able to perform it, the interviewers asked what they had actually been doing during the one-week period covered in each survey. Thus they obtained answers to the willing-and-able questions without asking them directly. The surveys made it possible to calculate the number of persons who were looking for work for the first time, and to keep track of others who would not be included in estimates based on unemployment-insurance data, such as the long-term jobless who had exhausted insurance benefits. The survey could also be designed to yield data about persons who were not part of the work force but who might decide or be induced to enter it, along with much other information. Canada and Japan soon adopted the survey technique, and most of the other industrial nations used it periodically as a check on their conventional ways of counting the unemployed, chiefly through easily available statistics on the numbers collecting unemployment insurance and making use of government employment offices. It was not more widely employed primarily because it was very expensive.

The existence of monthly survey data encouraged economists to draw finer distinctions among the unemployed, who could now easily be grouped according to age, sex, race, education, and other variables, and also according to why they were not working. This kind of fragmentation produced among other things a number of new categories of joblessness. To older concepts such as frictional and seasonal

[1] Ewan Clague, *The Bureau of Labor Statistics* (New York, 1968), pp. 49–54; National Bureau of Economic Research, *The Measurement and Behavior of Unemployment* (Princeton, 1957), pp. 65–66. The size of the sample has since been increased. Currently 58,834 households are surveyed each month.

unemployment were added such types as "search" and "precautionary" unemployment, "search" referring to persons who could be seen, as it were, as employed in gathering information about possible jobs, "precautionary" to those who rejected jobs so as to be free to accept better ones. The American economist Milton Friedman spoke of a "natural rate" of unemployment reflective of an equilibrium between the advantages of idleness (tax-free insurance payments, free time, the chance to look for a better place) and the loss of income involved. Since one had to be actively seeking work to be counted as unemployed, some economists even argued that good times *increased* the number of the jobless by enticing housewives, retired persons, and students to look for work. On the other hand, whether bad times caused more people to enter the labor market (the "additional worker theory," based on the reasoning that when breadwinners lost their jobs other members of their families began to look for work) or led to a decline as the long-term jobless gave up hope and stopped looking for work was also much debated in the mid-1950s.[2]

It was a measure of the prosperity of the times that such concepts could come to mind, but so many definitional nuances, and also the fact that the household-survey method called attention to the degree to which individuals decided for themselves whether or not to be unemployed,[3] probably raised as many questions as they answered. More detailed knowledge, in other words, drew attention to the ambiguity of the term.

The statistical breakdowns that the household surveys facilitated also pointed up certain social and economic problems. No matter how low the general level of unemployment, rates were higher among the young, the uneducated, and various disadvantaged minorities. To some extent these differences could be explained on the basis of prejudice (as in the case of American blacks, among whom unemployment was commonly twice as high as the white rate), but they also called into

[2] S. L. Wolfbein, *Unemployment in the United States: A Study of the American Labor Force* (Chicago, 1964), pp. 22–23; J. L. Palmer, *Inflation, Unemployment and Poverty* (Lexington, Mass., 1973), pp. 36–37, 131; R. L. Miller and R. M. Williams, *Unemployment and Inflation: The New Economics of the Wage Spiral* (St. Paul, 1974), pp. 30–31; *Measurement and Behavior of Unemployment*, pp. 30–31.

[3] No one was counted as unemployed who was not a member of the labor force, and people often entered and left the labor force voluntarily. A count made during a bitter winter storm in the industrial regions of the United States in January 1977, for example, recorded a drop of half a percentage point in unemployment, almost certainly produced by the unwillingness of large numbers of "nonworking" people to brave the elements in search of work. The condition of such people remained unchanged, but for official purposes they ceased to be unemployed. Arthur M. Ross, a leading authority on the subject, wrote in 1964: "The border of the labor force is not really a definite line but a shifting and shadowy area." *Unemployment and the American Economy* (New York, 1964), p. 5.

question the effectiveness of Keynesian tactics in combatting some types of unemployment. Under modern conditions the complex industrial processes essential for the expansion of output, upon which prosperity and full employment depended, were reducing the need for unskilled labor and increasing the need for educated and highly trained personnel. Instead of producing full employment, some economists claimed, fiscal and monetary policies that caused effective demand to rise might create a shortage of skilled labor and a surfeit of unskilled. A "two-tiered" or "dual" labor market appeared to be developing.

This was not merely the argument that machines were making human labor superfluous. Although, despite the experience of two centuries of mechanization, that argument continued to be made, the weight of informed opinion rejected it. Summing up the controversy as it had evolved from the time of J.-B. Say and Ricardo to the 1960s, a Swiss economist, Kurt Gehri, concluded that while technological change might displace workers in the short run, other (Keynesian) forces really controlled the volume of employment. Gehri added, however, that "there was no mechanism in the economic system that spontaneously assured the reintegration of workers displaced by technological progress." Technological unemployment was indeed occurring all the time, and with the development of electronic computers, at a quickening pace, but for those who viewed the trend with alarm, this "automation" of industry was of an order different from that of any previous change. Aside from the rapidity and pervasiveness of the technological advances, which threatened at the very least to unsettle and inconvenience millions of workers, automation appeared to be producing both a "manpower bottleneck" and also "creeping unemployment," which, an ILO report warned, was "developing simultaneously with rising production and productivity."[4]

Charles C. Killingsworth of Michigan State University advanced the most convincing explanation of what was happening. According to Killingsworth, aside from the frictional unemployment that always resulted when workers were replaced by machines, modern conditions were creating a new type of structural unemployment. Manufacturers were introducing labor-saving machines and techniques not so much, as had usually been the case in past times, to increase output, as to reduce costs. (What Ricardo in the famous chapter added to the third edition of his *Principles* had conceived of as theoretically possible but

[4] Kurt Gehri, *Du chômage technologique* (Zurich, 1970), p. 260; U.S. Department of Labor, *Labor Experience of Other Countries in Dealing with Technological Unemployment* (Washington, 1963), p. 5; Stanley Lebergott, ed., *Men Without Work: The Economics of Unemployment* (Englewood Cliffs, 1964) p. 67.

unlikely was at last coming to pass!)[5] Moreover, the new technology was focusing the demand for labor on the educated and highly skilled. Killingsworth showed that in 1962 unemployment was almost nonexistent among American college graduates, whereas over 9 percent of those without an eighth-grade education were out of work. If Keynesian stimulants were applied in such a situation, he warned a Senate committee, the effect would only be to produce "a severe shortage of workers at the top of the educational ladder."[6]

Although the Soviet Union was also experiencing a shortage of skilled labor and an oversupply of unskilled, radicals in the capitalist nations saw in this reasoning evidence that employers were trying "to balkanize the labor market" by increasing class differences within the work force, and also proof of the Marxist doctrine that the capitalist system contained within itself the seeds of its ultimate collapse. Those economists who looked to increasing demand to solve all problems sought to refute Killingsworth by calling attention to the fact that when demand did rise sharply, unemployment among supposedly incompetent workers fell rapidly; as one labor economist put it, "if demand were driven up to a sufficiently high level, the lame, the halt, and the blind would find employers camping on their doorsteps." This argument was similar to Hobson's point that the decline of unemployment during the boom periods of the late nineteenth century proved that the jobless were not morally or physically incapable of work.

Killingsworth and many other "establishment" economists, however, believed that the problem was real and could be solved by making "very large increases in our investment in human beings." All the industrial nations, and some of the "developing" ones undertook ambitious "manpower programs" designed to fit their unemployed for the work of the new electronic age, most of them as part of broad efforts to reduce frictional unemployment and iron out geographical imbalances between the supply of and the demand for labor. In addition to vocational retraining, the European industrial nations offered loans, tax relief, or other subsidies to encourage manufacturers to build factories in areas of labor surplus, and made grants to displaced workers to help them relocate where work could be more easily found. France, for example, set up a vocational retraining program as early as 1946 and in 1954 began to subsidize factory construction in selected districts. After 1951, West Germany provided assistance in resettling refugees where jobs were available. Belgium passed a comprehensive

[5] See above, pp. 72–73.
[6] Lebergott, *Men Without Work*, pp. 55–58; Arthur Okun, ed., *The Battle Against Unemployment* (New York, 1965), p. 36.

Regional Development Act in 1959 involving loans, tax incentives, and even public construction of factories.[7]

The United States lagged in adopting such devices. The famous GI Bill of Rights subsidized vocational education and training programs for countless veterans, but this had been, from the perspective of the so-called manpower problem, inadvertent. Only with the passage of the Area Redevelopment Act of 1961 and the Manpower Development and Training Act of 1962 did the government make a conscious effort to reduce structural unemployment, and these programs were too small to have much statistical impact. On the surface this appeared paradoxical, because Americans were much more worried about the effects of automation than the Europeans, who tended to think that any technological advance was good because it would speed up economic growth. The explanation of the apparent paradox lay in the fact that from the mid-1950s to the mid-1960s, a period of hectic expansion in western Europe, unemployment there seldom exceeded 2 percent, while the American jobless rate was two or three times as high. The situation was, however, ironic, because American capital investments, principally through the Marshall Plan, had triggered the European boom, and because American technology was the most advanced in the world.

Getting governments to tackle the manpower problem was relatively easy, although in retrospect it is clear that most of their efforts were at best only modestly effective. Political resistance to truly forceful use of monetary and fiscal policy to regulate the economy in the interest of controlling unemployment was often much stiffer, principally because of persisting concerns about the danger of inflation. These concerns were greater in some countries than in others—in Germany, for example, memories of the great inflation of the early 1920s acted as a perpetual check on expansive policies. But no nation was prepared to ignore the risks of soaring prices; in a sense the Keynesian tools were seen as too effective. In the 1950s no nation would reject its commitment to full employment in principle either, but it was often difficult to persuade governments to state precisely what full employment meant to them. In 1956 the International Labor Organization did

[7] Moshe Lewin, *Political Undercurrents in Soviet Economic Debates* (Princeton, 1974), pp. 156, 347; Walter Galenson, *A Primer on Employment and Wages* (New York, 1970), p. 106; D. M. Gordon, *Theories of Poverty and Underemployment: Orthodox, Radical, and Dual Labor Markets* (Lexington, Mass., 1972), pp. 53–81, esp. p. 78; Lebergott, *Men Without Work*, pp. 65–66; R. C. Wilcock and W. H. Franke, *Unwanted Workers* (Glencoe, 1963), pp. 261–66; Ross, *Unemployment*, pp. 182–84; Department of Labor, *Labor Experience of Other Countries*, pp. 9–13; E. M. Bussey, "Assistance to Labor Surplus Areas in Europe—Belgium," *Monthly Labor Review*, 83 (1960), 573–74; H. R. Bowen and G. L. Magnum, *Automation and Economic Progress* (Englewood Cliffs, 1966), pp. 159–67.

a study of this problem and its analysts came to the conclusion that the reason for the hesitancy and vagueness was the fear of inflation— "governments want to be sure that they do not become obliged to increase demand to such an extent that inflation will result as well as a higher level of employment."[8]

Albeit with misgivings, most of the industrial nations, and most economists, "accepted" a certain amount of inflation in the postwar years because there was so little unemployment. Still-vivid recollections of the 1930s and the developing prosperity after the privations of war made that happy situation seem to be well worth the inflationary price. In the United States, however, especially during the presidency of Dwight Eisenhower, more concern was expressed about rising prices and (as economists were wont to put it) the government was willing to "tolerate" a certain amount of unemployment in order to check the rise. In the late fifties the American unemployment rate, which had exceeded 4 percent only during brief periods for a decade after the war, began to fluctuate between 4 and 7 percent. From 1958 through 1962 it never fell below 5.5 percent. As late as 1955 *Fortune* could still refer to unemployment as no more than "a cloud on the economic horizon" and focus its discussion on the question of why the cloud did not "evaporate entirely," but soon thereafter the cloud began to become more ominous.[9] Yet the consumer price index rose by an alarming 3.3 percent in 1956, despite the fact that unemployment had fluctuated throughout the year around the 4 percent mark. The following year, when unemployment soared to 7 percent, the price index again rose by over 3 percent.

These developments caused the first stirrings of doubt about the Keynesian analysis of unemployment. "Economists were bafflled," one of their number recalled a few years later. "Here was no relatively simple case of inflation *or* depression; the two appeared simultaneously."[10]

If, as seemed logical, price inflation reflected an excess of demand over the supply of goods and services, that excess demand ought to cause an increase in production and thus reduce unemployment. So Keynes had reasoned in the *General Theory* and indeed in most of his

[8] A separate controversy developed over *how* to determine full employment, whether by simply counting the unemployed, by measuring the length of time it took the jobless to find work (the turnover approach), or by comparing the number of unemployed with the number of job vacancies. A Swedish economist, Bertil Ohlin, suggested defining full employment in terms of price stability, which clearly would put the objective of avoiding inflation ahead of providing the maximum number of persons with work. *Measurement and Behavior of Unemployment*, pp. 16–40.

[9] "Why Unemployment Persists," *Fortune*, 51 (May, 1955), 32.

[10] Morris Singer, "Inflation without Full Employment," *Social Research*, 26 (1959), 1–2.

writing during the interwar period. Although in the dark days of the depression he had enjoyed goading mossbacks by describing inflation as a positive social good, a way to "disinherit" established wealth, he was aware of the danger of overstimulating an economy that was already functioning at or near full employment. In *How to Pay for the War* (1940) he explained what he called the "ridiculous system" by which inflation had in fact compelled wage earners to pay a heavy share of the costs of World War I by reducing their real income despite the large wage increases they had obtained. "Inflation," he wrote, "allows [wage earners] to spend and deprives them of the fruit of spending." In World War II, he argued, inflation could be prevented by a policy of deferring a part of the wages paid to workers, thus reducing aggregate demand at the time and also piling up a reserve of future demand that would prevent a possible postwar slump. But that inflation might occur while substantial numbers of workers were unemployed in Keynesian terms made no sense.[11]

Economists endeavored to explain this strange phenomenon in two ways. In practical terms, they attributed it to the influence of large corporations and labor unions. Giant, oligopolistic industries were finding it simpler to grant large wage increases to powerful unions and recoup by raising prices than to risk strikes that might paralyze their operations for protracted periods. In such industries price competition was minimal; higher costs *could* be passed on with relative impunity, producing what was called "cost-push" inflation (as distinct from the conventional "demand-pull" variety). "At levels below those corresponding to reasonably full employment," wrote Paul Samuelson, "our institutions of wage bargaining and price settling may . . . lead to a price and wage creep, a creep which can be lessened by conventional depressing of demand by monetary and fiscal policy measures but only at the cost of creating greater unemployment." A British white paper put the problem more simply: "If the . . . conditions necessary to maintain full employment are exploited by trade unions and business men, price stability and full employment become incompatible."[12]

On the theoretical level, A. W. Phillips of the London School of Economics hypothesized in 1958 that there was a relationship between unemployment and the rate at which wage levels changed. He studied British wage and unemployment statistics during the period from 1861 to 1957. By plotting on graphs the annual percentage change of money wages and the unemployment rate, he produced the so-called Phillips curve, which reflected a "tendency for the rate of change of money

---

[11] J. M. Keynes, *How to Pay for the War* (New York, 1940), pp. 70–73, 49, 46.

[12] Robert Lekachman, ed., *Keynes' General Theory: Reports of Three Decades* (New York, 1964), p. 339; *International Labour Review*, 74 (1956), 4.

wages to be high when unemployment is low and to be low or negative when unemployment is high." Furthermore, the rate of change at any level of unemployment was swifter when unemployment was declining than when it was increasing. In themselves these conclusions were not particularly striking—like any commodity, the price of labor tended to fluctuate with changes in the demand for it, and workers were known to be more likely to resist wage cuts when demand was declining than employers were to resist increases when it was on the rise. But, Phillips announced the evidence of nearly a century of British experience also suggested that to hold wage rates stable required an unemployment rate of about 5½ per cent.[13] The implication, of course, was that to maintain full employment one must put up with a certain amount of inflation. Inflation could be curbed, therefore, only by "tolerating" an increase in unemployment. (This word, so smug, so arrogant, appeared in the literature with increasing frequency in the late fifties.)

If Keynes had been the shepherd of full employment, a French economist remarked, Phillips was the wolf.[14] The Phillips curve did not, however, suggest that Keynesian monetary and fiscal techniques did not function as the master had claimed. Rather, the curve indicated that there was, so to speak, a certain amount of friction in the system that inhibited the smooth functioning of monetary and fiscal techniques.

Phillips's theory was soon tested against different data by other researchers, who discovered roughly similar relationships. In 1959 Paul Samuelson and another economist plotted a Phillips curve based on twentieth-century American data and concluded that in order to end cost-push inflation the nation would have to accept an unemployment rate of from 5 to 6 percent. However interesting and intellectually satisfying their reasoning, this conclusion merely reflected current reality; the American inflation rate had subsided almost to zero by 1960 and unemployment ranged between 5 and 6 percent. No one could know in advance if more aggressive monetary and fiscal policies would cause prices to rise in this situation—Samuelson admitted that the Phillips curve was "a slippery concept"—but the Eisenhower administration was unwilling to risk the experiment. Bitter arguments raged in political and business circles as well as among economists as to the wisdom of this caution and, more broadly, about what was wrong with the economy and what could be done about it.[15]

Why did other industrial nations have much lower unemployment

[13] A. W. Phillips, "The Relation between Unemployment and the Rate of Change of Money Wage Rates in the United Kingdom, 1861–1957," *Economica*, 25 (1958), 283–99.

[14] Hughes Puel, *Chômage et capitalismes contemporains* (Paris, 1971), p. 25.

[15] Miller and Williams, *Unemployment and Inflation*, pp. 46–70; P. A. Samuelson and R. M. Solow, "Analytical Aspects of Anti-Inflation Policy," *American Economic Review*, 50 (1960), 192; Lekachman, *Keynes' General Theory*, p. 340.

rates? Was it merely because their methods of counting the jobless were less comprehensive? Or did different demographic trends, or the absence of despised and degraded racial minorities, or their larger percentages of agricultural workers, less likely to become unemployed, or the presumed hesitancy of foreign employers to lay off workers the moment business slackened explain the differences? Or did the Europeans and the Japanese simply care more about full employment than price stability, whereas Americans (at least the ones who controlled policy) gave a higher priority to preventing inflation?

Those who discounted the danger of inflation included economists as prestigious as Alvin Hansen, who in 1957 warned against "making a fetish of rigid price stability." In the early sixties, when John F. Kennedy, seeking to fulfill his campaign pledge to "get the country moving again," was pressing a reluctant Congress to approve fiscal stimulation, another economist wrote scornfully of the "remarkable spectacle of an administration laboring to convince its public that unemployment matters," adding that "strict canons of monetary behavior" were probably both unnecessary and unattainable. But the inflation problem aside, American economists were increasingly coming to recognize that eliminating unemployment would not be easy. When he took over as head of President Kennedy's Council of Economic Advisers in 1961, Walter Heller predicted that an 8 percent increase in GNP would bring unemployment down from its current rate of 6.4 percent to an acceptable 4 percent. But in reality an increase of 15 percent only brought the rate down to 5 ½ percent, and in June 1963 Heller estimated that reducing unemployment to 4 percent by the end of 1964 would require an increase of national output of $14 billion per quarter. The next year Professor Seymour Harris of Harvard claimed on the basis of a study of trends over the last decade that the amount of increase in GNP necessary to produce an additional million jobs had doubled, from 13 billion 1962 dollars to 26 billion.[16]

In retrospect it seems clear that, despite what may be called their theory-laden rhetoric, economists were allowing current reality to influence their most abstract analyses. With American unemployment apparently "stuck" above 5 percent, economists began to alter their definitions of full employment. The most commonly accepted figure during the 1950s was 4 percent, although 4 percent was roughly double the actual unemployment rate in western Europe and Japan.[17] The

[16] Okun, *Battle against Unemployment,* p. 56; Ross, *Unemployment,* pp. 162, 167; Seymour Harris, *Economics of the Kennedy Years* (New York, 1964), pp. 122–23.

[17] When Kennedy appointed a committee of experts to examine American methods of counting the jobless, it concluded that while European statistics underestimated unemployment as defined in the United States, the difference was not substantial. See President's Committee to Appraise Employment and Unemployment Statistics, *Measur-*

more industrialized nations of Europe were attracting millions of new workers from the poorer lands of the Mediterranean basin. Soon German movie houses were showing films in Turkish and there were North African quarters in most large French cities. In 1963, while Walter Heller, an optimist by American standards, was still describing 4 percent unemployment as acceptable, Swedish economists were claiming that a 2 percent rate was no more than "comfortably low" and indicating that still lower rates were attainable. West German government economists, who in the mid-fifties, when the German *Wirtschaftswunder* was just beginning, had defined full employment as anything below 5 percent unemployment, were calling that figure "obsolete" by the end of the decade when the unemployment rate was 2 percent, and soon thereafter, with immigrant "guest workers" pouring into Germany by the hundreds of thousands, they reduced the upper limit to under 3 percent. And Heller, as has been suggested, was more sanguine than most American experts. After a conference of specialists on unemployment in 1963, Arthur M. Ross of the University of California noted a "tendency to relax the criteria" as unemployment increased, adding somewhat ruefully, that it was "academic to debate whether 3 per cent or 4 per cent should be the goal, while the rate drifts along indefinitely at 6 per cent."[18]

Acting on the recommendation of Heller and other economists, Kennedy sought to stimulate consumer demand by reducing taxes, his thought being that a tax cut would seem a more palatable form of fiscal stimulation to conservatives than an increase in government spending. A "tax multiplier" could be as effective as a public-works multiplier. With so much unemployment, administration economists argued, the resulting budget imbalance would not cause inflation, and the stimulus to the economy provided by the tax cut would increase government income and soon bring the budget back into balance. Congress balked, however, and it was not until 1964, after Kennedy's assassination, that an $11 billion reduction was enacted.

Late 1964 marked a low point in the morale of American economists. "Millions of words had been spoken about unemployment and related problems," wrote Arthur M. Ross. "Innumerable conferences on automation had been held; countless boards, commissions, committees, and task forces had been appointed." The tax cut had gone through and massive new funds had been appropriated for retraining workers displaced by technology and upgrading the education of

---

ing Employment and Unemployment (Washington, 1962), and A. M. Ross, ed., *Employment Policy and the Labor Market* (Berkeley, 1965), pp. 27–28.

[18] Lebergott, *Men Without Work,* p. 160; Ross, *Employment Policy,* pp. 26–27; Ross, *Unemployment,* pp. 19–20.

disadvantaged groups. But unemployment had not declined significantly. "Now the questions were becoming more difficult."

The nation had "moved into [a period of] underemployment equilibrium," another leading student of unemployment, Stanley Lebergott, wrote in 1964. Lebergott was particularly worried by the growth
of long-term unemployment; the number of persons idle for more than
15 weeks had tripled since 1957. Except perhaps for short periods
during booms, the best that could be hoped for, he indicated, was an
unemployment rate of 4.5 percent. On the other hand, Ross's col-
league at Berkeley, Robert A. Gordon, although equally disconsolate,
blamed public opinion for the persistence of unemployment. "Congress and the American people seem to be prepared to live indefinitely
with unemployment of more than 4 percent," he complained, adding
as "a wild guess" that between 6 and 7 was the limit of what was
"tolerable." No European government, he claimed, would give up
"any significant degree of employment or growth" merely to slow
down the inflation rate.[19]

By the end of 1965, however, the effects of the 1964 tax cut were
being felt; without triggering any substantial increase in prices, the tax
cut had brought unemployment down to about 4 percent. The confidence of Keynesian economists was swiftly restored. "The right level
of demand is a narrow line between the specter of inflation from too
much demand and the danger of excessive unemployment from too
little," Arthur M. Okun explained in *The Battle Against Unemployment.*
"In retrospect, most economists would conclude that unemployment
—not inflation—has been our major economic problem since 1957.
With 20–20 hindsight, most of us would conclude that our policies
tolerated excessive unemployment and [we] should have taken more
expansionary risks." The American unemployment rate leveled off just
below 4 percent in 1966 and 1967, while the inflation rate hovered
around the 3 percent level. By the latter year Robert A. Gordon, who
in 1964 had feared that 7 percent unemployment was in the cards, was
saying that a rate of 3 percent or even of 2 percent was possible.
Progress at reducing the structural unemployment among young people, blacks, and other groups had not been very great, he confessed,
but Kennedy's manpower legislation and Lyndon Johnson's Great Society program had accomplished something. The problem was at least
"manageable." Somewhat more conservatively, Stanley Lebergott
now proposed 3.5 percent unemployment as the maximum tolerable
in the United States, and another economist spoke of "fine tuning" the
economy, delicately manipulating monetary and fiscal policy to achieve

[19] Ross, *Employment Policy,* pp. 6–8, 29, 35, 48.

exactly the right mix. Garth L. Magnum of the Upjohn Institute for Employment Research expressed this new confidence in particularly florid language:

> The jet transport of economic growth has not yet touched down at the haven of full employment where it needs to reverse its engines [he wrote]. . . . The landing place of full employment is buried in a fog of inexperience, but we have sufficient statistical radar to reduce the danger of feeling our way toward it. . . . The economy [is] within shooting distance of solving the problem of general unemployment.[20]

During the late 1960s the industrial nations again experienced the heady pleasures of prosperity—rapid economic growth combined with negligible unemployment. Once more Keynesian techniques had proved capable of controlling the complex forces surging through the world economy. Prices *were* rising more rapidly by 1966 and especially by 1968, but overall the economic picture was sunny and the prestige of economists particularly high. In 1965, laying out its economic policy for the last half of the 1960s, the French government had spoken of "*two* objectives of fundamental importance, stability and full employment," and set a goal for growth by 1970 that envisaged "a slight slackening of the demand for labor" *(une légère détente sur le marché du travail)*. However, in its next five-year plan drafted at the end of the sixties, the government rejected the idea of "accepting" higher unemployment. "No one," a French economist wrote in 1971, "any longer dares invoke the argument of necessary unemployment." In 1970 the American economist Walter Galenson wrote in a "primer" designed for use in college economics courses that even 3.5 percent unemployment was "indefensible as a national target." Two years later in the second edition of his widely read book, *Keynes and After*, Michael Stewart, a British economist, admitted that there was "cause for complaint" about the steady inflation that Great Britain and other countries were experiencing, but he dismissed as "hard to take seriously" the argument that inflation might be a greater evil than unemployment. Anxiety about the current state of the economy, Stewart insisted, was "basically misguided."[21]

But while prosperity was inspiring these and similar expressions of confidence, the inflation characteristic of the postwar era and indeed of the entire period since the end of the recession of 1937–38 shifted

[20] Lebergott, *Men Without Work*, pp. 2, 34, 47; Okun, *Battle against Unemployment*, pp. x–xi; R. A. Gordon, ed., *Toward a Manpower Policy* (New York, 1967), pp. 2–7, 24–25.

[21] M. F. Mouriaux, *L'emploi en France depuis 1945* (Paris, 1972), pp. 60–61; Puel, *Chômage et capitalismes*, pp. 13, 270; Galenson, *Employment and Wages*, p. 114; Michael Stewart, *Keynes and After* (London, 1972), pp. 211, 224, 281.

in velocity. The huge American expenditures on the war in Vietnam, unaccompanied either by price controls or by tax increases, was a major cause of this shift, both in the United States and elsewhere, too. Wage rates began to rise faster, particularly in western Europe and Japan, where by 1970 the annual increases were averaging more than 10 percent. Next, in 1972, began an ever-more-dramatic explosion of commodity prices, many of which doubled and tripled in a year and a half. But the ultimate inflationary pressure came in 1974 when most of the major oil-producing nations decided to quadruple the price of crude petroleum. Except for oil, supplies of which were ample for current use, these price increases were caused by real or anticipated shortages resulting from crop failures and the heavy demand for raw materials resulting from the industrial expansion of the period.

These events, especially the sudden increase in the price of the petroleum products so essential to industrial production, caused a worldwide recession in 1974 and 1975. (The word "depression" had apparently disappeared from the lexicon of economists and politicians.) The unemployment rate in the United States exceeded 5.5 percent in 1974, touched 9 percent in 1975, and fell back only to between 7 and 8 percent during the "recovery" of 1976–77. More ominously, German, French, British, Italian, and other European rates climbed into the 5 to 6 percent range during the recession, and failed, like the American, to drop back to earlier levels when the recovery took hold. Germany had the strongest economy in Europe, yet in early 1976 nearly 6 percent of its labor force was idle. The flow of labor from the Mediterranean basin to northern and western Europe slackened. By 1977, more Italian workers were returning to their native towns and villages than were leaving.

The "creeping" inflation of the 1960s had become the "galloping" and "double-digit" inflation of the 1970s, but the inflation was strangely independent of the ebb and flow of economic activity and therefore of unemployment. In the United States, which was less affected than most of the other industrial nations, prices rose during 1970 by more than 5 percent while the unemployment rate was going up from 4 percent to 6. Between 1970 and 1977, through good times and bad, the American consumer price index rose by 50 percent, the Japanese doubled, the British more than doubled. Even in Germany prices increased by about 40 percent in these years.

With unemployment high and output declining, the Keynesian formula called for economic stimulation—some combination of lower taxes, more public investment, make-work programs, easy credit. But with prices soaring the formula required government belt tightening, high interest rates, stiffer taxation. These approaches were self-canceling. The one obvious alternative, fiscal stimulation combined with wage and price controls, known as an "incomes policy," found favor in some quarters (John Kenneth Galbraith of Harvard was a leading American advocate), but was unpopular with both labor and business groups and was indeed viewed generally as too drastic and likely to produce a cumbersome and ineffective bureaucracy. As a short-run policy, critics argued, an incomes policy would cause producers to hold back goods and only dam up price and wage increases that would burst forth in a flood when controls were removed.[22] As a permanent policy it would mean the end of free-enterprise capitalism, a prospect most people either rejected on principle or were afraid to face. Economists, in short, had no convincing or even hopeful proposals for reducing unemployment very substantially.

In desperation, some turned to the tactic, practiced during the Great Depression in less sophisticated ways, of trying to define a portion of the unemployment out of existence. The sample survey method of counting the jobless enabled the statistically inclined to turn a single unemployment rate (say, the official American total of 7.5 percent in June 1976) into a maze of percentages for different kinds of people, ranging from a modest 4.4 percent for married men to a horrendous 18.4 percent for teenagers. Such figures could be used to point up the seriousness of unemployment but also to minimize it, for example by stressing the low rate among heads of families, the bulwark of the society, or by discounting the problem of unemployment among the young on the ground that the young suffered relatively less when out of work than older people. Focusing attention on long-term unemployment (defined as persons out of a job for fifteen weeks or more) also could lead to the conclusion that only these 2.2 million were *really* suffering. There was also a school of thought that argued for downplaying unemployment rates and stressing instead the number of people employed; since that number was increasing rapidly during 1976 —in the United States by some 4 million persons in six months—the conclusion could be drawn that unemployment was not a significant social problem. These manipulations amounted to a revival of discussions of structural unemployment and as such tended to deflect attention from the immediate problem of getting competent workers back on private payrolls to even more difficult questions relating to the most efficient use of national resources, human and material. And neither the discussions nor the statistical legerdemain satisfied anyone.

[22] In the United States, the ninety-day price and wage freeze decreed by President Nixon in the summer of 1971 and the efforts to limit increases thereafter by regulatory boards provided ammunition to these critics, for there was great opposition to the controls and large price and wage increases as soon as they were lifted.

Although "free market" economists of the school of Milton Friedman insisted that doing away with artificial restrictions on economic activity would solve the unemployment problem, most prestigious members of the profession were losing confidence in their ability to manage the world economy, and their reputations suffered accordingly. "Stagflation," the name given to the baffling new condition, was impossible according to the general theory but only too real. "The Keynesian conceptualization of the problem is being torn to shreds," an American labor-union economist noted glumly in the spring of 1975. Paul Samuelson, who had been awarded a Nobel prize in 1970 in recognition of his contributions to economic understanding, confessed meekly five years later, that "experts feel less sure of their expertise," the problem being that "the system is now so biased toward inflation."[23]

By 1976 economics was in what could almost be described as a state of disarray; many in the profession found cause to criticize current policies, but no substantial group had the confidence to claim, let alone the arguments to persuade others, that a different set of policies would bring back full employment quickly. Typical was the comment of a Washington-based economist who announced that "the purely Keynesian era is over," and then called for "not . . . a revolution in economics but . . . an evolution," an indirect way of admitting that he did not know what should or would follow the defunct Keynesian era. In Great Britain, the *New Statesman* published a "definition" of an economist similar in tone to that employed by Keynes in his remarks about the classical writers in the *General Theory:* An economist is "an inhabitant of cloud-cuckoo land; one knowledgeable in an obsolete art; a harmless academic drudge whose theories and laws are but puffs of air."[24] During the 1976 American presidential election campaign, the candidates strove mightily to distinguish their proposals for reducing unemployment one from the other, but the economists who were advising them, Democratic and Republican alike, were pessimistic about reducing unemployment very much. Alan Greenspan, chairman of President Ford's Council of Economic Advisers, claimed to have studied dozens of proposals for reducing hard-core unemployment without discovering one that seemed likely to accomplish anything, and the Democratic experts were not much more sanguine. "The economics profession just doesn't know as much about this issue as it should," the economic policy coordinator of Jimmy Carter's campaign complained to a reporter.[25]

[23] *New York Times*, April 21, 1975.
[24] *Ibid.*, April 21, 1976.
[25] *Ibid.*, August 18, 1976.

The dilemma was clearly described by Charles L. Schultze of the Brookings Institution shortly before he replaced Greenspan on the Council of Economic Advisers after Carter's election as President:

> Every time we push the rate of unemployment toward acceptably low levels, by whatever means, we set off a new inflation. And, in turn, both the political and economic consequences of inflation make it impossible to achieve full employment.[26]

Some pessimists in late 1976 were going still further, arguing that inflation, far from tending to stimulate the economy and reduce unemployment, was actually a depressant of economic activity and thus a cause of unemployment. And if it did not increase unemployment directly, by squeezing the real income of many families inflation encouraged additional persons to look for work to help make ends meet; the rapid growth of the labor force was a major reason why it was so difficult to bring the unemployment rate down even when the number of new jobs was rising.

That the deliberate unbalancing of governmental budgets would produce disastrous inflation was the central fear of Keynes's critics in the 1920s and 1930s, and indeed of classical economists long before Keynes was born. (Many thinkers, struggling to devise ways of stimulating flagging economies, had come to the brink of recommending inflation only to back off at once when they realized where their thoughts were leading them.) But although Keynes himself recognized the danger of excessive inflation once full employment had been achieved, he discounted it, probably because he was living and working in a country suffering from particularly virulent forms of unemployment and deflation. In any case, he devoted little space to the question in the *General Theory*,[27] and in his popular writings he disparaged the risks with the insouciance typical of his manner of dealing with orthodox views. He taught that a little inflation was a good thing, that it made optimists of us all and sparked economic growth, thus a better life. Until full employment was achieved, he stated in the *General Theory*, "rising prices will be associated with an increasing aggregate real income."[28]

[26] *Ibid.*

[27] "When full employment is reached, any attempt to increase investment still further will set up a tendency in money-prices to rise without limit." This was for Keynes a theoretical point, related to R. F. Kahn's reasoning that in a closed system the multiplier effect of hiring one man "would then place all the remainder of the unemployed into secondary employment." *General Theory*, p. 118; Kahn, "Relation of Home Investment to Unemployment," pp. 189–90.

[28] J. M. Keynes, *The General Theory of Employment, Interest, and Money* (New York, 1964), p. 119.

In the mid-1970s, this association no longer held true. Like many medicines, when taken repeatedly inflation required larger doses to achieve the desired effect, soon became addictive (making withdrawal too painful to bear), and ultimately failed to perform its curative function at all. In 1972 economists Otto Eckstein and Roger Brinner showed that the smug assumption inspired by the Phillips curve, namely, that it was possible to "trade off" a particular volume of unemployment by "accepting" a particular rate of inflation, was incorrect once a certain rate of inflation had been reached. When prices rose by more than 2½ percent annually, they explained, "the price coefficient rises gradually to unity." Translated into everyday language, this meant that at low rates of inflation consumers buy more than they can afford and thus stimulate the economy, but that as prices rise more rapidly they recognize only too well what is happening and cut down on their purchases.[29] Put differently, the popular acceptance of Keynesian economics weakened the effectiveness of its fiscal and monetary techniques. The truths that Keynes had explicated remained, just as those of Adam Smith and Ricardo and the other pioneers of the science remain, but it was becoming increasing likely that the general theory was not really general after all, but rather, as Keynes had said of classical theory, a special case, applicable only to certain conditions at a certain time. If so, the brief golden age of full employment has ended.

[29] Miller and Williams, *Unemployment and Inflation,* pp. 51–52.

13

Unemployment Today

In a world again plagued by substantial unemployment, what will life be like? It is reasonable to assume, first of all, that the loss of work can no longer be the mass material and psychological catastrophe that it was during the Great Depression or at any earlier time. Unemployment insurance is everywhere quite comprehensive and unrestricted by actuarial limits. When unemployment becomes more widespread and prolonged, the periods of coverage are extended by legislative or executive fiat; when benefit payments are ravaged by inflation, they are increased in the same manner. French industrial workers are now guaranteed full pay for a year when laid off. Many jobless Americans are entitled by contract to supplemental benefits from their former employers to buttress insurance payments. The generous size of German insurance grants have "drawn much of the sting from unemployment."

Moreover, the internalization of what may be called the Keynesian value system has altered the psychology of unemployment. If, in order to cool an overheated economy, a government may deliberately cause workers to lose their jobs—and all governments claim and occasionally exercise this right, which is an essential weapon in the Keynesian arsenal—then those who lose their jobs are unlikely to feel either personally inadequate or the hapless victims of an inscrutable fate. And even when the state is not applying the brakes to the economy, being unemployed cannot logically seem the fault of the jobless because maintaining full employment is (again by official declaration) the responsibility of the state. The force of this logic has permeated the consciousness of thousands who have never read Keynes's *General Theory*. As a result, the irrational tendency of so many of the unemployed of the thirties to blame themselves for their unfortunate condition, the tendency that puzzled social scientists like E. Wight Bakke and Siegfried Kracauer, and vexed radicals like George Orwell and Matthew Josephson, is fast disappearing among the unemployed of the seventies.

Germans are supposedly an especially work-oriented people, but during the recession of 1975 a reporter interviewing large numbers of idle German workers characterized their mood as "carefree." Unemployment "no longer seems dreadful," he wrote. "The loss of dignity that used to accompany the loss of a job has been remedied." The collection of benefits has been so routinized in Germany that while the expression *stempeln gehen* (to go to be stamped) persists as a colloquialism for "to be unemployed," the jobless worker need no longer even put up with the inconvenience of reporting periodically at a labor exchange. Instead a computer directs unemployment credits to his bank account. In 1972 a French economist, somewhat troubled by the increase in the number of the jobless, commented that unemployment insurance and other social changes had "altered the image of unemployment and made it seem less inadmissible *(mois inavouable)*, a normal part of an expanding economy."[1]

While being unemployed for any length of time is certainly no joke, it seems clear that the malaise felt and expressed by persons thrown out of work nowadays rises from fear that some sacrifice of living standards may result rather than from any imagined stigma attached to being dependent upon unemployment compensation. This is so despite the fact that the payments are to a considerable extent a form of public charity. The trend that so alarmed William Beveridge when he followed the development of British unemployment policy in the 1920s has everywhere continued until there is no longer much relationship between what workers and their employers pay into the systems and what the unemployed take out of the systems (or, better, are given by the state).

These new attitudes and policies, which are in keeping with the realities of industrial capitalism, are of course a great gain for all concerned, but they are not without disadvantages. Although it may appear to make social sense not to adhere to narrow standards when the unemployed "exhaust" their benefits, insurance funds that depend upon outside resources do not really insure in the sense "make certain." Increasingly open-ended systems dispensing larger sums than the funds taken in are also inflationary, and while the payments do increase aggregate demand and thus help create jobs, the inflationary effects make necessary still larger supplements, which further exacer-

[1] *New York Times*, January 19, 1975; Claude Fontaine, "Population et chômage," *Revue d'économie politique*, 85 (1972), 1025.

bate the inflation and push the system still further from its actuarial base.

This aspect of modern insurance systems also tends to reduce the zeal with which discharged workers seek reemployment. That insurance would have this effect seemed axiomatic to the classical economists, and the point was raised vociferously by such twentieth-century critics as Jacques Rueff when national unemployment insurance was first being introduced. It could be dismissed as of no practical and very small theoretical importance if the systems were still self-sustaining. Obviously society can better tolerate the laggards than leave all of the jobless without support when unemployment strikes. But as presently constituted most unemployment-insurance systems come close to encouraging idleness. By extending benefit periods and raising payments —all to good social purpose when the economy lags and prices soar —they inadvertently remove that goad to effort, the knowledge that support is limited and will be cut off at a predetermined point. In the commendable interest of reducing anxiety, they foster the element in human nature that prefers leisure to labor, an element that requires in many persons relatively little encouragement to assert itself. Most systems also permit the unemployed to reject proffered jobs that are not as good as those just lost, a policy desirable in principle but not the one best calculated to reduce unemployment and, in a period of genuine economic decline, impossible of achievement for all.

In short, by fostering the illusion of security, unemployment insurance supplies both workers and the state with a little more psychological comfort than is good for either. Workers view it not so much as a system for sharing a risk, as in the case of fire or life insurance, but as a right derived from their participation in a complex, manipulative political system. The state uses unemployment benefits as part of the welfare system, a relatively noncontroversial form of relief disguised as insurance earned and paid for by the recipients. The effect in both cases is to divert attention from the fundamental fact—much emphasized by Keynes—that unemployment impoverishes not only the idle workers but also society, which it deprives of the workers' product and the economic stimulation thereof. If unemployment insurance benefits were based only on the contributions of workers and employers, they would have to be supplemented by public welfare if the jobless were to be sustained at present levels. Such a system would be no more costly than what now exists, and by compelling the recipients to recognize the true character of the payments, it might encourage them to seek new jobs more actively.

It is often suggested that instead of supporting the unemployed until they can find new jobs the state should create jobs for them, the argument being that the work would be socially useful and have a potent multiplier effect on the economy, and that the employed individuals would profit psychologically and emotionally from being purposefully occupied. The heartening effect of New Deal employment programs and the boost that Nazi public works gave to the German economy are advanced as examples of the benefits of job-creation schemes. History, however, offers few other illustrations of successful make-work programs. The French experiments of 1789–91 and 1848 were disasters, and English efforts over the centuries to occupy the jobless fruitfully, while persistent, varied, and sometimes ingenious, were only less spectacular failures. The state can put unemployed people on its payroll easily enough; finding tasks that they can usefully perform is another matter. The political institutions of free-enterprise economies are not designed to organize and supervise the employment of masses of labor. Choosing socially valuable projects is not beyond their capacities, but fitting the people who need work into the kinds of jobs that these projects provide is not so simple. Even in the regimented yet rootless world of modern industry, labor is not an unspecialized force like steam or electricity, or an interchangeable part like a spark plug that can energize one machine or another according to need. Unemployed assembly-line workers do not ordinarily make adequate bricklayers, nor are laid-off bricklayers likely to make capable (or willing) ditchdiggers.

The New Deal arts, theater, and writers projects proved that it is not impossible to create make-work programs for particular types of skills. However, these projects employed only a relative handful of very specialized people, and these, so to speak, "outside" the basic economy. Setting up comprehensive make-work programs with the previous occupations of the unemployed in mind would be next to impossible administratively and not even necessarily in the public interest; after all, that interest may well have caused those workers to lose their jobs. For the state to build steel mills and automobile factories because steel and automobile workers have been laid off would be economic nonsense, the practical difficulties aside.

Under ordinary circumstances, make-work projects are based upon a superficially plausible but incorrect assumption: that since those to be employed want to work, any work that is honest and decently paid will suffice. In practice this has usually meant projects that require large numbers of unskilled laborers, a kind of lowest-common-denominator approach based on the assumption (also plausible but incorrect) that anyone who can work at all can handle an "unskilled" job. Putting aside the facts that most such jobs are unpleasant, boring, and require more physical strength than the average unemployed worker can muster, there is often a contradiction between the objective of creating labor-intensive projects and projects that are socially useful. Modern industrial societies have relatively little need for unskilled labor, a fact which goes far toward explaining the growth of structural unemployment that all of them have experienced. Traditionally, road building and road repair were the typical make-work activities, but roads are no longer built with shovels and wheelbarrows, putting aside this time the question of whether the world needs more roads. And what the world does need—more housing for example—would require large investments in materials, often in materials already in great demand, with the risk that programs large enough to occupy significant numbers of the unemployed would push price levels still higher.

The idea of the government stepping in as employer of last resort is extremely appealing, but it is an impractical idea and one that obfuscates the central problem of the incompatability of full employment and stable prices. After all, if massive public-works programs could reduce unemployment without harmful inflationary side effects they would not be needed, since monetary and fiscal policies would then be able to accomplish the same objective without the risks and inefficiencies involved in state-administered business ventures. It is largely because fiscal and monetary stimulants *do* seem to produce "unacceptable" inflation that the unemployment problem exists.

Moreover, under modern conditions it is difficult to envisage work programs that would not be punitive in effect, if not in intent. To offer pick-and-shovel, leaf-raking, and other laborious or dull jobs to persons without any means of support is one thing, but quite another when the jobless can draw upon unemployment insurance or even welfare. The spectacle of WPA officials distributing snow shovels during blizzards to gaunt and ragged men was somehow heartening in the America of the 1930s because the men had no other source of income; in the 1970s the idle are less gaunt and ragged and are unlikely to accept such work unless threatened with the loss of available public assistance; only the absence of the workhouse would distinguish such a system from the discredited nineteenth-century British system based on the principle of less eligibility.

If unemployment is a disease that is particularly prevalent in modern industrial societies, and experience certainly suggests that it is, inflation appears to be an inherent characteristic of all modern societies, and the relationship between unemployment and inflation is, unfortunately, intimate. In the best of all possible worlds there would be neither unemployment nor inflation, but this world is not it. Unless and until some new Keynes shows us how to manipulate our affairs so as to avoid them—and this new savior is, alas, not in sight—these twin scourges seem destined to harass us indefinitely. Put less apocalyptically, it does not seem that either full employment or price stability is in the cards, given the present state of technology and economic knowledge. How, therefore, does the prospect of an eternal erosion of the value of money affect attitudes toward unemployment?

Keynes liked to say that inflation was a fact of life. In 1923, for example, he described history as "an almost unbroken chronicle in every country . . . back to the earliest dawn of economic record, of a progressive deterioration in the real value of . . . money."[2] Like most of the historical judgments in Keynes's work, this one was something of a distortion, designed to buttress an argument, although understandable in the context of the deflation of the interwar years, which to him seemed a kind of historical aberration. Keynes also claimed that inflation produced important social benefits: in the twenties he focused upon its supposed capacity to redistribute wealth more equitably by "disinheriting" bondholders; later he stressed the psychological boost that gradually increasing prices gave to investment. But like all economists, Keynes knew too that inflation tended to lower real wages, which could not be justified in his system unless full employment was achieved.

At the time that Keynes was constructing his general theory it was widely believed that the tremendous economic growth associated with the industrial revolution had run its course. "The era of easy expansion has ended," the French poet-philosopher Paul Valéry wrote in 1931. "All habitable territory has been discovered, surveyed, divided up. . . . The age of stagnation (*du monde fini*) has begun." In England a few years later, Joan Robinson, one of Keynes's most influential disciples, was justifying the need to apply "powerful stimulants" to the economy on the grounds that the Western world was fast approaching the time when its population would cease to grow, and that technological advances comparable to those of the nineteenth century were "scarcely to be hoped for." That "powerful stimulants" might cause inflation alarmed conservatives but seemed beside the point to Keynes and his followers because of the persistent deflationary trend of the period. As Keynes, always ready with a clever remark, put it in 1929, "to bring up the bogy of Inflation . . . at the present time is like warning a patient who is wasting away from emaciation of the dangers of excessive corpulence." In 1937 Robinson called it "a stock bogy," adding, "In times of peace with a stable government and a competent monetary authority it is little to be feared."[3]

[2] J. M. Keynes, *Essays in Persuasion* (New York, 1963), p. 86.

[3] *Ibid.*, pp. 124–25; Paul Valéry, *Regards sur le monde actuel* (Paris, 1931), p. 28; Joan Robinson, *Introduction to the Theory of Employment* (New York, 1937), pp. 120–23.

Keynes thus devised a theory and suggested policies for implementing it that discounted the danger of inflation and put great emphasis on stimulating economic growth. Circumstances, however, change—nowadays, it would take a greater iconoclast than Keynes to refer to inflation as a "bogy." Logically, continuous inflation ought always to stimulate consumption and thus increase employment, since money in hand will never be worth as much again and since anything purchased on credit can be paid for with depreciated currency. In practice this is not always the case—rising prices cause some persons to reduce expenses in order to have enough for future needs, or merely to refrain from buying because their sense of what goods are "worth" has been shaped by earlier, lower nominal values. Rapid inflation sometimes leads to panic buying, sometimes to hoarding—its effects on economic activity are quite unpredictable. To the extent that the unpredictability makes it difficult to forecast economic trends, rapid inflation undermines the efficiency of policies aimed at controlling the economy.

Since money supposedly represents a fixed value, in a narrow sense *any* inflation is a kind of breach of contract, a fraud perpetrated by the state that prints the money against the citizens who accept it in exchange for their labor. Up to a point the fraud is not worth bothering about; it can be perhaps justified as a price paid for the convenience provided, comparable in a way to the seigniorage charged by mints for coining precious metals. But under recent conditions the fraud has become more serious; money has depreciated so rapidly that it is impossible for a prudent person of ordinary means to hold on to what he has. In the United States, an annual rate of inflation of 5 percent would now be considered modest, but even 5 percent more than wipes out the earnings of a savings account after income tax is paid on the interest. The situation varies from country to country, but banks rarely pay interest equal to the local inflation rate—never when tax charges are considered. In addition to its immorality and its psychologically upsetting aspects, this erosion of accumulated wealth reduces investment and thus contributes to unemployment.

Rapid inflation also makes any system of social security a chimera, because the amounts that can reasonably be paid in by workers and their employers at one level of prices and wages do not accumulate and appreciate enough during a lifetime of labor to provide adequate income for workers after retirement at the price levels then in effect. After all, the beneficiaries of old-age insurance and other pension funds are quite literally *rentiers,* and as Keynes so shrewdly pointed out, inflation is a neat device for reducing the value of the assets of the *rentier* class. When the economy and the working population are expanding fast enough a social security system can continue to function despite inflation, since current contributions cover the difference between what the retired have paid in and what they must be allowed to withdraw if they are to live decently. This hypothecation of the future cannot, however, long continue if the growth rate of the economy slackens or if the work force ceases to expand at a fast enough pace. The state can step in when insurance funds are depleted and it can and does increase insurance payments to "compensate" for inflation. In doing so, however, the state must either divert government resources from other presumably useful purposes, or increase general taxation (counterproductive so far as reducing unemployment is concerned), or resort to further inflation, which merely postpones the reckoning.

That both unemployment and inflation are undesirable goes without saying. What *is* often said is that unemployment is more damaging to society than inflation, and a powerful case can be made for this view. Unemployment is nearly always undeserved; it strikes certain individuals down while passing by others no more skillful or hard-working; it focuses losses instead of distributing them. Inflation on the other hand, attacks its victims gradually and erodes the worth of everyone's money equally.

However, reducing unemployment drastically, if possible at all, would appear to require more massive inflation. And, whatever may be said about the subject, it is not necessarily true that unemployment is more damaging to society than inflation. We have learned how to live with unemployment, at least after a fashion. It should be possible to parcel out the economic losses more equitably and to compensate for the psychological burdens unemployment imposes still better. But can society, in the long run, survive the effects of continuous inflation?

When this question was asked in the 1930s Keynes had a devastating answer: "In the long run we are all dead." To grant that Keynes was correct in advocating inflationary policies at that time, however, does not mean that his tactics are the right ones for every situation. Keynes saw stagnation as the root cause of unemployment and devised and justified methods of stimulating economic growth. When he did his work, energy was cheap and vast sources of energy remained undeveloped. Raw materials were a glut on the market; conservation meant chiefly protecting rare animals, cutting down trees scientifically, preventing soil erosion, and the like. As a result of Keynes's insights, modern societies have become dependent upon, indeed addicted to growth. Their search for growth has led to inflation, and reciprocally, inflation has increased the public's expectation of growth, if only by causing numbers to become larger. A *monde fini* such as Paul Valéry envisaged has become almost inconceivable.

But is economic growth currently desirable? I leave aside such issues as overpopulation, pollution, and the quality of life as being principally matters of taste or, at most, less immediately crucial economically than most of those who are especially concerned about these issues claim. How, under modern conditions, can output be expanded while the use of energy is curbed? ("Saving" energy by designing lighter automobiles and turning down thermostats does not really come to terms with the kind of growth rates necessary to achieve full employment as society is now organized.)

If the reduction of unemployment requires an increase of consumption, and if increasing consumption requires not only large public deficits that result in skyrocketing inflation but also an increase of production which will perforce place greater pressures on scarce raw materials and energy, leading to still more inflation, is the reduction of unemployment in the public interest?

No one wants to settle for less than he now has. This is a human characteristic, much strenghtened, as I have just indicated, by continuous inflation. Not to face reality, however, can result in successful adaptation only by chance. Less now does not have to mean less tomorrow, certainly not less forever. It might be better to accept more circumscribed material conditions for the short run, for if the social cost of growth is higher than its worth, the industrial world needs to learn to endure substantial unemployment for a season. Perhaps, therefore, the expression "to be unemployed" had best be understood in the archaic sense of *chômage*, to take one's ease, sheltered from the burning heat. In the long run a new way to grow will surely be discovered—in technology, or in a new way of understanding and managing the contemporary economic system, or if need be in a new system.

Actually, it is not necessary to "accept" more unemployment than was "tolerable" during the golden age. "More" unemployment exists and no one whose opinion carries much weight has offered a convincing proposal for bringing the rate down to the levels of the last decade, with or without inflation. What to do about the victims of structural unemployment is one of the great challenges of modern times. In the 1950s structural unemployment seemed a uniquely American phenomenon, but by the late 1970s it had taken on world dimensions. In the summer of 1977, well over a million and a half western Europeans below the age of 25 were unable to find work. Substantial numbers of these young people were well educated and possessed of valuable skills, as, of course, were many jobless young Americans. However, the preponderant majority were unskilled and poorly educated.

The process of industrial growth had given rise to a paradox, indeed, to a dilemma. In order to increase output, more efficient means of production were devised. These techniques improved the productivity of labor, justifying wage increases. Higher wages, however, encouraged the further substitution of machinery for human labor. Thus improved productivity made necessary still greater output if the prevailing level of employment was to be maintained. But since more advanced technologies required still more highly skilled and disciplined workers (qualities for which the young are not famous), the demand for youthful workers lagged. In the United States and to an increasing degree in Europe too, declining educational achievement levels exacerbated the problem. It was no coincidence that among ghetto youths in the big American cities both employment and scores on standard academic achievement tests were well below the national averages. The meager results that manpower programs have achieved indicate that educational and training efforts have not been of much value.

At the same time higher wage rates elevated the expectations of workers in all the industrial nations; the unskilled and unlettered became progressively more reluctant to accept unpleasant or arduous or "dead end" jobs, or ones that paid little because the work was not very productive. And minimum-wage laws, however desirable as a way of assuring *workers* a certain standard of living, also tended to increase structural unemployment. Although legal minimums were in no country more than marginally adequate, they made it prohibitively expensive for employers to hire people to do many useful but relatively unproductive tasks. The employers therefore either left the tasks undone or found ways of doing them with machines, even though in many instances human labor could perform the tasks better.

Nineteenth-century classical economists believed that all forms of social insurance, even what we call welfare, are counterproductive because they cause unemployment and serve as a disincentive for hard work. According to modern theory, society's devices for dealing with poverty and involuntary idleness increase employment by putting money in the pockets of people who will spend it promptly, thus stimulating demand and causing idle people to be put to work. The paradox is that under modern conditions both the theories accurately describe reality. Welfare and unemployment insurance benefits surely stimulate output, but minimum-wage laws cause employers to make decisions that reduce employment, and welfare and unemployment insurance payments cause many potential workers to refuse certain kinds of jobs or to search less enegetically for employment when out of work. Clearly, the problem calls for social restructuring as well as (probably much more than) economic change. How that can be brought about no one can say with confidence, but efforts to bring it about are more likely to reduce structural unemployment than more direct approaches.

Workers idled by cyclical fluctuations present a different and more easily understood problem. The injustice resulting from cyclical unemployment lies in its arbitrary character—some workers suffer all the loss, the rest escape unscathed, and those who suffer are selected not because they are less efficient or less reliable or less in need of work than their fellows, but because they are newcomers. If, instead of 6 or 8 or 10 percent of the work force being unemployed and the rest fully occupied, everyone in the work force were to suffer an equivalent reduction of the hours of labor, this injustice would be avoided.

Since economic conditions vary from one industry to another and since workers in one industry are not readily interchangeable with those in others, an arrangement of this sort could function only on the plant or corporation level, but that is the level at which employment decisions already are made. If such an arrangement was possible, unemployment insurance would be unnecessary, or rather the arrangement would itself be insurance against unemployment. There would still be a place for insurance, but it would properly be called wage insurance rather than unemployment insurance.

Work sharing has never, unfortunately, been much practiced. Since organized labor rejected the idea during the Great Depression when real wages were rising and public aid for the unemployed was mostly inadequate, it is not likely that labor will look upon the idea more favorably today, when the jobless are better protected and inflation is eroding the purchasing power of full-time workers' paychecks. And if the loss of work is not to be shared equally, seniority is a plausible standard—objective and in accord with most persons' view of equity if the basic premise, that some must bear all the work loss, is sound. But is the premise sound?

When the demand for automobiles or refrigerators or steel wire slackens, manufacturers reduce output and lay off some of their hands. They often could with some effort keep all employed on reduced schedules, without affecting either the volume produced or the size of the wage bill. When state or city budgets are cut back, policemen, firemen, teachers, and clerks are laid off. Presumably all could be kept at work if all would accept reduced wages and benefits.

The practical difficulties of work sharing are large. Manufacturers can often reduce output most efficiently by closing a plant in one city entirely and keeping another somewhere else on full time. If government workers agreed to pay cuts in order to prevent discharges, they would relieve taxpayers of the inconveniences that reduced services cause and thus give up a major weapon in their struggle to have the cuts restored. Issues between capital and labor and between the state and its employees are seldom clear cut. To expect workers to accept less money without a contest would be unreasonable. Factory hands naturally believe that manufacturers should cut profits or reduce their other expenditures instead of lowering wages. Civil servants think that the citizens they serve ought to pay higher taxes or find other sources of revenue.

The virtue of unemployment for both employers and those workers who escape the ax is that it provides a way to avoid confrontations. Labor leaders believe that unemployment is a social and personal calamity and they strive earnestly to discover and put into effect the means of reducing it, but their attitude toward the unemployed remains essentially dispassionate. In the last analysis, theirs is an adversary relationship. Unions often call strikes over a few cents an hour in wages but rarely to try to prevent reductions in the work force. This may be perfectly logical but it is also conventional. Employers recognize the predisposition of organized labor in this regard and react accordingly. Reducing wages by lowering wage rates usually means breaking a contract, reducing wages by shortening the hours worked antagonizes the entire work force. But layoffs affect only a minority, and that the least powerful.

In Japan and to a lesser extent in western European countries, employers were supposed to be more hesitant than their American counterparts to discharge workers when demand slackened. Recent unemployment statistics from these countries demonstrate that this forbearance has limits. On the other hand, American steelworkers and some other union groups are beginning to make lifetime job guarantees a subject for collective bargaining. The future of job sharing is uncertain. So too is the future of unemployment, but if there is a lesson to be learned from the history of this phenomenon, it is that sound attitudes and policies are responses to particular conditions, which change over time. Inflation was the bogy of the age of John Maynard Keynes; fear of it caused a quarter of the world's work force to suffer unemployment. Fear of unemployment must not become the bogy of modern times.

Index